VOLUME 559

THE ANNALS

of The American Academy *of* Political
and Social Science

ALAN W. HESTON, *Editor*
NEIL A. WEINER, *Assistant Editor*

THE CHANGING EDUCATIONAL QUALITY
OF THE WORKFORCE

Special Editors of this Volume

ROBERT ZEMSKY
PETER CAPPELLI
University of Pennsylvania
Philadelphia

 SAGE Periodicals Press *THOUSAND OAKS LONDON NEW DELHI*

Origin and Purpose. The Academy was organized December 14, 1889, to promote the progress of political and social science, especially through publications and meetings. The Academy does not take sides in controverted questions, but seeks to gather and present reliable information to assist the public in forming an intelligent and accurate judgment.

Meetings. The Academy occasionally holds a meeting in the spring extending over two days.

Publications. THE ANNALS of the American Academy of Political and Social Science is the bimonthly publication of The Academy. Each issue contains articles on some prominent social or political problem, written at the invitation of the editors. Also, monographs are published from time to time, numbers of which are distributed to pertinent professional organizations. These volumes constitute important reference works on the topics with which they deal, and they are extensively cited by authorities throughout the United States and abroad. The papers presented at the meetings of The Academy are included in THE ANNALS.

Membership. Each member of The Academy receives THE ANNALS and may attend the meetings of The Academy. Membership is open only to individuals. Annual dues: $56.00 for the regular paperbound edition (clothbound, $82.00). Add $12.00 per year for membership outside the U.S.A. Members may also purchase single issues of THE ANNALS for $11.00 each (clothbound, $16.00). Add $2.00 for shipping and handling on all pre- paid orders.

Subscriptions. THE ANNALS of the American Academy of Political and Social Science (ISSN 0002-7162) is published six times annually—in January, March, May, July, September, and November. Institutions may subscribe to THE ANNALS at the annual rate: $250.00 (clothbound, $295.00). Add $12.00 per year for subscriptions outside the U.S.A. Institutional rates for single issues: $44.00 each (clothbound, $51.00).

Periodical postage paid at Thousand Oaks, California, and additional offices.

Single issues of THE ANNALS may be obtained by individuals who are not members of The Academy for $19.00 each (clothbound, $29.00). Add $2.00 for shipping and handling on all prepaid orders. Single issues of THE ANNALS have proven to be excellent supplementary texts for classroom use. Direct inquiries regarding adoptions to THE ANNALS c/o Sage Publications (address below).

All correspondence concerning membership in The Academy, dues renewals, inquiries about membership status, and/or purchase of single issues of THE ANNALS should be sent to THE ANNALS c /o Sage Publications, Inc., 2455 Teller Road, Thousand Oaks, CA 91320. Telephone: (805) 499-0721; FAX/Order line: (805) 499-0871. *Please note that orders under $30 must be prepaid.* Sage affiliates in London and India will assist institutional subscribers abroad with regard to orders, claims, and inquiries for both subscriptions and single issues.

Printed on recycled, acid-free paper

THE ANNALS
© 1998 *by* The American Academy *of* Political *and* Social Science

Editorial Office: 3937 Chestnut Street, Philadelphia, PA 19104.

For information about membership* (individuals only) and subscriptions (institutions), address:

SAGE PUBLICATIONS, INC.
2455 Teller Road
Thousand Oaks, CA 91320

From India and South Asia,	*From the UK, Europe, the Middle*
write to:	*East and Africa, write to:*
SAGE PUBLICATIONS INDIA Pvt. Ltd	SAGE PUBLICATIONS LTD
P.O. Box 4215	6 Bonhill Street
New Delhi 110 048	London EC2A 4PU
INDIA	UNITED KINGDOM

SAGE Production Staff: LISA CUEVAS, ERIC LAW, DORIS HUS, and ROSE TYLAK

*Please note that members of The Academy receive THE ANNALS with their membership.

Library of Congress Catalog Card Number 98-60537
International Standard Serial Number ISSN 0002-7162
International Standard Book Number ISBN 0-7619-1735-7 (Vol. 559, 1998 paper)
International Standard Book Number ISBN 0-7619-1734-9 (Vol. 559, 1998 cloth)
Manufactured in the United States of America. First printing, September 1998.

The articles appearing in THE ANNALS are indexed in *Academic Index, Book Review Index, Combined Retrospective Index Sets, Current Contents, General Periodicals Index, Public Affairs Information Service Bulletin, Pro-Views,* and *Social Sciences Index.* They are also abstracted and indexed in *ABC Pol Sci, America: History and Life, Automatic Subject Citation Alert, Book Review Digest, Family Resources Database, Higher Education Abstracts, Historical Abstracts, Human Resources Abstracts, International Political Science Abstracts, Managing Abstracts, Periodica Islamica, Sage Urban Studies Abstracts, Social Planning/Policy & Development Abstracts, Social Sciences Citation Index, Social Work Research & Abstracts, Sociological Abstracts, United States Political Science Documents,* and/or *Work Related Abstracts, Westlaw,* and are available on microfilm from University Microfilms, Ann Arbor, Michigan.

Information about membership rates, institutional subscriptions, and back issue prices may be found on the facing page.

Advertising. Current rates and specifications may be obtained by writing to THE ANNALS Advertising and Promotion Manager at the Thousand Oaks office (address above).

Claims. Claims for undelivered copies must be made no later than twelve months following month of publication. The publisher will supply missing copies when losses have been sustained in transit and when the reserve stock will permit.

Change of Address. Six weeks' advance notice must be given when notifying of change of address to ensure proper identification. Please specify name of journal. Send address changes to: THE ANNALS of the American Academy of Political and Social Science, c/o Sage Publications, Inc., 2455 Teller Road, Thousand Oaks, CA 91320.

THE ANNALS

of The American Academy *of* Political *and* Social Science

ALAN W. HESTON, *Editor*
NEIL A. WEINER, *Assistant Editor*

FORTHCOMING

THE FUTURE OF FACT
Special Editors: Jeffrey J. Strange and Elihu Katz
Volume 560   November 1998

EMOTIONAL LABOR IN THE SERVICE ECONOMY
Special Editors: Ronnie J. Steinberg and Deborah M. Figart
Volume 561   January 1999

THE EVOLVING WORLD OF WORK AND FAMILY:
NEW STAKEHOLDERS, NEW VOICES
Special Editors: Bradley K. Googins and Marcie Pitt-Catsouphes
Volume 562   March 1999

See page 2 for information on Academy membership and
purchase of single volumes of **The Annals.**

CONTENTS

BOOK DEPARTMENT CONTENTS

INTERNATIONAL RELATIONS AND POLITICS

AFRICA, ASIA, AND LATIN AMERICA

EUROPE

UNITED STATES

SOCIOLOGY

ECONOMICS

PREFACE

Contemporary interest in the relationship between education and the economy, broadly defined, has been driven by two different academic perspectives. The first and arguably more important was the development within labor economics of research focusing on investments in worker training and skills as well as more general investments in human capital. Pioneering research by Theodore Schultz, Gary Becker, and Jacob Mincer used these investments to explain, among other things, the labor market outcomes of individuals. The second, closely related perspective sought to explain the economic development of nations in terms of investments in human capital. Most of this research viewed education and skill development as something of a black box. What interested most researchers were the outcomes of investments in human capital, not the characteristics of what occurred during education and training that actually made a difference.

By the mid-1980s, however, the interest in peeking inside that black box had begun to grow, in large part because of changes in the labor force, shifts in the economy, and the emergence of arguments about the relationship between the two. *Workforce 2000*, the 1987 report sponsored by the U.S. Department of Labor (Johnson and Packer 1987), predicted that the United States faced a substantial "skills gap," arguing that a shift toward higher-skilled jobs might outstrip the rise in education levels. While the merits of the report's technical conclusion would be debated by academics over the next decade, *Workforce 2000*'s substantial impact on public policymakers yielded a host of initiatives, each designed to make education and training more readily available to the American workforce.

In part, *Workforce 2000* struck a responsive chord because it reinforced the growing perception that the nation's schools were failing, as measured by the performance of their students, to provide both academic and job-related skills. That was the indictment underlying the 1983 report *A Nation at Risk* (National Commission 1983). In 1985, *The Forgotten Half*—the work of a special commission created by the W. T. Grant Foundation—focused on how little is done in the United States to prepare school leavers for the labor market. Several of the commission's studies concluded, for example, that the main benefit of vocational education programs was simply that they helped some students obtain jobs after they graduated with the same employers who provided the work experience. *America's Choice: High Skills or Low Wages!* (National Center 1990), a third major report to explore the links between work, school, and economic productivity, made the argument that the gap between rising skill demands and potentially declining workforce skills would threaten the ability of the U.S. economy to remain competitive. The subsequent body of research on rising income inequality has similarly pointed to

8

issues associated with skills as the potential, though admittedly indirect, cause.

In the public arena, these arguments have led to a broad set of policy initiatives, often at the state and local levels, where most educational policy is made in the United States. Some of these initiatives have concentrated on traditional educational experiences. Others have invested resources in new pedagogies designed to improve student performance in school as well as at work. Another, highly related set of initiatives has concentrated more directly on relationships between traditional schooling and the labor market, especially for students who do not enroll in higher education.

In 1994, these efforts culminated in the passage of the School-to-Work Opportunities Act and more than $300 million in grants to the states in support of grassroots innovations in the way in which schools and employers relate to each other. At the same time, arguments about the need for firms to restructure and the breakdown of traditional systems of employment relationships suggest that the problem of making transitions from school to work may no longer be a one-shot phenomenon but one that follows individuals throughout their lifetimes.

The seriousness, as well as the tangled nature, of these issues concerning education and the economy make it inevitable that researchers and students will look increasingly inside the black box of education as they seek to understand the policy themes that have been developing over the last two decades. The articles in this volume provide excellent guides to those issues, as well as offer direction for future research.

The articles are organized around three themes. The first focuses on long-standing questions associated with the economics of education. Jere Behrman, Lori Kletzer, Michael McPherson, and Morton Owen Schapiro examine the fundamental issue of the economic payoff to human capital investments and the underlying assumptions that are required about human behavior to estimate those payoffs. They examine student decisions about college choice—which themselves are partly a function of past choices and also partly a function of expectations about future opportunities and alternatives—using microeconomic models.

John Bishop summarizes the research on occupation-specific versus general education and training, arguing against the recommendation that policy should focus on general academic skills. He believes that academic skills are not good substitutes for occupation-specific skills, and he raises the question of what would happen if schools stopped offering job-related training.

David Card and Alan B. Krueger examine how school resources affect students' educational attainment and earnings. They conclude, on balance, that the amount of money schools spend does not necessarily affect the earnings and educational attainment of their students.

Finally, Nevzer Stacey examines the social benefits of education that extend beyond the traditional labor market returns associated with human capital models. She suggests that including an assessment of these benefits as part of discussions around educational policies might lead to better policy decisions.

The second theme addresses current trends in educational policies and practices. Marvin Lazerson establishes the context for this discussion by describing the unprecedented growth of higher education in the years following World War II and its transformation from a "public good" to a "private benefit" that confers economic rewards. He then discusses how its current problems have emerged during the 1980s and 1990s, as the costs of attending college began to outpace the economic returns.

Robert Zemsky discusses what happens when higher education becomes the norm in a society and when this arrangement comes under duress, forcing a restructuring of the educational enterprise. Trends such as declining economic returns to college with rising costs and the bifurcation of higher education providers into outlets and up-market medallions are reshaping the landscape of higher education.

Jerry A. Jacobs and Scott Stoner-Eby examine the growth of adult enrollment in recent decades in the United States and its impact on the educational attainment of the population, highlighting the role of the baby-boom generation in the growth of adult enrollment. They also show that the enrollment of adult students contributes significantly to the increase in the overall educational attainment of the U.S. population.

The volume's third theme examines the relationships between school and the workplace. Peter Cappelli, Daniel Shapiro, and Nichole Shumanis describe the problem of securing employer participation in programs designed to help school leavers make the transition into the workplace. Arguments suggesting that employers do not participate in these activities were central to policy initiatives such as the School-to-Work Opportunities Act, which provided support for work-based learning programs. However, the authors find that participation in school-to-work partnerships and work-based learning programs is substantial.

As somewhat of a contrast, Harold Salzman presents an analysis of the role of the firm in workforce skill development, describing how employers are losing the capacity to provide this investment in human capital for their workforces. Stephen R. Barley examines the extent to which the U.S. military serves as a provider of skills in the civilian economy, concluding that the economic returns to service are primarily due to access to further education. The implications are especially important in the context of the recent drawdown of military enlistments in the United States.

Daniel Shapiro and Maria Iannozzi use recent survey data to examine the benefits that result from an improved articulation between the nation's economic and educational systems. They find that individual employers benefit from participating in activities related to school reform and the educational process.

Finally, Ralph S. Saul examines the more typical view that few American employers see schools as effective partners in their search for skilled workers.

This growing disconnection between the nation's schools and its businesses threatens to undermine the educational quality of the workforce, on which American productivity depends. The challenge is to develop initiatives that require neither new funds nor another government agency; rely on the market to create incentives for firms to invest in human capital; and lower the costs to employers of screening and hiring workers.

PETER CAPPELLI
ROBERT ZEMSKY

References

Johnson, William and Arnold Packer. 1987. *Workforce 2000: Work and Workers for the 21st Century*. Washington, DC: Hudson Institute, for the U.S. Department of Labor.

National Center on Education and the Economy. 1990. *America's Choice: High Skills or Low Wages!* Rochester, NY: National Center on Education and the Economy.

National Commission on Excellence in Education. 1983. *A Nation at Risk: The Imperative for Educational Reform*. Washington, DC: National Commission for Excellence in Education.

W. T. Grant Foundation. Commission on Work, Family, and Citizenship. 1985. *The Forgotten Half*. Washington, DC: W. T. Grant Foundation.

ANNALS, *AAPSS*, **559**, September 1998

Microeconomics of College Choice, Careers, and Wages

By JERE BEHRMAN, LORI KLETZER, MICHAEL McPHERSON, and MORTON OWEN SCHAPIRO

ABSTRACT: Understanding the economic payoff to human capital investments is very important from the standpoint both of individuals and of society. However, this article argues that correctly estimating these impacts necessitates having a well-developed idea of the microeconomic determinants of human behavior. Without this, empirical analyses of such topics as career choice, college choice, or wage determination will be flawed. The authors begin the article with a discussion of why these choice models are important—using examples of similar attempts that do not capture sufficient information—and illustrate their usefulness in a variety of contexts. They also describe the results of their attempts to examine college choice using microeconomic models.

Jere Behrman is professor of economics and director of the Population Studies Center at the University of Pennsylvania.

Lori Kletzer is associate professor of economics at the University of California, Santa Cruz.

Michael McPherson is professor of economics and president of Macalester College.

Morton Owen Schapiro is professor of economics and dean of the College of Letters, Arts and Sciences at the University of Southern California.

NOTE: The research reported on here was supported by grants from the Andrew W. Mellon Foundation and the National Science Foundation (grant number SED-9115440).

MICROECONOMIC analyses of educational investment and career choice examine how the influence of personal and family background characteristics, actual and expected market conditions, and economic incentives interact to shape individuals' choices about the sequence of decisions that result in an educational and occupational outcome. Sophisticated analyses of college and career choice at the microeconomic level emphasize the heterogeneity in various respects (academic aptitude, family resources, and so on) of the populations studied and the interactions between these varied characteristics and various opportunities and incentives in producing observed choices.

The underlying conception of behavior in the kinds of microeconomic models we have in mind is longitudinal and sequential. That is, college and career destinations are seen as the result of the individual's moving along a path over time. Choices made along the way are influenced by the person's characteristics, which themselves are partly a function of past choices and also partly a function of expectations about future opportunities and alternatives. The facts that these choices are extended over time and that choices at a given time are responsive to the results of past choices and to expectations about the future have crucial implications for empirical modeling strategies in this area.

First, empirical estimation of such models virtually requires the availability of longitudinal data on individuals—that is, observations of the choices made by individuals at various stages in the evolution of their educational and career paths. Second, the complex temporal interdependence of choices made at different times introduces serious complexities in the empirical analysis of such data.

Two particular implications should be underscored. First, it is clear in sequential modeling that the alternatives available at time t_1 are dependent on choices made at an earlier time t_0—for example, the decision to go to Juilliard for college certainly conditions one's later choice of major. But, with this kind of interdependence, it becomes very easy to believe that attendance at Juilliard has a causal impact on one's likelihood of majoring in piano when in fact it may be that a disposition to major in piano produced both the decision to go to Juilliard and the decision to major in piano. In principle, if one could accurately measure the disposition to major in music at, say, age 16, one could control for this factor in estimating the impact of Juilliard attendance on choice of major. (Equivalently, one could achieve such control by having good measures of all the factors that determine the disposition at age 16.) Unfortunately, one is likely to lack complete measures. In that case, the omitted variables that influence both the tendency to go to Juilliard and the tendency to major in piano are likely to lead to overestimating the Juilliard effect on choice of major.

The second, and related, problem is the influence of expected future opportunities on choices at a particular time. Here the essential difficulty is posed by the fact that individuals' characteristics will influence their expectations—a highly talented mathematics student, for example, would expect greater returns from the pursuit of a mathematics career than would someone with limited mathematical aptitude. If the researcher possessed a good independent measure of the individual's expectations and of the individual's relevant characteristics, this dependency could be explicitly modeled and would not be problematic. In the absence of such measures, there are great difficulties in sorting out the effects on career choice that operate through influencing earnings expectations from effects that operate in other ways.

The proper analysis of sequential choice in longitudinal data sets remains a difficult analytical and empirical issue. Fortunately, however, the last 20 years have brought real improvements in our capacity to perform such analyses. Several large longitudinal data sets on individuals—with good information on personal and family characteristics, educational histories, and employment histories—have been developed with federal support. Over the same period, improved statistical techniques to cope with the temporal interdependence of choices have been developed.

Next we will examine as a case study a career with special significance for a nation's economic future, science and engineering, before turning to a broader discussion of career choice. We will then report more briefly on some original empirical results regarding college choice and future wages that result from the type of estimation methods suggested here.

CAREER CHOICE: THE CASE OF SCIENCE AND ENGINEERING

Only the foolhardy defend economic models on the grounds of their realism. Yet the simplifications inherent in many models of the labor market for scientists and engineers seem particularly unsettling. Many of these models, including some rather influential ones, are almost purely mechanical: with fixed proportions of students grinding through high school, some other fixed proportion grinding through college, some percentage of them going into scientific or engineering careers, some fraction of others going to graduate school, and so on. The proven ability of these models to be quite spectacularly and consistently wrong has not been enough to discourage their production.

More sophisticated models recognize the interaction of supply and demand in determining labor market outcomes.[1] Increases in demand raise wages and, with a lag, yield an increase in quantity supplied. While it has proved difficult to come up with stable and believable parameters for such models, they highlight an important adjustment mechanism that is bound to play a role and is almost sure to be important.

Yet even these models overlook or oversimplify aspects of the operation of markets for educated labor that intuitively seem quite important. While the presence of lags in the adjustment process in aggregate supply-demand models recognizes that some rather complicated behavior is taking place, which involves learning and the adjustment of plans, the details of that process are very much behind the scenes.

By contrast, microeconomic models of career choice put these matters of planning, choosing, learning, and adjusting at center stage. It is illuminating, we think, to view the process of career choice explicitly as a sequential process, marked by uncertainty at every step. In contrast to aggregate supply-demand models, which tend to suppress recognition of differences in the characteristics of labor market participants—and thus of differential response to changes in external conditions—microeconomic models of career choice highlight the differences in background, aptitude, and circumstances and permit the testing of hypotheses about whether these differences matter.

To clarify the following discussion, consider two stories about how the market for some group of scientists—say, microbiologists—responds to variation in the wages and opportunities in that field. Suppose wages and job opportunities for microbiologists experience a rather abrupt drop but one that is widely believed to be likely to persist for some years. Imagine that we can successfully categorize potential microbiologists according to ability. The question we want to ask is, How will the relative supply of students to the field of microbiology vary according to the ability of the students?

Scenario I is that the most promising students in microbiology have a real passion for the subject and feel something of a calling to it. In less

prosaic terms, we might say that their relative advantages as microbiologists, compared to their prospects in other fields, are quite high. In this scenario, most of the top-quality students stick with microbiology, while the poorer wages and job prospects scare the less promising students away. Most of the decline in the entry of microbiologists to the profession occurs at the low end in terms of quality, with the result that the average quality of microbiologists actually rises as total numbers fall.

Scenario II reverses this. Top microbiology students have excellent alternatives and can, with relative ease and little sacrifice, migrate from microbiology to other fields of study, such as law or banking. Less capable students, although subject to the same pressures, face less good alternatives and are, on the margin, less likely to leave the field. As a result, the average quality of entering microbiologists falls with declining demand. The economic and social significance of a decline in the number of entering microbiologists is likely to be quite different depending on which of these scenarios prevails.

The issue raised by these two stories illustrates one class of questions that is naturally studied under the rubric of the microeconomics of career choice. In general, models of science and engineering labor markets, particularly those that aim at forecasting or policy analysis, completely neglect the kinds of considerations suggested by these stories. Here, we raise the following question: can insights and evidence from the microeconomic analysis of career choice be used effectively to improve the usefulness of forecasts and policy analyses of markets for educated labor in science and engineering?

Recent controversies have focused considerable attention on the adequacy of current models of science and engineering labor markets. In the late 1980s, the National Science Foundation (NSF) produced forecasts of substantial "shortfalls" of scientists and engineers at both bachelor's and advanced levels through the 1990s and beyond. Although the producers of these analyses introduced various qualifications into their analyses, policy advocates both inside and outside NSF relied on these forecasts in arguing for programs that would increase the number of scientists and engineers in coming years.[2]

In the last several years, a variety of circumstances have resulted in substantial declines in the demand for scientists and engineers, leading many observers to conclude that the nation faces a surplus instead of a shortfall of qualified science and engineering personnel. Congressional hearings have focused on the inadequacies of the NSF modeling efforts, and substantial efforts have been undertaken to produce more adequate models.

Some of the limitations of existing models lie on the demand side. The controversial NSF models, for example, measure demand for new scientists and engineers simply as the number of newly produced scientists and engineers in a benchmark period that is judged to be one of rough supply-demand balance. Whether or not the number of science and engineering personnel produced in that year could be taken as a good measure of demand in that year, it is certainly quite arbitrary to suppose that the same level of production would be suitable in other years. An adequate model of demand would need to take into account the influence of underlying economic factors, such as changes in the industrial mix and changes in technology, on demand for scientists and engineers.

More directly pertinent to issues of career choice are limitations on the treatment of supply in existing models. The NSF model derives a supply of new college graduates by applying a coefficient to the size of the college-age population. This coefficient is determined judgmentally on the basis of recent experience; the model does not make the coefficient sensitive to variation in the supply-demand balance. The yield of scientists and engineers from the college graduate pool is similarly determined by a judgmental coefficient, which again is not sensitive to supply-demand consideration. Wages are not included in the model.

Many other models of science and engineering labor markets share major characteristics with the NSF model, although some are more elaborate in various ways. Thus some models disaggregate fields within science and engineering more finely; some recognize more stages in the educational pipeline—introducing a separate step from college entry to college completion, for example.

Perhaps the most significant departure from the NSF type of model is found in those models that explicitly incorporate feedback between supply and demand. Richard Freeman has contributed a number of studies for various markets for educated labor that explicitly model lagged wage adjustments and lagged responses of supply and demand to changes in wages as part of the adjustment process (see, for example, Freeman 1975). Other analysts have produced models in which an adjustment of supply to demand is assumed to occur but which do not explicitly incorporate wages or other mediating variables into the analysis.

It is a controversial question whether these simple aggregate models, whether or not they incorporate lagged adjustment processes, can capture enough of reality to shed light on likely future developments in science and engineering labor markets. There cannot, however, be much doubt that these analyses fall woefully short of allowing analysts to assess the effects of various policy issues that are brought forward in response to diagnoses of shortages or surpluses in these labor markets.

Consider, for example, the influential analyses of the market for scientists and engineers published by Richard Atkinson (1990, 1988) almost a decade ago. Atkinson cited the NSF forecasts of shortfalls in scientists and engineers in making a case for increased support for the education of people in those fields. Yet both the nature of the problem as he diagnosed it and the policies he advocated in response to the shortfall assumed knowledge of behavioral relationships that are not included in typical aggregate models of these labor mar-

kets. He argued, for example, on the basis of evidence that is not integrated into these aggregate models, that the majority of the interested and qualified students who are "lost" to science and engineering between their freshman and senior years of college switch to other areas because they find other fields more promising and believe they would have better job prospects elsewhere. He emphasized the importance for policy purposes of interesting women and minorities in scientific and engineering careers, while the aggregate models shed little light on how determinants of the decision to enter science or engineering differ between race and gender groups.

Atkinson's policy proposals also presupposed facts about behavioral responses that are not explored in typical supply-demand models. He proposed in particular that increases in fellowship opportunities, especially when targeted at women and minorities, would elicit a strong supply response.

A second set of issues that figures prominently in policy discussions but is largely absent from modeling efforts is the matter of the quality of scientists and engineers. It is commonly alleged, with at least some empirical support, that the quality of students in undergraduate engineering programs fluctuates sharply with fluctuations in the state of the engineering labor market. When the market is strong, both the number and quality of engineering students rise, with the rise in quality being due partly to the interest of more able students in engineering and partly to engineering departments in universities rationing access to their programs by quality.

Although the relation between quality as measured by conventional academic standards and quality as measured by workplace performance is by no means clear, it seems plausible to many observers that fluctuations in the academic quality of persons entering the science and engineering professions matter significantly to productivity. In the limited context of research science, for example, Levin and Stephan (1991) have argued that the absence of growth in the publication productivity of recent cohorts of scientists, despite the fact that they have a larger knowledge base to work with, may reveal a decline in the quality of the research personnel. They speculate that such a decline might be related to the relatively weak labor market for academic scientists and engineers in recent times.

The quality issue assumes added importance in policy discussions for two reasons. First, it seems quite plausible that, at the margin, adjustments in the employment of scientists and engineers occur through quality. It is less likely that jobs will go unfilled than it is that they will be filled by less qualified personnel—a fact that has been shown strikingly in the case of high school teachers of science and mathematics. Second, programs to recruit students to science and engineering are often very quality oriented, as is the case with fellowship programs of the kind Atkinson advocates. The issue is generally not only one of attracting enough students or workers but of attracting the right students and workers—and this is an issue that aggregate models of supply and demand barely address at all.

CAN MICROECONOMIC ANALYSIS
OF CAREER CHOICE HELP?

We suggest four categories of questions where aggregate models of supply and demand quickly run into severe difficulties.

1. How large is the response of individuals to changes in the incentives for pursuing particular career paths? Incentives may include scholarships and fellowships, expected earnings, expected risks of unemployment, and the like. The impact of incentives may vary at different points in the career path. Once a student has chosen to attend a technical institute like Cal Tech for college, for example, he or she may be unlikely to become discouraged about pursuing a science or engineering career. Yet the decision for a student with particular characteristics to attend such an institution in the first place may well be more strongly influenced by incentives.

2. How do responses to incentives vary among students with differing characteristics? Are students with strong mathematical aptitudes more or less sensitive to fluctuations in science or engineering wage rates than those with weaker aptitudes?

3. How do various social and economic background characteristics influence persons' interests in science and engineering?

4. What is the interaction between these background characteristics

and incentives to pursue careers in science and engineering? For example, are students from low-income families more likely to be influenced by fellowship opportunities in their choice of majors and careers? An affirmative answer would provide a reason for aiming to target fellowship money on such students.

It should be clear enough that aggregate supply and demand models are very limited in their ability to respond to these questions. Some worthwhile evidence about responses to wages and labor market conditions can be obtained from time-series models that incorporate response lags. Such studies are bound to be handicapped, however, by the limited number of observations available in the time series and by the confounding effects of other economic and social changes that are correlated with the labor market variables of interest.

To push further with aggregate time-series models, by trying to detect effects of changes in fellowship or financial aid policies or by examining differential responsiveness to wage changes of different population groups, is almost certainly too ambitious. Convincing analyses of differential behavior of different population groups are similarly very difficult to achieve in the time-series context.

Do we have reason to believe that micro data sets and the kind of longitudinal analysis described earlier can do better? Plainly, the best way to answer this question affirmatively is to do the analyses and demonstrate their effectiveness. Still, there may

be some purpose to trying to describe the reasons why conceptually this approach seems to hold promise.

The first point to emphasize is that it is very plausible to believe that behavioral responses vary importantly both at different stages of the life cycle and across groups with different characteristics. This variation is important in its own right, we have suggested, for policy purposes, but it also suggests advantages to the use of micro data sets. Time-series analyses will inevitably require aggregating people with quite different characteristics and collapsing different segments of the sequential career path. Such aggregation is certain to add to the imprecision of estimated behavioral effects and can easily lead to biases. A sequential approach, by contrast, makes it possible to design the model so that it permits the extent of behavioral response to, say, expected wages to vary along the career path, affecting the decision to go to college, the choice of major, the decision to complete, and so on in potentially different ways.

Similarly, an analysis based on micro data can make explicit the possibility that men and women or people of different ethnic, social, or economic backgrounds may respond differently to differences in the incentives they face.

The opportunity to study interactions between people's characteristics and their response to variations in expected wages adds an important dimension to what can be learned from aggregate studies.

In the following two sections, we report briefly on studies we have undertaken that apply the kind of sequential microeconomic analysis described here to questions about college choice and about the impact of college attendance on wages.

MICROECONOMIC ANALYSIS OF COLLEGE CHOICE

There is a large literature concerning college attendance decisions (a selected review of this literature is in Behrman et al. 1995). These decisions are naturally thought to be influenced strongly by family background. But previous studies of the impact of family background on college attendance generally suffer from the selectivity problem we have described previously: if they include high school achievement as a determinant of college choice, they treat it as predetermined in a statistical sense rather than determined in part by observed and unobserved components of family background as part of a longer-run educational strategy. But family background may affect college decisions indirectly through effects on high school achievement as well as through direct effects. Previous estimates, by treating high school achievements as predetermined, may be biased and are not informative about the importance of direct versus indirect effects of family background.

In Behrman et al. (1995), we show statistically that high school achievement is determined jointly with college investment decisions; that is, students' decisions about working to achieve in high school are influenced by their college ambitions. We find evidence that high school achievement depends on many of the same background variables that influence college educational investments and that failure to account for this interdependence leads one mistakenly to attribute part of the effect of high school achievement to family background variables that influence achievement levels. Thus, treatment of high school achievement as an endogenous component of a longer-run educational strategy rather than as predetermined has substantial effects on the estimated magnitudes of some responses of interest and permits the identification of direct versus indirect effects of family background.

Another improvement on the existing literature is that we focus on qualitative differences between colleges rather than merely on the quantitative nature of college choice (enrollment in two-year versus four-year schools, for example). School quality variations between four-year colleges and universities are large and appear to affect post-schooling outcomes. Studies that focus exclusively on the quantitative aspect of college choices miss the important qualitative dimension of those choices on which family background may also have direct and indirect influences.

We estimate the effects of family background on both the qualitative choice of whether to enroll in a two-year versus a four-year school and, for those who enroll in four-year colleges and universities, on the qualitative choice between those schools. The inclusion of this qualitative dimension of choice affects our understanding of the nature and magnitude of family background effects on college in some important respects. For example, family income has but limited direct impact on whether students enroll in postsecondary colleges and universities, but it has strong direct effects on the quality of educational institution selected for those who attend private four-year colleges.

This discussion is far from being the final word on the determination of college choice. Instead, it is intended to indicate that the type of methodology described earlier can be usefully applied in analyzing how students select between colleges and universities.

MICROECONOMIC ANALYSIS OF WAGE DETERMINATION

The greatest effort economists have made in studying the impact of college attendance on the economy has undoubtedly been in terms of estimating the returns to human capital. Again, the methods described here can shed new light on a much-discussed topic.

There has been a rising interest in understanding better the impact of college choices on wages, an interest motivated by concerns about increasing wage inequalities, about increasing costs of elite private colleges, and about the perceived increasing roles of highly educated individuals in maintaining international competitiveness. As in the case of college choice, previous studies have been subject to several limitations (this literature is reviewed in Behrman et al. 1996). For one, they have not considered possible differential impacts for different demographic groups identified by race and gender. In addition, once again, with few exceptions, they have not considered the choice dimensions with regard to time in college and college quality.

Behrman et al. (1996) address both of these limitations. Estimates are obtained of the impact of time in college and of college quality choices on wages for four demographic groups based on an explicit dynamic framework. These estimates suggest that treating time in college and college quality as choices within a dynamic framework affects fairly substantially the estimated effects. Based on these results, most previous studies may have overestimated the impact of both college quality and time in college because of the failure to deal with such choices and, in a lesser but still substantial number of cases, because of the failure to control for the quality dimensions of pre-college education.

The estimates also suggest that there are important demographic differences in the wage benefits of college. The estimated wage benefits from higher college quality and more time in college tend to be highest for nonwhite males, next for nonwhite females and then white females, and least for white males. For some members of all groups, there appear to be some incentives for increasing college quality (by paying somewhat higher tuition, and so on), more so for those who are in college longer because of interactions between college quality and time in college. But these incentives differ strongly across groups, being much higher for nonwhite males and much lower for white males, with females in between. For nonwhites, there also appear to be incentives (again stronger for males than females) to increase time in college. For whites, in contrast, the estimated net gains do not appear to create such incentives (at least at a reasonable real discount rate of 4 percent)—a result that contrasts with common interpretations of estimated earnings equations.

The results for nonwhites raise important questions regarding why there is unrealized potential for reaping net benefits from more time in college or attending higher-quality colleges. A number of possible answers to this question—poor information about the impact of college, imperfect capital markets for financing college, poor information about college quality differentials, discriminatory admissions—may have important policy implications on both equity and efficiency grounds.

CONCLUSION

Understanding the economic payoff to human capital investments is very important from the standpoint both of individuals and of society. But it is our view that to estimate these impacts correctly necessitates having a well-developed idea of the microeconomic determinants of human behavior. Without this, empirical analyses of such topics as career choice, college choice, or wage determination will be flawed. Our intention here has been to lay out our reasoning as to why these choice models are important and to illustrate their usefulness in a variety of contexts.

Notes

1. Leslie and Oaxaca (1993) review this literature. See also Stapleton (1989), Ehrenberg (1991, 1992), Levin and Stephan (1991), Freeman (1975), and Levy (1988). Stephan (1996) presents an excellent overview of the economics of science.

2. National Science Foundation (1988, 1994), National Science Board (1993), National Research Council (1979), and National Academy of Sciences (1995) present data on a variety of science and engineering indicators.

References

Atkinson, Richard C. 1988. Bold Steps Are Needed to Educate the Next Generation of Scientists. *Chronicle of Higher Education* 34(25):B1.

———. 1990. Supply and Demand for Scientists and Engineers: A National Crisis in the Making. *Science* 248 (Apr.):425-32.

Behrman, Jere R., Jill Constantine, Lori G. Kletzer, Michael S. McPherson, and Morton Owen Schapiro. 1996. Impact of College Quality Choices on Wages: Are There Differences Among Demographic Groups? Williams Project on the Economics of Higher Education. Discussion paper no. 38.

Behrman, Jere R., Lori G. Kletzer, Michael S. McPherson, and Morton Owen Schapiro. 1995. How Family Background Sequentially Affects College Choices: High School Achievement, College Enrollment and College Quality. Duplicated.

Ehrenberg, Ronald G. 1991. Academic Labor Supply. In *Economic Challenges in Higher Education*, ed. Charles Clotfelter et al. Part 2. Chicago: University of Chicago Press.

———. 1992. The Flow of New Doctorates. *Journal of Economic Literature* 30(2):830-75.

Freeman, Richard. 1975. Supply and Salary Adjustments to the Changing Science Manpower Market: Physics,

1948-1973. *American Economic Review* 65(1):27-39.

Leslie, Larry R. and Ronald L. Oaxaca. 1993. Scientist and Engineer Supply and Demand. In *Higher Education: Handbook of Theory and Research*, ed. John C. Smart. Vol. 9. New York: Agathon Press.

Levin, Sharon G. and Paula E. Stephan. 1991. Research Productivity over the Life Cycle: Evidence for Academic Scientists. *American Economic Review* 81(1):114-32.

Levy, David M. 1988. The Market for Fame and Fortune. *Historical Political Economy* 20(4):615-25.

National Academy of Sciences. 1995. *Reshaping the Graduate Education of Scientists and Engineers*. Washington, DC: National Academy Press.

National Research Council. 1979. *Research Excellence Through the Year 2000: The Importance of Maintaining a Flow of New Faculty into Academic Research*. Washington, DC: National Academy of Sciences.

National Science Board. 1993. *Science and Engineering Indicators—1993*. Washington, DC: Government Printing Office.

National Science Foundation. 1988. *Doctoral Scientists and Engineers: A Decade of Change*. Washington, DC: National Science Foundation.

———. 1994. *Characteristics of Doctoral Scientists and Engineers in the United States: 1991*. NSF #94-307. Arlington, VA: National Science Foundation.

Stapleton, David C. 1989. Cohort Size and the Academic Labor Market. *Journal of Human Resources* 24(2):221-52.

Stephan, Paula E. 1996. The Economics of Science. *Journal of Economic Literature* 34(3):1199-1235.

Occupation-Specific Versus General Education and Training

By JOHN BISHOP

ABSTRACT: In this article, John Bishop summarizes research from many sources concerning the current debate over occupation-specific versus general education and training. He argues against a recommendation made by the *Economist* magazine that government scale back its support of school-based occupation-specific training and instead focus on academic education. Research shows, to the contrary, that productivity derives directly from social abilities (such as good work habits and people skills) and cognitive skills that are specific to the job and occupation, not from reading, writing, and mathematics skills. Old skills are becoming obsolete more rapidly, so new skills must be learned more frequently. This implies a greater overall need for occupational training, not a reduced need. The rise in job turnover has made employers more reluctant to hire inexperienced workers and provide them skill training, so the need for school-based vocational training has never been greater. Occupational turnover has been declining, so the payback period of occupational skills has been rising.

John Bishop is a professor at the New York State School of Industrial and Labor Relations and chair of the Human Resources Studies Department at Cornell University.

NOTE: This article summarizes research that received support from many sources. The sources include grants to the National Center on the Educational Quality of the Workforce (agreement #R117Q00011-91) and to the Consortium for Policy Research in Education, as administered by the U.S. Office of Educational Research and Improvement; grants from Cornell University's Center for Advanced Human Resource Studies; and a grant to Cornell from the National Association of State Directors of Vocational Technical Education Consortium. The findings and opinions expressed in this report do not reflect the position or policies of the Office of Educational Research and Improvement or the U.S. Department of Education.

GLOBALIZATION and automation have increased the relative demand for skilled workers. Governments have responded by expanding and improving education and training. But what kind of education or training should get priority—generic academic skills or occupation-specific skills? The *Economist* (Training for Jobs 1994) argues that occupation-specific education should be dropped and generic skills should be taught instead:

Economists have long argued that the returns on general education are higher than those on specific training, because education is transferable whereas many skills tend to be job-specific. Today this case is becoming more compelling still as jobs become less secure, the service sector expands and the life-cycle of vocational skills diminishes and the market puts an even greater premium on the ability to deal with people and process information. (26)

This policy recommendation, however, is based on three false premises:

1. Academic skills are good substitutes for occupation-specific skills.
2. Accelerating skill obsolescence has reduced the payoff to occupational training.
3. Rising job turnover has reduced payoffs to occupational training by schools.

This article examines what research tells about each of these issues.

EVIDENCE THAT OCCUPATIONAL SKILLS ARE ESSENTIAL

In most jobs, productivity derives directly from social abilities (such as good work habits and people skills) and cognitive skills that are specific to the job, the occupation, and the occupational cluster—not from reading, writing, and mathematics skills. When the small and medium-sized employers who provide most of the new jobs in the American economy are asked which skills they look for when hiring, they cite work habits and occupational skills ahead of reading and mathematics skills. In 1987, the owners of small and medium-sized businesses who were members of the National Federation of Independent Business (NFIB) were asked, "Which abilities influence hiring selections the most?"[1] Forty percent ranked "occupational skills (already has them)" as the first choice, and another 14 percent ranked these skills as number two (Table 1).

By contrast, only 6 percent of these American employers ranked "reading, writing, math and reasoning ability" as their first choice, and another 13 percent ranked these skills as second. Leadership and people skills were also seldom ranked at the top. The trait that most directly rivaled occupational skills was "work habits," which was ranked most important 29 percent of the time and ranked number two 36 percent of the time. Only 3 percent of the employers ranked "work habits" in fifth or sixth place. Clearly, good work habits are an important hiring criterion for just about every job.

There is greater disagreement about the importance of already developed occupational skills. For 20 percent of the jobs offered by these employers, previous occupational

TABLE 1
ABILITIES SOUGHT WHEN HIRING

	Percentage Ranked			Mean Rank by Skill	
	#1	#2	#5 or #6	High	Low
Occupational/job skills (already has them)	40	14	20	2.36	3.01
Ability to learn new occupational and job skills	15	26	13	2.96	2.84
Work habits and attitude (trying hard, enthusiasm, punctuality)	29	36	3	2.30	2.20
People skills (teamwork, appearance, getting along with others)	9	15	33	3.79	3.49
Leadership ability (organize, teach and motivate others/solve problems)	1	2	54	5.16	5.33
Reading, writing, math and reasoning ability	6	13	39	5.65	3.83

SOURCE: Analysis of a 1986 survey of members of the National Federation of Independent Business. See Bishop 1995.

skills ranked fifth or sixth. They tended to be the jobs requiring less skill—service and clerical workers, operatives, and sales clerks. In these lower-wage jobs, work habits were the number-one consideration; "ability to learn new occupational and job skills" ranked number two; and "occupational skills (already developed)" ranked number three. "Reading, writing, math and reasoning" was ranked last for the more highly skilled jobs and second from last in the less skilled jobs (Bishop 1995).

From this data, it can be surmised that American high school graduates who are good at reading and mathematics do not get much better jobs than their less accomplished peers in the years immediately after graduation (Bishop 1992). The best starting jobs tend to go to graduates who took vocational courses and/or worked part-time during the school year (Bishop 1995). However, reading and math skills do pay off eventually. They help graduates get into and complete college, and, at work, they help new hires learn the job and

occupational specific skills necessary for high productivity.

SUCCESS ON THE JOB

Once hired, which abilities predict success on the job? The NFIB survey also provides insight into this question. The responding business owners supplied information on the background and on-the-job success of two employees (A and B) who had recently occupied the same job.[2] After the two employees had been at the firm for a year or more, the employers were asked:

Which of the two employees (A or B) proved better on each of the following: "occupational and job skills," "ability to learn new occupational and job skills," "work habits and attitudes," "people skills (teamwork, appearance, getting along)," "leadership ability (organize, teach and motivate others)" and as a group "reading, writing, math and reasoning ability"?

They were asked to evaluate whether employee A was "much better" than, "better" than, or "no different" from

FIGURE 1
WAGE AND PRODUCTIVITY EFFECTS OF ABILITIES

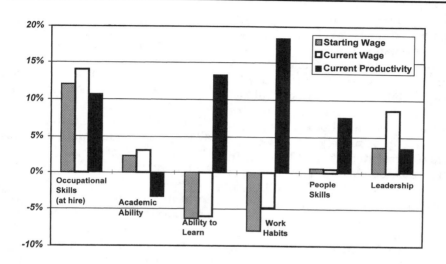

SOURCE: Analysis of a 1986 survey of members of the National Federation of Independent Business. See Bishop 1995.

employee B or whether B was "better" or "much better" than A. Since the firms were small, the owners had contact with each worker, and their judgments were probably quite well informed.

In most cases, business owners perceived important differences in ability between their employees. In 78 percent of the cases, the occupational skills of one of the two workers were judged to be "better" or "much better" than the other's. Reading, writing, math, and reasoning skills were judged to be different 58 percent of the time. Generally, those who were strong along one dimension of ability were strong along other dimensions as well.

Which trait contributes most to overall job performance was deter-mined by regressing relative starting wage rate, current (or most recent) wage rate, and global ratings of relative productivity for workers A and B, according to their ranking on each of the six different worker abilities. The analysis controlled for gender, ethnicity, and marital status. For current employees, wage and productivity reports reflected the date of the interview, which was an average of one year after the employee was hired. For separated employees, the productivity report took place "two weeks before leaving the firm" and the wage report took place "at the time of separation." The results for all three labor market outcomes are presented in Figure 1. The bars in Figure 1 represent the percentage differential in wage rates or productivity that results from one worker being "much better" than another along one of the six ability dimensions, while holding other abilities, tenure, ethnicity, gender, and marital status constant.

Ex-post assessments of relative occupational skill, learning ability, work habits, and people skills all had significant positive relationships with relative global productivity ratings at approximately one year of tenure (represented by the black bar in Figure 1). Employer assessments of a worker's academic skills and leadership ability, by contrast, had no relationship with current overall job performance ratings. Holding demographics and employer evaluations of other traits constant, workers thought to have "much better" occupational skills were judged to be 10.7 percent more productive after about one year on the job.

The impacts of occupational skills on relative wage rates are even more striking. Occupational skills were the only ability that had large positive effects on relative wage rates. Workers thought to be "much better" in occupational skills started with a 12 percent higher wage and were making 14 percent more after a year or so on the job.

Academic skills had no significant effects on wage rates. People skills also had no effects on wage rates. Leadership had modest positive effects on wage rates and initial productivity but not on productivity a year later. The two abilities with the largest impacts on productivity one year later—ex-post assessments of work habits and the ability to learn new occupational and job skills—had

significant negative relationships with wage rates (Bishop 1995).

CORRELATIONS BETWEEN
JOB KNOWLEDGE AND
JOB PERFORMANCE

A third way to assess the importance of occupational skills is to measure them directly and then examine their correlation with ratings of overall job performance. Meta-analyses of the hundreds of empirical validity studies have found that content-valid paper-and-pencil job-knowledge tests are good predictors of job performance. Dunnette's meta-analysis (1972) of 262 studies of occupational competency tests found that their average correlation with supervisory ratings was .51, which is higher than any other predictor, including tests of generic reading and mathematics skills. Vineberg and Joyner's meta-analysis (1982) of studies done in the military came to similar conclusions. Tests assessing job knowledge are also considerably better predictors of ratings of overall job performance than are measures of the personality constructs associated with good work habits (Hough 1988).

When paper-and-pencil tests of occupational knowledge appropriate for the job compete with reading and mathematics tests to predict supervisor ratings of job performance, the job-knowledge tests carry all of the explanatory power, while the reading and mathematics tests carry none. When judged performance on a sample of critical job tasks is the measure of job performance, the beta coefficient on the job-knowledge test is two to four times larger than the beta coefficient on a basic-skills composite (Hunter 1983).

To summarize, in almost all jobs, productivity derives directly from social abilities (such as good work habits and people skills) that are generic and cognitive skills specific to the job, occupation, or industry—not from reading, writing, and mathematics skills. Reading and math skills contribute to productivity by helping the individual learn the occupation and job-specific skills that are directly productive. Since large improvements in job knowledge are easier to achieve than equivalent (in proportions of a standard deviation) improvements in verbal and mathematical skills, occupation-specific training is highly desirable—if the student is likely to put the knowledge to use by working in the occupation or a closely related one.

SKILL OBSOLESCENCE AND THE DEMAND FOR TRAINING

Skills are becoming obsolescent more rapidly than in the past. But those who argue that this implies a reduced need for occupation-specific skill development have the story exactly backward. Obsolescent occupational skills must be replaced by new occupational skills. If old skills become obsolete more rapidly, then new skills must be learned more frequently. This implies a greater overall need for occupational training, not a reduced need.

Skill obsolescence is greatest in fast-changing fields that are close to the frontier of knowledge, such as the computer industry. It is precisely in these fields that the payoff to skill development is the greatest. Mane's study of data from the National Educational Longitudinal Study of 1988 found that recent high school graduates who had taken computer courses in high school earned significantly more in 1993 than those who had not (Mane 1997). People who use a computer at work are paid 10 percent more per hour than those who do not, even when industry and occupation are held constant (Krueger 1993).

While high rates of obsolescence mean the payoff period is short, they also mean that the supply of workers with the new skills is small, because previous generations of trainees did not learn them. This is a major reason why engineers receive higher starting salaries than violinists. Each violinist competes with a large stock of already trained violinists. Newly minted engineers, by contrast, have skills not taught to earlier generations, so they are competing primarily with others of the same vintage, not also with previous generations of engineering graduates. Graduates of training programs that impart the latest skills gain skills that are in short supply and therefore are well rewarded. In fact, graduates of such training programs may be valued precisely because they bring new ideas to the firm and can teach new skills to coworkers. Thus the labor market responds to high rates of skill obsolescence by paying a higher premium for the new skill.

JOB TURNOVER AND INCENTIVES TO PROVIDE TRAINING

Has the need for expanded, recurrent training been fully met by employers? Probably not. High rates of job turnover are a major disincentive for employers who are considering training investments. The job turnover of American workers has increased over the past 25 years, making it more costly for firms to provide training. The proportion of the workforce with fewer than 25 months of tenure at their companies rose from 28 percent in 1968 to 40 percent in 1978 and has remained high since. The average tenure of male workers fell 5 percent between 1963 and 1981 (holding age composition constant) and then fell another 8 percent between 1983 and 1987 (Bishop 1995).

The *Economist* cites the high rates of job turnover as justification for scaling back school-based occupational training. Here, again, the argument is exactly backward. The social returns to occupational training are influenced by occupational turnover, not job turnover. Occupational mobility rates in the United States have moved in the opposite direction from job mobility. Occupational mobility fell by 13 to 20 percent between 1978 and 1987 (Markey and Parks 1989), and this drop has raised the social returns on occupational skill development. Since the rise in job turnover rates has reduced employer willingness to finance training, the need for school-based occupational training has increased.

SHOULD SCHOOLS STOP OFFERING TRAINING IN OCCUPATION-SPECIFIC SKILLS?

A good case can be made that workers would be better off if employers, rather than schools, assumed a greater share of the responsibility for providing occupational training. When employers provide training, trainee-time costs tend to be minimal, and productivity increases tend to be large and immediate. There is a high probability that the trainee will use the training in his or her job and be rewarded for doing so. Incentives to keep costs (including trainee-time costs) down, to select effective trainers and training strategies, and to learn the new material are strong and well aligned.

Most of the costs of employer-sponsored training are paid by employers, not by employees in the form of lower wages during training (Bishop 1994). Nevertheless, trainees receive substantial wage increases after such training. This training is a "great deal" for the worker. The sum of the benefits of training accruing to employers, employees, and others in society (for example, the social benefits) are much larger than the social costs (Bishop 1995).

The problem with employer training is that there is too little of it. The major beneficiary of training—the worker—is often poorly informed about costs and benefits and lacks the resources and access to capital markets necessary to pay for training. Employers pay most of the costs of the training provided at workplaces, but many of the benefits accrue to others: the worker and future employers of the worker (Bishop 1994). Because trainees are generally paid while receiving training, and because trainers frequently interact with trainees one on one, hourly costs are very high. High costs also result because most employers are too small to achieve economies of scale and specialization in providing training. Finally, public subsidies are generally not available when occupational training is provided by an employer.

Since the hourly costs of providing training in occupational skills are very high for employers, employers quite naturally seek to have others—schools or other employers—do it for them. They prefer to hire already trained and experienced workers. When such workers are unavailable, they select relatives and family friends for trainee positions to reduce turnover and fulfill family obligations. This situation, of course, means that young people who are not part of social networks that include small business owners and managers are unable to get their foot in the door. Since costs are high and turnover substantial, most American employers pursue a just-in-time training strategy, where training is only in the skills needed for the current job. Training is undertaken only when it is expected to quickly yield very high returns.

When making training investment decisions, employers are comparing the costs they incur to the increase in productivity (net of resulting wage increases) of the workers expected to remain at the firm. Benefits received by other employers or the worker will have zero weight in their calculation. The result inevitably is underinvestment (from society's point of view) in employer training that develops general skills.

WHAT WOULD HAPPEN IF SCHOOL-BASED TRAINING WAS ELIMINATED?

If schools were to withdraw from the occupational training market, employers would become the sole provider of occupation-specific training. Since separation rates are high for most American companies, employers would not be willing to assume this task without some inducement. Government could offer employers training subsidies, but such a scheme would be difficult to administer and would probably cost more than the current school-based occupational training system.

In the absence of massive subsidies of employer training, shortages of skilled labor would develop, and wage premiums for occupational skills formerly learned in school would rise. Lacking immediately useful skills, school leavers would find it more difficult to find work and would have to accept lower wage rates. Some employers would substitute less skilled workers for the now more expensive skilled workers, and let the quality of the service they provide deteriorate. Others would find ways to substitute machines for people or arrange for workers located in other countries to perform the work (for example, many American companies now have software-writing subsidiaries in Bulgaria, Russia, and India). Eventually, the scarcity of skilled workers would become so severe and the wage differential between unskilled and skilled workers so large that employers would find it profitable to provide occupational skill training. In the new equilibrium, however, the society would have fewer skilled workers, a lower standard of living, and a more unequal distribution of earnings.

The *Economist* made its case for general, rather than occupation-specific, education on a priori grounds. The a priori argument is unconvincing, however. In societies with high rates of job turnover such as the United States, employers cannot be expected to pick up the entire burden of teaching occupational skills. Schools and colleges need to be a part of the occupational training picture.

But mounting effective occupational training programs is not an easy task. The rapid obsolescence of occupational skills makes it more difficult to keep curricula, equipment, and teaching staff up to date. Graduates of vocational programs are often unable to—or simply choose not to—locate jobs in the occupation for which they prepared. This is apparently the price one pays for allowing students to select the occupation for which they will prepare, rather than having employers select who will receive training, as occurs in apprenticeship systems. Is the price paid too high? How successful are American vocational-technical education programs in preparing young people for skilled work?

HOW EFFECTIVE ARE AMERICAN
VOCATIONAL-TECHNICAL
SCHOOLS AND COLLEGES?

What has research taught us about the effectiveness of vocational education in the United States? This summary of that research is organized around eight questions.

How large are the economic benefits of postsecondary vocational education? In 1992, 25- to 34-year-old full-time, full-year workers with two-year associate's degrees earned 21-28 percent more than high school graduates. Those with some college but no degree earned 14-15 percent more than high school graduates (U.S. Bureau of the Census 1993, tab. 30). Percentage impacts were generally larger for African Americans and females than for white males. Seventy percent of associate's degrees and 98 percent of other nonbaccalaureate certificates are awarded in vocational lines of study (National Center for Education Statistics 1993, 245). Workers who report that training from a two-year college helped them qualify for their current job earned 13 percent more in 1991 than other workers with the same amount of schooling, tenure, and potential work experience (Bowers and Swaim 1992).

How large are the benefits of government-sponsored vocational training programs targeted on high school dropouts and other economically disadvantaged youths? Solid evidence on the impact of government training programs on dropouts under the age of 22 comes from studies with strong randomized designs. During the 2.5-year follow-up period, young men with arrest records prior to entering training programs under the Job Training Partnership Act (JTPA) earned $6800 less than arrestees who were randomly assigned to not receive JTPA training. Subsidized on-the-job training lowered the earnings of those without an arrest record by $578 for women and $3012 for men. The only positive finding for JTPA youths was a 9 percent increase in the earnings of women receiving classroom training. The stigmatizing character of the programs may be one of the reasons for their failure. Although JTPA training fails to help young people, adults benefit substantially. For adults, payback periods were generally less than two years. The second-chance government training programs that work best are the ones that focus on teaching occupation-specific skills (integrating any basic skill teaching with occupational training) and that are well connected to the labor market.

Does high school vocational education lower dropout rates? The answer is yes. Kulik's review (1994) of the literature concludes that participating in vocational education lowers dropout rates.

How large are the economic benefits of secondary vocational education? Graduates of vocational training programs in secondary schools are not paid as well as those who have earned postsecondary diplomas and associate's degrees. Nevertheless, they earn substantially more than other high school graduates who do not go to college. Altonji (1988) found that four trade and technical courses substituted for a mix of academic courses raised wage rates by 5-10 percent, depending on specification. Kang and Bishop (1989) found that, in 1981, males who completed four trade and technical courses earned 21-35 percent more one year after graduation than those who took academic courses only. Young women with four credits of

business and office courses earned 40 percent extra. However, the benefits of high school vocational education diminish with time (Campbell et al. 1986). The fact that high school vocational education is successful with an age group that second-chance programs are unable to help suggests that priority needs to be given to keeping educationally disadvantaged youths in school, where they can benefit from mainstream vocational training programs.

Do the benefits of getting a vocational education depend on getting a training-related job? The answer to this question is yes. All of the studies that have examined this issue (Campbell et al. 1986; Rumberger and Daymont 1982; Grubb 1992, 1997; National Center for Education Statistics 1993) have found that the economic benefits of taking vocational rather than academic courses are much greater when a training-related job is obtained. This was true for all levels of occupation-specific education: secondary, community college, and four-year baccalaureate programs. Effects were particularly positive for those who entered the field they trained for and stayed in that field. Campbell et al. (1987) found that graduates of high school vocational programs who spent 100 percent of their time after high school in the field for which they trained earned 31 percent more than those who never had a training-related job. Training programs for sales clerk jobs were the exception. Graduates of distributive education programs earned less if they obtained training-related sales jobs. For trainees, the benefit of vocational education largely comes from the access it confers to higher-wage occupations. This suggests that school-based vocational education programs should avoid training young people for low-wage, low-skill jobs, even when high training-related placement rates can be guaranteed.

To what extent are occupation-specific skills learned in school being used in the labor market? Forty-three percent of employed graduates who completed two or more vocational courses in a specific field had jobs at the time they were interviewed in 1985 that matched their field of training (Campbell et al. 1987). Using a similar procedure of matching training fields against the jobs of 25- to 64-year-olds, Grubb (1997) found that jobs matched an individual's vocational major 61 percent of the time for bachelor's degree recipients; 47 percent of the time for male, and 63 percent of the time for female, associate's degree recipients; 55 percent of the time for certificate holders; and generally between 40 and 50 percent of the time for those with some college but no degree. Mangum and Ball (1989) found that employer-sponsored training had higher utilization rates: 85 percent for company training and 71 percent for apprenticeship. Apprenticeship training in Germany is also more likely to lead to relevant jobs. Six months after completing their training, 68 percent of those with civilian jobs were employed in the occupation (much more narrowly defined) for which they

were trained (Federal Institute for Vocational Training 1986). These results suggest that one way to increase training-related placement rates is to have employers cooperate with schools in the delivery of training. Other ways to increase the proportion of students who work in the occupation for which they train is to improve career guidance, offer training in expanding occupations, and upgrade the quality and relevance of the training.

Does studying occupation-specific skills in school lower achievement in the academic arena? At the end of high school, the gap between vocational and academic students is about one standard deviation, or about 3.5 grade-level equivalents. Much of this gap, however, preexisted the student's entry into vocational education (Kulik 1994). Indeed, students who have difficulty with academic subjects often seek out vocational courses precisely because they offer different settings and different modes of learning. Kulik concluded that "80% of the difference in test scores of academic and vocational students at the end of high school is due to the difference in aptitude of the students who enter the programs" (1994, 47). The key determinant of learning is the rigor of the courses taken, not the total number of academic courses or the total number of hours spent in a school building during a year. Thus, vocational students learn less mathematics and science than many academic students primarily because they take less demanding academic courses, not because they take fewer academic courses.

How many occupation-specific courses should non-college-bound high school students take? American vocational education has a modular structure. In high schools, the basic modular unit is typically a one-year course containing about 150 hours of classroom or shop time. Students need not complete a full program of four or more vocational courses to benefit from occupation-specific education. Among students who graduated in 1980 and did not attend college, those who took just two vocational courses in upper-secondary school earned 36 percent more in the year following graduation than those who took no such courses. Those who took four vocational courses earned 16 percent more than those who took two courses, and those who took six or more vocational courses earned 6 percent more than those who took four such courses (Kang and Bishop 1989). Mane's analysis (1997) of the early labor market success of 1992 high school graduates yields similar conclusions. These results suggest that (1) just about every student without definite plans to attend college full-time should take at least two—although four appears to be best—vocational courses before graduating, and that (2) vocational students should be counseled against taking an excessive number of vocational courses in high school. For occupations requiring more than 600 hours of classroom or shop time to attain proficiency, tech-prep programs integrating high school in-struction into a postsecondary program will generally be necessary.

CONCLUSION

Knowledge is exploding, and new skills are emerging every day. Our economy has become completely dependent on the expertise of others. Because of this dependence, we are willing to pay good wages to people who have skills and expertise that we lack. Rewards for specific skills are determined by the law of supply and demand. Abundant skills tend to be poorly rewarded. Scarce skills tend to be well rewarded. New skills in growing demand receive the highest compensation.

Most of a student's educational career is spent learning generic skills such as reading, writing, and arithmetic that are in abundant supply. Success in developing these skills does not, however, make one a highly competent worker or ensure a well-paid job. As Ralph Waldo Emerson observed in 1831, "The things taught in colleges and schools are not an education, but a means of education" (Tripp 1970, 173). These generic skills are tools for developing the scarcer skills and expertise that determine productivity in particular jobs and that are, therefore, well rewarded by the labor market.

It is unwise to devote one's entire education to learning things that most everyone else already knows. One must select a vocation for which one has talent and for which there is market demand and then pursue expertise and excellence within this niche. Expertise and excellence are impossible without specialization. Or, as Euripides put it, "The same man cannot well be skilled in everything; each has his special excellence."

Since individuals cannot achieve excellence without specialization, an education system that does not accommodate and indeed encourage specialization becomes a barrier to real excellence. People have diverse interests, diverse talents, and diverse learning styles. Employers are similarly diverse in the skills and talents they seek. A one-size-fits-all upper-secondary education is bound to fail the majority of students.

Occupational knowledge is cumulative and hierarchical in much the same way that mathematics and science are cumulative and hierarchical. Everyone must start at the bottom of the ladder of occupation knowledge and work his or her way up. The spread of information technology and of high-performance work systems is forcing workers to learn new skills, but the new skills are generally additions to, not replacement for, old skills. While learning a new skill is easier when the worker has good basic skills, a foundation of job knowledge and occupational skills is usually even more essential. At some point, every individual must start building his or her foundation of occupational skills. For the great majority of youths who do not have an uncle willing to take them on as an apprentice for a well-paid occupation, the foundation building should begin at least two years before the individual plans to leave school.

Students planning to work full-time when they graduate should not be forced or advised to focus solely on academic classes during their final years in high school. Such students should be advised to start building their foundation of occupational skills and knowledge while they are still in school. The option of returning to school or college in the future should be retained by certifying the skills attained and offering opportunities for further higher-level training at local community colleges.

Notes

1. The 500,000 members of NFIB were stratified by employment, and large firms were oversampled. Salaried managers in charge of subunits of large publicly owned corporations are not eligible for membership in NFIB, so the sample does not contain data on employment outcomes at large multiestablishment firms. A four-page questionnaire was mailed to approximately 11,000 firms, and, after three follow-up waves, 2599 responses were obtained. The survey focused on a single job—the job for which employers "hired the most people over the last two or three years."

2. After a series of general questions about the character of the job and the worker qualities that were sought when filling that job, the manager was asked to select two individuals who had been hired for this job and answer all subsequent questions specifically with reference to those two workers. The selection was made in response to the following question: "Please think of the last person hired for this job (job X) by your firm prior to August 1986 regardless of whether that person is still employed by your firm. Call this individual person A. The individual hired for job X immediately before person A is called person B. Do not include rehires of former employees." Information of varying degrees of completeness was obtained for 1624 person A's and 1403 person B's.

References

Altonji, Joseph. 1988. The Effects of High School Curriculum on Education and

Labor Market Outcomes. Chap. 3 of a report to the U.S. Department of Education from the National Center on Education and Employment, Department of Economics, Northwestern University, December.

Bishop, John H. 1992. The Impact of Academic Competencies on Wages, Unemployment and Job Performance. *Carnegie-Rochester Conference Series on Public Policy* 37(Dec.):127-94.

————. 1994. The Incidence and Payoff to Employer Training. Center for Advanced Human Resource Studies Working Paper 94-17, Cornell University, Ithaca, NY.

————. 1995. Expertise and Excellence. Center for Advanced Human Resource Studies Working Paper 95-13, Cornell University, Ithaca, NY.

Bowers, Norman and Paul Swaim. 1992. Probing (Some of) the Issues of Employment Related Training: Evidence from the CPS. U.S. Department of Agriculture, Economic Research Service. Duplicated.

Campbell, Paul B., Karen S. Basinger, Mary Beth Dauner, and Marie A. Parks. 1986. *Outcomes of Vocational Education for Women, Minorities, the Handicapped, and the Poor.* Columbus: Ohio State University, National Center for Research in Vocational Education.

Campbell, Paul B., Jack Elliot, Larry Hotchkiss, Suzanne Laughlin, and Ellen Seusy. 1987. *Antecedents of Training-Related Placement.* Columbus: Ohio State University, National Center for Research in Vocational Education.

Dunnette, Marvin D. 1972. *Validity Study Results for Jobs Relevant to the Petroleum Refining Industry.* Washington, DC: American Petroleum Institute.

Federal Institute for Vocational Training. 1986. *The Transition of Young People into Employment After Completion of Apprenticeship in the "Dual System."* West Berlin: Federal Institute for Vocational Training.

Grubb, W. Norton. 1992. Post-Secondary Education and the Sub-Baccalaureate Labor Market. *Economics of Education Review* 11(3):225-48.

————. 1997. The Returns to Education in the Sub-Baccalaureate Labor Market, 1984-1990. *Economics of Education Review* 16(3):231-45.

Hough, Leaetta M. 1988. *Personality Assessment for Selection and Placement Decisions.* Minneapolis, MN: Personnel Decisions Research Institute.

Hunter, J. E. 1983. Causal Analysis, Cognitive Ability, Job Knowledge, Job Performance, and Supervisor Ratings. In *Performance Measure and Theory*, ed. S. Lundy, F. Zedeck, and S. Cleveland. Hillsdale, NJ: Lawrence Erlbaum.

Kang, Suk and John Bishop. 1989. Vocational and Academic Education in High School: Complements or Substitutes. *Economics of Education Review* 8(2):133-48.

Krueger, Alan. 1993. How Computers Have Changed the Wage Structure: Evidence from Micro Data, 1984-1989. *Quarterly Journal of Economics* (Feb.):33-60.

Kulik, James A. 1994. *High School Vocational Education and Curricular Tracking.* Ann Arbor: University of Michigan.

Mane, Ferran. 1997. The Changing Labor Market for Recent High School Graduates. Cornell University. Duplicated.

Mangum, Steve and David Ball. 1989. Military Provided Occupational Training and Skill Transfer in the Post Draft Era. *Industrial and Labor Relations Review* 42(2).

Markey, James and William Parks. 1989. Occupational Change: Pursuing a Different Kind of Work. *Monthly Labor Review* (Sept.):3-12.

National Center for Education Statistics. 1993. *Occupational and Educational*

Outcomes of Recent College Graduates 1 Year After Graduation: 1991. Washington, DC: Department of Education.

Rumberger, R. W. and T. N. Daymont. 1982. The Impact of High School Curriculum on the Earnings and Employability of Youth. In *Job Training for Youth,* ed. R. Taylor, H. Rosen, and F. Pratzner. Columbus: Ohio State University, National Center for Research in Vocational Education.

Training for Jobs. 1994. *Economist,* 12 Mar.

Tripp, Rhoda Thomas, comp. 1970. *The International Thesaurus of Quotations.* New York: Harper & Row.

U.S. Bureau of the Census. 1993. *Money Income of Households, Families and Persons in the United States: 1992.* Current Population Reports, ser. P60-184, Department of Commerce, Sept.

Vineberg, Robert and John N. Joyner. 1982. *Prediction of Job Performance: Review of Military Studies.* Alexandria, VA: Human Resources Organization.

ANNALS, *AAPSS*, **559**, September 1998

School Resources
and Student Outcomes

By DAVID CARD and ALAN B. KRUEGER

ABSTRACT: In this article, David Card and Alan Krueger review the literature examining how school resources affect students' educational attainment and earnings. After addressing the challenges that researchers face in studying such a connection, the authors describe the theoretical framework they used to interpret the literature on schooling, school quality, and earnings. The framework is guided by four propositions: that earnings rise with educational attainment; that the marginal payoff to additional schooling is higher for those who attend quality schools; that, if the monetary payoff to an additional year of schooling rises, some students will attend school longer; and that a portion of the observed association between earnings and education is due to unobserved factors. After an account of the empirical findings in these studies, the authors conclude that there is some evidence that school resources affect earnings and educational attainment, although much uncertainty remains in the literature.

David Card is a professor of economics at the University of California, Berkeley. He was previously a professor of economics at Princeton University. Alan B. Krueger is Bendheim Professor of Economics and Public Affairs at Princeton University. He also served as chief economist of the U.S. Department of Labor from 1994 to 1995. They both have published extensively on the economics of schooling and serve as research associates for the National Bureau of Economic Research.

NOTE: This article was funded in part by a grant from the National Institute of Child Health and Development.

39

THIRTY years after the publication of the Coleman report in 1966 (Coleman et al. 1966) marks a fitting time to reassess the connection between school resources and student achievement. Coleman's original study and much of the literature it spawned are widely interpreted as showing that higher levels of school resources, such as lower class sizes, have no effect on student test scores. For example, Hanushek's influential survey of the literature concluded, "There appears to be no strong or systematic relationship between school expenditures and student performance" (1986, 1162).

The conclusion that schooling inputs such as class size and teacher pay have no impact on student achievement has come under renewed scrutiny for two main reasons. First, several recent meta-analyses—quantitative summaries of the estimates in the literature—suggest that greater resources do in fact lead to higher test scores. The authors of these studies argue that the literature contains too many positive estimates of the effect of resources on test scores to have occurred by chance, if resources truly do not matter (see Glass and Smith 1978; McGiverin, Gilman, and Tillitski 1989; Hedges and Stock 1983). Observe, for example, that Hanushek (1996) counts more than twice as many positive as negative estimates of the effect of expenditures per pupil on student achievement among the 141 studies that report their signs. If each estimate had a 50-50 chance of being positive or negative, the odds of observing so many positive estimates by chance is less than one in a million.[1] The low power of the individual estimates may explain why the preponderance of studies find statistically insignificant effects, while the combined literature points in the opposite direction. Meta-analysis also provides methods for accounting for the magnitude of estimated effects in the literature, as well as their signs. Hedges, Laine, and Greenwald (1994) conducted a meta-analysis of the studies surveyed by Hanushek (1986) and concluded that "the data are more consistent with a pattern that includes at least some positive relation between dollars spent on education and output, than with a pattern of no effects or negative effects" (5).

Second, and more germane to this article, is a body of literature that shifts attention away from test scores and focuses instead on how school resources affect students' educational attainment and earnings. Studying the impact of school resources on these long-term outcomes is critical because test scores are an imperfect measure of the value of school outputs. For example, Murnane, Willett, and Levy (1995) find that adding a standardized mathematics test score to a wage equation for male workers increases the explanatory power of the model by only about 2 percentage points. Heckman (1995) concludes, "Neither g [a measure of generalized intelligence] nor AFQT [the Armed Forces Qualifying Test] explains all that much of the variance in log wages" (1106). In sharp contrast to the literature on test scores, a number of studies have found a positive and statistically significant association between educational resources and students' educational attainment and earnings.

Researchers face a number of obstacles in studying the connection between school resources and economic outcomes. One difficulty is the need to wait until students finish school and enter the labor market. Consequently, researchers must have access to data sets that report not only the current earnings or completed education of adults but also information on the resources available in the schools they attended. Furthermore, since differences in the structure of the labor market may affect the reward to skills, and thus the measured impact of school resources, evaluations of the economic returns to school resources may require nontrivial identification assumptions, complex econometric modeling, or both. Another problem is that, compared to test score outcomes, the variance in earnings is large, making it more difficult to detect modest effects of school quality.

Omitted variables, such as parental background or state-level political variables, may bias the measured effect of school resources. (Of course, a parallel problem arises in nonexperimental studies of the effect of school resources on test scores.) Since the children of wealthier parents often attend schools with smaller class sizes and better-paid teachers, and since family background is thought to exert an independent effect on children's economic outcomes, there may be a spurious positive association between school resources and measured outcomes, even if school resources have no effect per se. On the other hand, students with weaker backgrounds may be assigned to remedial classes with higher resources per student, inducing a spurious negative correlation between school resources and student outcomes.

A study of economic outcomes requires a theoretical framework that incorporates the diverse interactions between family background, school inputs, educational attainment, and earnings. We therefore begin this article by outlining the key implications of such a model. This framework is then used to interpret estimates of the effect of school resources on educational attainment and earnings. Our reading of the empirical literature is that school resources tend to be positively associated with earnings and educational attainment but that the relationship is not always robust to specific features of the data set or empirical specification.

A difficult problem for most studies in the literature, including our own, is the presence of omitted variables that may be correlated with school quality. A potentially confounding problem is that many studies rely on aggregated (that is, school district or state-level) school-quality data rather than school- or classroom-level data. One way to overcome these problems is to follow students who were exposed to dramatically different educational resources for reasons having little to do with their own ability or their parents' wealth. The vastly different treatment of black and white students during the segregation era provides such a setting, and we have explored this issue in a longer version of this article (see Card and Krueger 1996b).

THEORETICAL FRAMEWORK FOR INTERPRETING THE LITERATURE

A useful framework for interpreting much of the literature on schooling, school quality, and earnings can be summarized by four theoretical propositions.[2]

Proposition 1: Earnings rise with educational attainment. If two individuals are otherwise identical, the one with more education tends to earn more. This proposition is based on one of the most firmly established empirical regularities in economics. A positive association between earnings and education holds across individuals even if one controls for other factors, such as IQ, family background, and work experience (Griliches 1977). It also holds across identical twins with different levels of education, and between groups who obtained different levels of schooling because of compulsory schooling laws or because they grew up near a college (Ashenfelter and Krueger 1994; Angrist and Krueger 1991; Harmon and Walker 1995; Kane and Rouse 1993; Card 1995). Although some of the observed correlation between earnings and education may be due to omitted variables—for example, those with more education may end up with higher earnings because of unobserved ability or family background factors—our reading of the literature is that this component is relatively small, on the order of 10 to 15 percent of the total effect. Furthermore, ran-

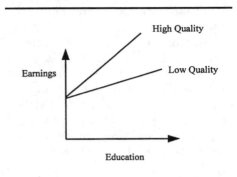

FIGURE 1
HYPOTHETICAL RELATIONSHIP

dom measurement errors in self-reported schooling may bias downward the observed slope between earnings and education by a similar magnitude.

Proposition 2: The marginal payoff to additional schooling is higher for those who attend higher-quality schools. This proposition is almost tautological: one would expect students who have access to higher-quality schools to benefit more per year of schooling than students who have access to lower-quality schools.[3] Figure 1, which shows the earnings-education profile rotating counter-clockwise from the y-intercept for those who attend higher-quality schools, illustrates the notion that higher-quality schooling increases the slope of the earnings-schooling relationship. Note, however, that it is an open question whether measured school resources (such as the pupil-teacher ratio) are related to the more abstract concept of school quality.

Proposition 3: If the monetary payoff to an additional year of schooling rises, some students will attend school longer. The observed relationship between school quality and earnings that emerges from a complete model of schooling and earnings is more complicated than that depicted in Figure 1 for several reasons. Importantly, as school quality increases, some students will attend school longer. This response may arise because students react to the economic incentives created by a higher payoff to schooling, or because school is more pleasant if quality is higher. In either event, a wide class of economic models predicts that improved school quality benefits some students by inducing them to stay in school longer, and this increase in educational attainment leads to higher pay.

Proposition 4: A portion of the observed association between earnings and education is due to unobserved factors that are jointly correlated with both variables. In other words, those who select higher-quality education tend to have greater earnings ability, irrespective of their education. Moreover, students who attend school longer in response to improved school quality (the implication from Proposition 3) will tend to be drawn disproportionately from the pool of more able students at lower grade levels. An interesting implication of this proposition is that the *observed* earnings-education profile will not rotate around the y-intercept at a zero level of education, as in Figure 1, but at a higher level of education, as illustrated in Figure 2. To understand why, consider what happens to the group of workers with the lowest level of education. If school quality

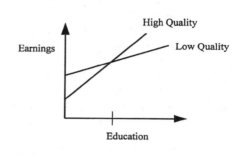

FIGURE 2
OBSERVED RELATIONSHIP

improves, the more able workers of this group will attend school longer, lowering the average earning ability of those who remain at a low level of education, and thus lowering the y-intercept in Figure 2. As school quality improves, the shrinking group of students with a low level of education will increasingly consist of less able individuals, who will appear to earn less, on average.

Omitted factors such as family background or student ability complicate the observed relationship between earnings and measured school quality in other ways as well. Suppose, for example, that students from wealthier families tend to stay in school longer and that these students would tend to earn more later on because of their family connections, regardless of their higher-quality education. In addition, suppose that wealthier families demand smaller class sizes, even though class size has no effect on actual school quality (that is, suppose there is no causal effect of school spending on education or earnings). In this case, the data will show a positive association between school spending and both educational attainment and earnings, although both correlations are spurious and merely reflect the failure to account for the independent effect of family wealth.

Nevertheless, the presence of omitted family background effects will not necessarily bias the correlation between measured school quality and the slope of the earnings-schooling relationship. To understand why, continue to suppose that children from wealthier family backgrounds in a given school or school district tend to have higher-quality education and higher earnings, so that part of the measured payoff to each additional year of schooling reflects omitted-variables bias. Under reasonable conditions, the magnitude of this bias will be similar for students from high-quality and low-quality school systems. Thus, comparing across school systems, the measured return to each additional year of schooling would be biased upward by a similar amount. In this case, differences in the slopes of the earnings-schooling relationship across higher- and lower-quality school systems will reflect true differences in the quality of schooling.

EMPIRICAL FINDINGS

For a detailed survey of the empirical literature on the link between school quality and economic outcomes, the interested reader might begin with Card and Krueger 1996a and Betts 1996. In the former, we concentrate on summarizing the effect of two particular educational inputs—expenditures per pupil and the pupil-teacher ratio—on educational attainment and earnings. We emphasize the pupil-teacher ratio because differences in class size account for close to one-half of the variation in expenditure per pupil across school districts and because changes in class size are the object of many educational reform proposals.

The theoretical framework outlined previously suggests two empirical strategies. In one approach, the structural earnings-schooling relationship illustrated in Figure 2 can be estimated, along with the effect of school quality, as measured by expenditures per pupil or the pupil-teacher ratio, on educational attainment. Alternatively, one can estimate the reduced form relationship between earnings and school resources—that is, a regression of earnings on measures of school quality like expenditures per pupil or the pupil-teacher ratio, without holding educational attainment constant.

The earliest wave of studies on school resources and economic outcomes, conducted in the late 1960s and 1970s, followed a third approach: researchers simply added measures of school quality to a standard human capital wage equation. Such models typically used educational attainment, work experience, parental education, urban residence, and, in some cases, IQ as explanatory variables. Earnings were based on individual observations. When a variable representing school quality was added, it was usually measured by average expenditures per pupil at the state or district level. All of these studies found that spending per student was positively associated with students' subsequent earnings, and most of the estimates were statistically significant at conventional levels.[4] The estimated elasticities from this literature fall in a fairly tight range: a 10 percent increase in school spending leads to about a 1 to 2 percent increase in subsequent earnings.

These specifications imply that the earnings-education profile has a fixed slope and that differences in school quality make this relationship shift up and down in a parallel fashion, as opposed to the tilting of the profile shown in Figure 1. A potentially undesirable feature of this specification is that it implies that more school resources raise (or lower) earnings by the same amount, regardless of the length of time that students are exposed to the greater resources in school. Additionally, because the studies hold educational attainment constant, the possibility that improved school quality might lead to higher wages by encouraging students to attend school longer is missed.

A second wave of studies allowed for school resources to have a differential effect on the slope and intercept of the earnings-education relationship. For example, Akin and Garfinkel (1980) estimate several wage regressions using micro data from the Panel Study on Income Dynamics (PSID). The dependent variable in their specification is the log of the wage rate (averaged over five years). The key explanatory variables of interest are state expenditures per student (in the decade in which the workers would have attended school), expenditures per student times years of education, and years of education. Their results indicate that greater spending per student is associated with higher earnings, but, contrary to the prediction in Figure 2, the effect occurs from an upward shift in the y-intercept rather than a steepening of the education gradient. Link, Ratledge, and Lewis (1980) replicate Akin and Garfinkel's model with the PSID as well as with the National Longitudinal Survey (NLS) of Young Men and generally find similar results.[5] Interestingly, both studies also find that if school resources are constrained to affect only the earnings-education slope, the earnings profile rotates as in Figure 1. In a recent paper, Altonji and Dunn (in press) use within-family differences in school resources to estimate this type of model with data from the NLS. By looking within families, they adjust for differences in omitted family background factors. Their findings imply that a 10 percent increase in spending per student is associated with a 1.3 percent increase in earnings. Interestingly, they find the estimated effect of school resources is greater, not smaller, when family background characteristics are held constant.

A potential problem with these second-wave studies is that the reward to skills may vary systematically across geographic areas with varying levels of school resources, and workers tend to stay in the area where they grew up. For example, in the southern United States, the return to education historically has been relatively high, while wages and school spending per student have been relatively low. This pattern could make it appear that higher school spending depresses the return to education, when the truth is that the South has invested less in education, keeping its return relatively high, and North-South migration has been insufficient to reduce the differential. Thus the second-wave estimates may confound labor market effects and school resource effects.

A third wave of estimates attempts to overcome problems caused by differential labor market structures across regions.[6] The conceptual experiment underlying these estimates is straightforward. Consider the workers observed in a particular labor market, for example, Chicago. Some workers in Chicago were educated in states with higher-quality school systems and others were educated in states with lower-quality schools. Among those working in Chicago, we would expect the earnings-education gradient to be steeper for workers who were educated in states with higher-quality schools. A weakness of this strategy is that there may be something unusual about those who moved from one area to another that confounds the effect of school resources.

In Card and Krueger 1992, we find that, in a given set of labor markets, the earnings-education slope does tend to increase for students who were educated in states with fewer pupils per teacher, higher average teacher pay, or a longer school year. In other words, the payoff to each additional year of education is greater for workers who come from areas with more resource-intensive schools, within a fixed labor market. This finding is strongest when co-

horts from given states are compared over time, which removes any effect of permanent state effects (such as unchanging state-level political variables). Identification of school-resource effects in these fixed-effects models comes from comparing successive cohorts of individuals from states like Alabama, which raised their school spending relative to states like New York. Further analysis indicates that the earnings-intercept tends to decline as resources increase. In short, the earnings relationship appears to pivot around a mid-level of education, as illustrated in Figure 2. We found that the crossover point in Figure 2 occurs around the high school graduate level. Our analysis makes use of the large samples afforded by the 1980 census.

Heckman, Layne-Farrar, and Todd (1996) extend this analysis using the 1970, 1980, and 1990 censuses. When they estimate virtually the same models as ours, they find similar effects of school resources in 1980 and somewhat larger effects in 1970 and 1990. The finding of larger effects of school resources in 1970 and 1990 is perhaps not surprising, since the payoff to education in general was at a relatively low level in 1980. Heckman, Layne-Farrar, and Todd also find that the intercept of the earnings-education relationship declines as school resources increase.

Heckman, Layne-Farrar, and Todd (1996) expand our basic econometric specification in several important directions. When they include regional aggregate supply and demand variables, the general pattern of results holds up. But when they allow for differential school resource effects by level of education, they find that school resources have little effect on earnings for workers who have not attended school beyond high school. The only education group for which resources are significantly related to earnings are those with a college education or higher. As school resources are measured at the secondary or elementary school level, this result may seem perplexing. One interpretation, however, is that higher school quality induces the most promising students to go further in school at each grade level, so the sample at each level of education becomes more select as school resources change.[7] Nonetheless, the effects of selective educational attainment are just conjecture at this stage, and the interpretation of the earnings-quality relationship conditional on education is still an open question. The reduced form models, which do not condition on education, provide one way of sidestepping this issue.

Another assumption that Heckman, Layne-Farrar, and Todd (1996) relax is the restriction that school quality has the same effect on the earnings-education slope in all regions. Regional differences in supply and demand conditions may alter the payoff to skills, and hence school quality, across regions. A related issue that they address is nonrandom migration. Workers may selectively sort across regions based on their comparative earnings advantage. (As noted earlier, the identification of school resource effects in Card and Krueger 1992a relies on the fact that migrants from states with different levels of school quality end up working in a common labor market.) As a

partial control for selective migration, Heckman, Layne-Farrar, and Todd control for the distance between the workers' region of origin and destination. These extensions weaken the effect of school resources and suggest that the return to higher school quality, as measured by the pupil-teacher ratio, varies across regions.[8]

The finding that school quality raises wages is not found in every data set. For example, using data from the National Longitudinal Survey of Youth (NLSY), Betts (1995) finds a statistically insignificant effect of school resources (measured by the high school's teacher-pupil ratio, teacher salary, and so on) on the earnings of young workers—on either the slope or the intercept in Figure 2. These data have important limitations for this purpose, however. The standard errors of the estimates from the NLSY are large, making it difficult to rule out small positive effects with a reasonable degree of confidence.[9] In addition, the sample has an average age of just 23, which means that many of the individuals have not yet finished school or settled into their careers, so wage effects for those with higher levels of schooling may be difficult to find. Nonetheless, Betts and others have interpreted his findings as evidence that school resources do not matter when the resources are measured at the school level, as opposed to the state or district level. We return to this point later.

Recall that school resources may also influence educational attainment. A majority of the studies of which we are aware have found positive and statistically significant effects of smaller class size on educational attainment. Some of these studies use micro data on individual's educational outcomes and school resources, while others use state- or district-level data. For example, Sander (1993) relates high school graduation rates to the pupil-teacher ratio across 154 Illinois school districts and for a subsample of 86 school districts in which there is only one high school in the district. In both cases, he finds that a 10 percent decrease in the pupil-teacher ratio is associated with about a 1.5 percentage point increase in the graduation rate. Heckman, Layne-Farrar, and Todd (1996) likewise find that a reduction in a state's pupil-teacher ratio tends to reduce the fraction of high school dropouts from that state and to raise the fraction of individuals who graduate from high school and (especially) college.

An advantage of the reduced form estimation approach—which involves a regression of earnings on school quality measures without controlling for educational attainment—is that it incorporates all the possible effects of school resources: on educational attainment, on the earnings-education profile, and on the intercept of the earnings-schooling relationship. In Card and Krueger 1992, we estimate a reduced form regression of (log) weekly wages on the state's pupil-teacher ratio, the worker's age and marital status, and dummy variables for residence in a metropolitan area, the state where the worker lives, and, in some models, the state where the worker was born. These models are relatively parsimonious, and so they are particularly susceptible to confounding effects from omitted variables. Nevertheless, the reduced form models have the advantage of making less restrictive identifying assumptions and are probably the most comparable specifications estimated across papers in the recent literature. Our 1992 reduced-form estimates based on the 1980 census imply that a 10 percent reduction in the average pupil-teacher ratio is associated with a 1.1 percent increase in weekly earnings. Betts's estimates (1995), which are based on NLSY earnings data and high school–level schooling data, imply that a 10 percent reduction in the average teacher-pupil ratio leads to a 0.4 percent increase in earnings.[10] Using the High School and Beyond Survey, Grogger's reduced-form estimates (in press) imply that a 10 percent increase in mean spending per student leads to a 0.7 percent increase in wages.

To summarize, much of the literature finds evidence of a positive and statistically significant relationship between school resources and earnings. By our count, some two-thirds of the two dozen studies on the impact of school spending or class size on earnings have found a statistically significant, positive effect of school resources (Card and Krueger 1996a). Positive effects of class size on educational attainment are also typically found in the literature.

We do not wish to paint an overly optimistic picture, however. Several important studies find statistically insignificant effects of changing school resources. Heckman, Layne-Farrar, and Todd (1996) have shown that the effect of school resources measured in Card and Krueger 1992 break down when some of the identifying assumptions (for example, linear education) are relaxed. Moreover, there are always questions in observational studies regarding whether relevant variables have been left out. Because wealthier families tend to invest more in their children at home and to live in communities with better-endowed schools, omitted family background may be a particular problem.

Betts (1996) and Hanushek (1996) note that biases created by omitted variables are possibly larger in studies that measure school resources at a more aggregate level, such as the state or school district level. Hanushek, Rivkin, and Taylor (1996) argue that state political variables are a particular problem for aggregate studies. Although this is possible, the fact that the models reported in Card and Krueger 1992 and Heckman, Layne-Farrar, and Todd 1996 that include state-fixed effects tend to show larger, rather than smaller, effects of school quality suggests to us that omitted state-level variables may lead to the opposite bias. In any event, the argument that omitted variables are a bigger problem for studies that use aggregate school quality data would be stronger if such omitted variables could be identified and if their inclusion in the regression models was shown to attenuate the effect of aggregate school resource measures.

A related problem concerns the endogeneity of school resources within schools (or within school districts). Children who perform poorly may be assigned to smaller classes, for example. With individual-level resource data, this may lead to downward-biased estimates of the effects of school resources. On the other hand, highly motivated children may be attracted to magnet schools with higher resources per pupil, leading to upward-biased estimates. In either case, the use of aggregated school quality measures will tend to lessen the biases of endogenous school resources within schools or districts. Finally, measurement error in school resources should be a cause for concern. Even the best micro data sets tend to have school resource data for one year, providing only a snapshot of the student's educational career, while district- or state-level resource data are more likely to average out year-to-year fluctuations in resources. Aggregated data reduce or eliminate random measurement errors that make it difficult to detect school resource effects using micro-level school quality data.

Ideally, these sources of bias could be eliminated by a randomized experiment, in which students are assigned to classes with different pupil-teacher ratios (or differences in other resources) and then followed over time. We are aware of only one large-scale randomized experiment involving class size, which pertained to elementary students in Tennessee (Mosteller 1995). This experiment showed a positive effect of lower class size on test scores at the lowest grades. We know of no randomized experiment that has been used to evaluate economic outcomes of schooling. In the absence of a true random experiment, it may be useful to consider the evidence generated by natural experiments—situations in which large differences in school resources were provided to seemingly similar individuals for arbitrary reasons. One interesting example of such a situation is the experience of black and white students in North and South Carolina, which we have explored in another version of this article (Card and Krueger 1996b).

CONCLUSION

Does the literature on school resources, educational attainment, and earnings prove beyond a reasonable doubt that resources matter? We do not believe that the evidence justifies so strong a conclusion. The available evidence is not unambiguous or ubiquitous, and it suffers from all the standard criticisms of drawing causal inferences from observational data.

To some extent, interpreting the literature depends on the strength of one's expectations. If one starts from the position that school resources do not make a difference, then one can point to the bulk of the evidence on the lack of a statistically significant connection between school resources and test scores, and a handful of studies on economic outcomes, to support that view. On the other hand, if one starts from the view that resources do make a difference, then the available evidence on school quality and economic outcomes may be interpreted as generally supportive. Perhaps the strongest evidence that resources matter comes from an analysis of the vast differences in resources for blacks and whites who attended schools in the segregated states. We suspect that further re-

search focusing on particular episodes of large changes in school quality—such as our simple case study of North and South Carolina (Card and Krueger 1996b)—might be valuable.

Thirty years after the Coleman report (Coleman et al. 1966), it is unfortunate and frustrating that more is not known about the outcomes of schooling. While most of the literature on test scores points to little, if any, effect of school resources, some observational studies and one actual experiment have found a connection. Although an unfortunate proposition, decisions about educational resources and reform must still be made in an environment of much uncertainty.

Notes

1. If all the estimates with unknown signs are counted as negative, the odds are still less than 1 in 100. On the other hand, Hanushek finds a much weaker pattern for the teacher-pupil ratio. But one must wonder whether some of these studies controlled for both the teacher-pupil ratio and expenditures per student in their estimating equations.

2. This model is developed formally in Card and Krueger 1996a. Also see Lang 1993 for a related model.

3. This analysis ignores any general equilibrium effects of changing the endowment of human capital. This assumption can be justified if the school system under consideration is small relative to the rest of the economy, so the price of human capital is set exogenously in the market.

4. Examples of this literature include Morgan and Sirageldin 1968; Johnson and Stafford 1973; and Rizzuto and Wachtel 1980. An example that found an insignificant positive effect of school resources is Ribich and Murphy 1975.

5. School spending per student in the NLS data pertains to the average secondary school in the district where the worker lived.

6. A seminal paper of this genre is by Behrman and Birdsall (1983), which studies school resources in Brazil. Because the emphasis in the present article, however, is on the United States, we do not describe their findings in detail.

7. By analogy, a high-quality undergraduate economics program is likely to have its most beneficial effect on students who continue on to graduate school. Would any department chair want his or her program evaluated on the basis of a sample that explicitly excluded students who continued on to graduate school?

8. Although Heckman, Layne-Farrar, and Todd (1996) find that school resources have a varying effect on the earnings-education slope across regions, in most regions a smaller pupil-teacher ratio is associated with a higher payoff to additional education.

9. Betts (1995) does not adjust the standard errors of his estimates for the fact that there are as many as 10 wage observations per individual in the NLSY sample. Betts generously provided us with his data, and we have used his sample to calculate standard errors that account for the correlation across earnings observations for the same individual over time. This adjustment raises the estimated standard errors by up to 100 percent.

10. These elasticities are calculated at the means of their respective data sets. The t-ratio of the Card and Krueger estimate reported in this paragraph is 6.2; for the Betts estimate, it is 1.7. However, both t-ratios are probably overstated because of multiple earnings observations per worker or per state. In specifications that include cumulative work experience rather than age, Betts finds a weaker effect of the teacher-pupil ratio. Because work experience may be influenced by educational attainment, which in turn may be influenced by school resources, we chose to hold constant age instead of experience in the reduced form models in our 1992 article.

References

Akin, John S. and Irwin Garfinkel. 1980. The Quality of Education and Cohort Variation in Black-White Earnings Differentials: Comment. *American Economic Review* 70(Mar.):186-91.

Altonji, Joseph and Thomas Dunn. In press. Using Siblings to Estimate the Effect of School Quality on Wages. *Review of Economics and Statistics* 78(4):665-67.

Angrist, Joshua D. and Alan B. Krueger. 1991. Does Compulsory Schooling Affect Schooling and Earnings? *Quarterly Journal of Economics* 106:(Nov.):979-1014.

Ashenfelter, Orley and Alan Krueger. 1994. Estimates of the Economic Return to Schooling from a New Sample of Twins. *American Economic Review* 84(5):1157-73.

Behrman, Jere and Nancy Birdsall. 1983. The Quality of Schooling: Quantity Alone Is Misleading. *American Economic Review* 73(Dec.):928-46.

Betts, Julian. 1995. Does School Quality Matter? Evidence from the National Longitudinal Survey of Youth. *Review of Economics and Statistics* 77(2):231-50.

———. 1996. Is There a Link Between School Inputs and Earnings? Fresh Scrutiny of an Old Literature. In *The Link Between Schools, Student Achievement, and Adult Success*, ed. Gary Burtless. Washington, DC: Brookings Institution.

Card, David. 1995. Schooling, Earnings and Ability Revisited. In *Research in Labor Economics*, ed. Solomon Polachek. Vol. 14. Greenwich, CT: JAI Press.

Card, David and Alan B. Krueger. 1992. Does School Quality Matter? Returns to Education and the Characteristics of Public Schools in the United States. *Journal of Political Economy* 100(Feb.):1-40.

———. 1996a. Labor Market Effects of School Quality: Theory and Evidence. In *Does Money Matter? The Effect of School Resources on Student Achievement and Adult Success*, ed. Gary Burtless. Washington, DC: Brookings Institution.

———. 1996b. School Resources and Student Outcomes: An Overview of the Literature and New Evidence from North and South Carolina. *Journal of Economic Perspectives* 10(4):31-50.

Coleman, James S. et al. 1966. *Equality of Educational Opportunity*. Washington, DC: Department of Health, Education, and Welfare.

Glass, Gene and M. L. Smith. 1978. *Meta-Analysis of Research on the Relationships of Class Size and Achievement*. ERIC Document Reproduction Service no. ED 168 129.

Griliches, Zvi. 1977. Estimating the Returns to Schooling: Some Econometric Problems. *Econometrica* 45(Jan.):1-22.

Grogger, Jeff. In press. School Expenditures and Post-Schooling Earnings: Evidence from High School and Beyond. *Review of Economics and Statistics* 78(4):628-37.

Hanushek, Eric, Steven Rivkin, and Lori Taylor. 1996. The Identification of School Resource Effects. University of Rochester. Paper.

Hanushek, Eric A. 1986. The Economics of Schooling: Production and Efficiency in Public Schools. *Journal of Economic Literature* 24(Sept.):1141-77.

———. 1996. School Resources and Student Performance. In *Does Money Matter? The Effect of School Resources on Student Achievement and Adult Success*, ed. Gary Burtless. Washington, DC: Brookings Institution.

Harmon, Colm and Ian Walker. 1995. Estimates of the Economic Return to Schooling in the U.K. *American Economic Review* 85(5):1278-86.

Heckman, James J. 1995. Lessons from the Bell Curve. *Journal of Political Economy* 103(5):1091-1120.

Heckman, James J., Anne Layne-Farrar, and Petra Todd. 1996. Does Measured School Quality Really Matter? An Examination of the Earnings-Quality Relationship. In *Does Money Matter? The Effect of School Resources on Student Achievement and Adult Success*, ed. Gary Burtless. Washington, DC: Brookings Institution.

Hedges, L. V. and W. Stock. 1983. The Effects of Class Size: An Examination of Rival Hypotheses. *American Educational Research Journal* 20:63-65.

Hedges, Larry V., Richard Laine, and Rob Greenwald. 1994. Does Money Matter? A Meta-Analysis of Studies of the Effects of Differential School Inputs on Student Outcomes. *Education Researcher* 23(Apr.):5-14.

Johnson, George and Frank Stafford. 1973. Social Returns to Quantity and Quality of Schooling. *Journal of Human Resources* 8(Spring):139-55.

Kane, Thomas and Cecilia Rouse. 1993. Labor Market Returns to Two- and Four-Year Colleges: Is a Credit a Credit and Do Degrees Matter? Working paper no. 311, Industrial Relations Section, Princeton University, Princeton, NJ.

Lang, Kevin. 1993. Ability Bias, Discount Rate Bias and the Return to Education. Boston University. Paper.

Link, Charles, Edward Ratledge, and Kenneth Lewis. 1980. The Quality of Education and Cohort Variation in Black-White Earnings Differentials: Reply. *American Economic Review* 70:196-203.

McGiverin, J. D., D. Gilman, and C. Tillitski. 1989. A Meta-Analysis of the Relation Between Class Size and Achievement. *Elementary School Journal* 90(Sept.):47-56.

Morgan, James and Ismail Sirageldin. 1968. A Note on the Quality Dimension in Education. *Journal of Political Economy* 76(Sept.-Oct.):1069-77.

Mosteller, Fredrick. 1995. The Tennessee Study of Class Size in the Early School Grades. *Critical Issues for Children and Youths* 5(Summer-Fall):113-27.

Murnane, Frank, John B. Willett, and Frank Levy. 1995. The Growing Importance of Cognitive Skills in Wage Determination. *Review of Economics and Statistics* 77(2):251-66.

Ribich, Thomas I. and James L. Murphy. 1975. The Economic Returns to Increased Educational Spending. *Journal of Human Resources* 10(Spring): 56-77.

Rizzuto, Ronald and Paul Wachtel. 1980. Further Evidence on the Returns to School Quality. *Journal of Human Resources* 15(Spring):240-54.

Sander, William. 1993. Expenditures and Student Achievement in Illinois: New Evidence. *Journal of Public Economics* 52(Oct.):403-16.

ANNALS, *AAPSS*, **559**, September 1998

Social Benefits of Education

By NEVZER STACEY

ABSTRACT: The majority of research on the outcomes of education has focused on the effect of educational attainment on individuals' wages and on the level of skill in the economy as a whole. In this article, however, Nevzer Stacey argues that examining the social benefits of education beyond its economic impact would provide a more comprehensive informational basis for developing national educational policies. She reviews the literature that examines the impact of educational attainment on four areas of potential intervention: health; family structure, fertility, and child care; the environment; and crime. Although these studies report some statistics on education, virtually none uses measures of learning or inputs related to the learning process to estimate the effect of education. Stacey concludes that a more systematic analysis is needed to improve our understanding of the full effect of education on society in order to determine appropriate public policy.

Nevzer Stacey is a senior research analyst at the Office of Educational Research and Improvement (OERI), U.S. Department of Education. She is OERI's team leader for research on transitions from education to work and adult learning. She serves as the leader for U.S. participation in the Organization of Economic Cooperation and Development's Study on the Transitions from Initial Education to Working Life. From 1995 to 1997, she was special assistant to the director of the National School-to-Work Office.

FOR decades, the primary argument for justifying education has been driven by its direct economic effects. Yet it is widely perceived that the effects of education spread beyond direct economic effects to include noneconomic, or social, benefits for individuals and society at large. These benefits include a better way of taking care of ourselves and, consequently, creating a better society in which to live. Quantifying these social benefits is a difficult task, but analyzing them more systematically would improve not only our understanding of the full effects of education but also the informational basis for considering education policies.

An analysis of the social benefits of education requires three steps:

— development of a common set of measures with regard to what we mean by education and its benefits;
— assessment of the causal impact of education on these social benefits; and
— determination of whether these social benefits necessitate any public policy interventions.

Social-benefit issues have been explored at some length in certain fields, particularly in health. In other fields, however, a great deal of work remains to be done. To promote better understanding of these issues in education, the Office of Educational Research and Improvement of the U.S. Department of Education commissioned a series of papers by experts in four fields: health, parenting, the environment, and crime. Their research findings vary; the impacts are significant regarding health and minimal regarding the environment. The findings in each of the four areas are described next.

HEALTH

Michael Grossman and Robert Kaestner, who reported on the "effects of education on health" (1997), summarized trends in the educational attainment and health of the U.S. population since 1960. They focused on empirical research using U.S. data as they attempted to establish a causal relationship between more schooling and better health. They considered externalities and possible rationales for governmental interventions in the health care of its citizens, including better education.

Specifically, the evidence presented by Grossman and Kaestner shows that, in the last 30 years, much progress has been made in raising schooling levels and reducing infant mortality. For example, the number of white high school graduates approximately doubled between 1960 and 1990, and the corresponding number for African Americans tripled (U.S. Bureau of the Census 1993, tab. 231). Equally impressive results were reported in lowering the infant mortality rates in African American infants (U.S. Department of Health and Human Services 1994, tabs. 1-3 and 2-1).

A considerable number of studies in the United States suggest that the number of completed years of formal schooling is the most important predictor of good health (Auster, Leveson, and Sarachek 1969; Grossman 1972; Silver 1972; Grossman and Benham 1974). These studies also indicate that schooling is a more important correlate of health than is occupation or income. How is this association possible? One can argue that there is a causal relationship between health and education—that is, health improves as we increase schooling. Alternatively, we can hypothesize the inverse: healthier individuals are more likely to attain more schooling. Finally, we could state that there is no causal relationship at all. In other words, the state of a person's health could have nothing to do with the amount of schooling he or she has.

One way of looking at the effects of schooling on health is to focus on mortality rates. There are a few studies that challenge the importance of schooling as a determinant of mortality (Duleep 1986; Behrman et al. 1991; Menchik 1993). One study, in particular, concludes that low income has a significant effect on mortality (Duleep 1986). These results may be biased, however, since the sample was limited to married men, who have lower mortality and higher education than their single counterparts do. Another study, conducted in 1982 by Fuchs, also challenges the conclusion that schooling has a substantial causal impact on health. Fuchs states that the relationship may be due to a third factor—individuals' time preferences, which are choices made to invest in long-term payoffs rather than short-term benefits. Other studies have examined the effects of schooling on areas such as smoking, the use of seat belts, children's nutritional intake, good health, and cognitive development. There are numerous studies that have been supported by the World Bank that focus on the effects of mothers' schooling on infants' and children's health and nutrition.

In summary, the review of major studies indicates that education has a positive causal effect on good health. The question that remains to be answered is whether there is reason for government intervention to correct for externalities and capital market imperfections and the possibility to promote a more equal distribution of health outcomes. Until the mechanisms through which schooling affects health have been fully identified, the answer is no. Behavioral changes are difficult and costly to achieve; therefore, research based on national data on a variety of health outputs, and a complete set of health and schooling inputs, must precede any public policy intervention.

FAMILY STRUCTURE, FERTILITY, AND CHILD WELFARE

The second field that also appears to have a close relationship to education is discussed by Rebecca A. Maynard and Daniel J. McGrath in "Family Structure, Fertility, and Child Welfare" (1997). According to these authors, "The public school system, together with the family, is the main institution for socializing American children." With the rising entry of women into the labor market, the longer number of hours that children are away from home, and the growing number of families headed by a single parent, schools are carrying a larger responsibility in children's social development and welfare.

The review of literature shows us that there is an important relationship between education and national trends in family formation patterns, fertility patterns, parenting, and child welfare. Most studies on this topic indicate that students' investments in schooling and its educational outcomes—that is, academic performance and educational attainment—directly affect their future earnings and family patterns. There are many positive social outcomes associated with higher levels of school completion. For example, rates of poverty, out-of-wedlock childbearing, early family formation, and child abuse and neglect are all substantially lower among high school graduates than among dropouts (Moore 1994; Zill 1994). Other studies also indicate that child abuse and neglect are associated with lower levels of parental education (Finkelfor 1994; Roper and Weeks 1993).

Maynard and McGrath (1997) also review the literature that shows direct and enduring effects of education on the physical environment of the home, such as the amount and quality of time parents spend with their children, the number of children and spacing of their births, and changes in family status.

What appears to emerge from all these studies is the mediating role of education. Based on this knowledge, a large number of programs have been established to improve outcomes, but, unfortunately, the results have been disappointing. These are mostly due to our inability to create interventions that influence behavior. Even when the programs appear to be effective, the time period required to observe any changes in behavior is much longer than when

evaluations are expected to show beneficial gains. When justifying the investment of public funds, there is always a pressing need to provide evidence that a program is effective and is producing the intended outcomes. What rarely happens is the improvement of programs based on information gathered from performance measures. It is extremely difficult to evaluate the impact of such public interventions in the short term. As long as some studies on different aspects of family health and welfare continue to show encouraging results, it is imperative that societies make the necessary investment to capture the intergenerational effects of public investment in education.

ENVIRONMENT

Can education promote private behavior that enhances environmental quality for everyone or increases individuals' effectiveness in protecting themselves from negative environmental effects? In his "Feedback Effects and Environmental Resources" (1997), V. Kerry Smith attempts to address this question. Like others who have searched for direct or indirect evidence of the effects of education on behavioral responses, Smith finds no direct evidence. He also finds no literature on education's role in improving environmental quality.

In the absence of relevant research, the task becomes one of defining terms and interpreting existing models. For example, in the Becker-Mincer labor market model (Becker 1965), education is represented by the number of years of schooling completed by each individual. This model does not take into consideration the quality of education that is received, and it ignores any role education may play in contributing to other aspects of an individual's activities. One such model was developed by Haveman and Wolfe (1994). They use their calculation of the value of education through its impact on the attainment of desired outcomes, such as family size and child spacing. Even if these models were correctly to reflect an effect due to education, one could argue that the individuals did not choose to get education in order to accomplish these goals. Therefore, the lesson to be learned from examining existing models is that a certain amount of education can produce different behaviors.

But the interpretation of the behaviors is very complex and would depend a great deal on how clear-cut the signs for implied effects actually are. As indicated by studies by Smith and Desvousges (1987)—which were designed to estimate people's willingness to pay for reductions in the risk of being exposed to hazardous waste—it is not clear that the interpretation of education as enhancing people's understanding of the issues is quite accurate. Viscusi and Magat's research on product warnings (1987) does not find a significant role for education in enhancing the effects of a warning either. The number of years of schooling is again a positive contributor to the behavioral intention, but it is not significant.

One of the most interesting aspects of the findings for judging the effects of education is the differential impact of education on behavior. The

studies conducted by Ippolito and Mathios (1990) on women with no college and some college education show differences in the consumption of cereal related to advertising on the fiber content of the cereal. Once again, education plays a role in influencing people's performance in market and nonmarket tasks, thus opening the door to the recognition that these impacts can alter policy. The role for education as a complementary factor in improving the performance of public information and risk communication related to environmental resources becomes paramount. The increasing complexity of environmental problems warrants a better understanding and communication of information about environmental resources. Given that there is very little research on education's role in improving environmental quality, the question that is important to address is the role of education in environmental policymaking: how can education promote particular private behaviors and enable individuals to protect themselves from negative environmental effects? This may be a new perspective on the possible social benefits of education.

CRIME

In the search for determining the social benefits of education, the fourth area reviewed is that of crime. Ann Dryden Witte's review of the literature (1997) suggests possible crime-reducing effects of education, but the empirical evidence regarding the effects of education on crime is limited. The review of crime in the last 20 years shows that today's levels are lower than in the late 1970s and early 1980s. Donohue and Siegelman (1994) provide the most comprehensive review of crime statistics and data showing how the composition of crime has changed. Yet they conclude that there is a lack of evidence on how crime is related to education.

Models on understanding criminal behavior fall into three broad categories: economic, sociological, and psychological. In the early economic models developed by Becker (1965), education played no role at all. Earlier models also had limited relevance for juveniles, who play a substantial and increasing role in the crime problem today. Later on, economists began to develop time-allocation models where education, like work, became a substitute activity. These later models suggest possible ways of incorporating economic models of crime, based on psychological processes (David 1988; Flinn 1986; Tauchen and Witte 1995).

Flinn's model (1986) suggests that human capital formation decreases crime directly because it raises wages. More recently, economists have become interested in habit formation, addiction, and peer group effects. Some economists are also interested in consumer demand. This type of model incorporates education by having education impart information about a particular activity and by providing information on its costs and benefits.

Sampson and Groves (1989) developed a model that considers the effect of sociodemographic factors on measures of community disorganization and its effects on crime. Although this model does not directly take education's effects on crime into consideration, it uses social network theory to measure social organizations. It opens the door for exploring the effects of education on crime, if it can be argued that schools as social organizations can be a source for organizing the community.

Moffitt (1993) has developed an interesting psychological model that argues that persistent, long-term offenders exhibit a wide range of antisocial behaviors during their lifetimes. She sees adolescent-limited criminal behavior as pervasive and tied to a "maturity gap." She believes that teenagers now mature earlier, but their transition to adulthood is more delayed than ever before. To support this typology, Nagin, Farrington, and Moffitt (1995) identified a group of adolescent-limited offenders on the basis of official records. This group appears to have adopted traditional lifestyles. Self-reports indicate that this group continues to offend; however, these offenses are those with low probabilities of detection, such as employee theft and drug use. This work may suggest a number of possible anticrime roles for education. A few suggestions may be that schools need to have more adult-like environments, combine work and school, and facilitate the integration of adult and teen cultures.

The analysis of much experimental evidence suggests that programs that provide intensive education for preschool children and their parents result in the most persistent crime-reduction effects. Early childhood interventions have received much attention, and public policy dealing with prevention appears to be less expensive than dealing with the problems at a later date. Whether these early intervention programs can be adopted for juveniles is questionable. In the absence of evidence from experiments, the need to review correctional studies becomes imperative. Unfortunately, education's role in studies of crime has not been analyzed in great detail. A few studies incorporate the time spent in educational activities as an explanatory variable. They find that time spent at school and time spent working are associated with a significantly lower level of criminal activity (Gottfredson 1985; Farrington, Gallagher, and Morley 1986; Viscusi 1986; Witte and Tauchen 1994).

These results must be viewed with caution. Correctional studies of crime are difficult for a number of reasons, but a review of the literature provides a number of insights upon which an explicit model for the impact of education on crime might be constructed. The first is that most crime is committed by male adolescents. The second is that a disproportionate amount of the violent crime is committed by a relatively small group of persistent offenders who begin their antisocial behavior at a very early age. A third finding is that neither the number of years of schooling completed nor receipt of a high school diploma has a significant effect on an individual's level of criminal activity. Communities with larger numbers of unsupervised teenagers and little community involvement among residents have higher crime rates. These facts suggest a number of possible avenues for the crime-reducing effect of education. For example, among the many roles of education is the milieu it provides; the clear goals, rules, and firm discipline in schools may be an environment that can produce desired anticrime outcomes.

In summary, if education does help to reduce crime, it appears that the impact will arise from the educational programs' socializing and supervisory roles and not from their primary educational activities. However, there is great need for new correctional studies based on models that incorporate the role of education and use longitudinal data to bring new insights to some crucial questions.

CONCLUSION

Although in a number of fields, the social benefits of education are frequently discussed, the measurement of education, such as the use of schooling attainments with no information on school quality, may bias estimates of education effects in either direction. Virtually none of the studies in the current literature on the social benefits of education uses measures of learning or inputs in the learning process other than the number of years spent in school. While cognitive achievements represent an important product of schooling and an important dimension of education, there may be other dimensions—such as self-discipline, problem-solving capabilities, specific skills, general knowledge, and learning how to learn—that also are important in assessing the social benefits of education. Unfortunately, the reviews of the current literature have uncovered no efforts to assess such possibilities systematically.

The data on outcomes potentially affected by education are often very crude, may be available only for selected subsamples, and only partially represent the outcomes of interest. Such data problems can affect what we think we know about the social benefits of education and our choice of strategies for attempting to estimate them (Behrman 1997). The critical point is not whether some benefits or outcome indicators have more or less random measurement error than others, but whether there are systematic errors. These measurement problems, unfortunately, have been barely touched in the literature on the social benefits of education. Better measures of the multiple dimensions of the social effects of education may alter our perceptions of what the more important benefits are.

A serious problem is the difficulty of capturing the external effects of education. For example, a better-educated farmer may provide his neighbor with a better example of the application of new technology and thereby provide a positive externality. In addition, a better-educated farmer may find it easier to learn from a neighbor, so the transmission of the externality may be facilitated. Better longitudinal data on individuals and on their neighbors or co-workers from whom they may learn could permit the identification of some of the external social benefits of education.

Another measurement problem is that available data, with some excep-tions, primarily are nonexperimental, behavioral, or cross-sectional. Longitudinal behavioral data permit much better control for endogenous choices and unobserved factors such as preferences and abilities in the analysis of the social impact of education than do cross-sectional data, which are the data that primarily have been used in analyses to date. Longitudinal data, though more costly to collect, have the potential for substantial gains in our understanding of the social benefits of education. There would be gains in understanding if more efforts were made to obtain good experimental data, but, for some questions, experiments are precluded by costs or ethical concerns.

In addition to the measurement problems, there are serious concerns associated with determining the causal effect of education from behavioral data. Ascertaining the causal impact of education, as opposed to associations of education with various outcomes, is extremely difficult precisely because education reflects choices of individuals, families, communities, and policymakers. These choices are made in the presence of important factors that are not measured in most data sets used to analyze the effects of education.

Once the social benefits of education are determined, they may have important policy implications. That education may have some strong positive social benefits is not in itself an efficiency reason for policy intervention and support. In addition, there must be a presumption of market failure, in the sense that the total effects differ from the private effects, and some presumption that policy failures will not be of a magnitude that will swamp possible gains from policy interventions. But our opportunities to influence family environments are extremely limited. We can pump in resources, but we cannot be sure that those resources will get to the children. We can offer family support services, but we cannot be sure that parents will use them. It is virtually impossible to use public policy to induce parents to love and look out for their children. Public policy does, however, have direct access to children for significant periods of time when those children are in school. The basic policy question is whether we can use that time to enhance the futures of our children.

Finally, policies have to be made on the basis of imperfect information, but the very limited evidence on which to base such policies does mean that there are considerable potential gains from further research that addresses the issues outlined here.

References

Auster, R., I. Leveson, and D. Sarachek. 1969. The Production of Health: An Exploratory Study. *Journal of Human Resources* 4:411-36.

Becker, G. S. 1965. A Model of the Allocation of Time. *Economic Journal* 75:493-517.

Behrman, J., R. Sickles, P. Taubman, and A. Yazbeck. 1991. Black-White Mortality Inequalities. *Journal of Econometrics* 50:183-203.

Behrman, Jere. 1997. Conceptual and Measurement Issue. In *Social Benefits of Education*, ed. Jere R. Behrman and Nevzer Stacey. Ann Arbor: University of Michigan Press.

David, M. L. 1988. Time and Punishment Again: An Intertemporal Model of Crime. *Journal of Political Economy* 96:383-90.

Donohue, J. and P. Siegelman. 1994. Is the United States at the Optimal Rate of Crime? Working paper, School of Law, Northwestern University, Chicago.

Duleep, H. O. 1986. Measuring the Effect of Income on Adult Mortality Using Longitudinal Administrative Record Data. *Journal of Human Resources* 21:238-51.

Farrington, D., B. Gallagher, and L. Morley. 1986. Unemployment, School Learning, and Crime. *British Journal of Criminology* 26:335-36.

Finkelfor, D. 1994. Current Information on the Scope and Nature of Child Abuse. *Future of Children* 4:32-53.

Flinn, C. 1986. Dynamic Models of Criminal Careers. In *Criminal Careers*, ed. A. Blumstein, J. Cohen, J. Roth, and C. Visher. Washington, DC: National Academy Press.

Fuchs, V. R. 1982. *Time Preference and Health: An Exploratory Study*. Chicago: University of Chicago Press.

Gottfredson, D. C. 1985. Youth Employment, Crime, and Schooling. *Developmental Psychology* 21:419-32.

Grossman, M. 1972. *The Demand for Health: A Theoretical and Empirical Investigation*. New York: Columbia University Press.

Grossman, M. and L. Benham. 1974. Health, Hours, and Wages. In *The Economics of Health and Medical Care*, ed. M. Perlman. New York: John Wiley.

Grossman, M. and Robert Kaestner. 1997. Effects of Education on Health. In *Social Benefits of Education*, ed. Jere R. Behrman and Nevzer Stacey. Ann Arbor: University of Michigan Press.

Haveman, R. and B. Wolfe. 1994. *Succeeding Generations: On the Effects of*

Investments in Children. New York: Russell Sage Foundation.

Ippolito, P. M. and A. D. Mathios. 1990. Information, Advertising, and Health Choices: A Study of the Cereal Market. *Rand Journal of Economics* 21:459-80.

Maynard, R. A. and Daniel J. McGrath. 1997. Family Structure, Fertility, and Child Welfare. In *Social Benefits of Education*, ed. Jere R. Behrman and Nevzer Stacey. Ann Arbor: University of Michigan Press.

Menchik, P. L. 1993. Economic States as a Determinant of Mortality Among Black and White Older Men: Does Poverty Kill? *Population Studies* 47:427-36.

Moffitt, Terrie. 1993. Adolescence-Limited and Life-Course-Persistent Antisocial Behavior: A Development Taxonomy. *Psychological Review* 100:674-701.

Moore, K. 1994. Trends in Teenage Children. Paper presented at the seminar series in Persistent Poverty Conference on the Causes and Costs of Teen Motherhood, sponsored by the American Enterprise Institute.

Nagin, D., D. Farrington, and T. Moffitt. 1995. Life-Course Trajectories of Different Types of Offenders. *Criminology* 33:111-40.

Roper, P. and G. Weeks. 1993. *Child Abuse, Teenage Pregnancy, and Welfare Dependency: Is There a Link?* Olympia, WA: Evergreen State College, State Institute for Public Policy.

Sampson, R. and W. Groves. 1989. Community Structure and Crime: Testing Social-Disorganization Theory. *American Journal of Sociology* 94:774-802.

Silver, M. 1972. An Economic Analysis of Spatial Variations in Mortality Rates by Race and Sex. In *Essays in the Economics of Health and Medical Care*, ed. V. R. Fuchs. New York: Columbia University Press.

Smith, V. K. and W. H. Desvousges. 1987. An Empirical Analysis of the Economic Value of Risk Changes. *Journal of Political Economy* 95:89-114.

Smith, V. Kerry. 1997. Feedback Effects and Environmental Resources. In *Social Benefits of Education*, ed. Jere R. Behrman and Nevzer Stacey. Ann Arbor: University of Michigan Press.

Tauchen, H. and A. D. Witte. 1995. The Dynamics of Domestic Violence: Does Arrest Matter? *American Economic Review* 85:414-18.

U.S. Bureau of the Census. 1993. *Statistical Abstract of the U.S.: 1993*, 113th ed. Washington, DC: Government Printing Office.

U.S. Department of Health and Human Services. National Center for Health Statistics. 1994. *Vital Statistics of the United States*. Vol. 2, *Mortality*. Part A. Washington, DC: Government Printing Office.

Viscusi, W. K. 1986. Market Incentives for Criminal Behavior. In *The Black Youth Employment Crisis*, ed. R. B. Freeman and J. J. Holzer. Chicago: University of Chicago Press.

Viscusi, W. K. and W. A. Magat. 1987. *Learning About Risk: Consumer and Worker Responses to Hazard Warnings*. Cambridge, MA: Harvard University Press.

Witte, A. D. and H. Tauchen. 1994. Work and Crime: An Exploration Using Panel Data. *Public Finance* 49:155-67.

Witte, A. Dryden. 1997. Crime. In *Social Benefits of Education*, ed. Jere R. Behrman and Nevzer Stacey. Ann Arbor: University of Michigan Press.

Zill, N. 1994. Characteristics of Teenage Mothers. Photocopy of talking points for the conference "The Cost of Teenage Child Bearing," sponsored by the American Enterprise Institute.

ANNALS, *AAPSS*, **559**, September 1998

The Disappointments of Success: Higher Education After World War II

By MARVIN LAZERSON

ABSTRACT: From a historical perspective, Marvin Lazerson gives an account of the unprecedented growth of higher education in the years following World War II, its transformation from a public good to a private benefit that confers economic rewards, and the current problems that it faces during an era of retrenchment. He demonstrates how higher education's postwar success was built on three already established patterns and beliefs: vocationalism, public higher education, and multiple sectors of postsecondary schooling. He then discusses how the world of higher education changed after 1970, when critics began to voice concerns over unchecked expansion, and how its current problems emerged during the 1980s and 1990s, as the costs of attending college began to outpace the economic returns.

Marvin Lazerson is Carruth Family Professor at the Graduate School of Education, University of Pennsylvania. He is a widely published educational historian and commentator on current issues in higher education.

NOTE: I would like to thank Jesse Minier and Barbara Jaffe for providing much of the data, posing many of the most intriguing questions, challenging the interpretations, and aiding in the writing. The work reported herein is supported under the Educational Research and Development Center Program, agreement number R309A60001, CFDA 84.309A, as administered by the Office of Educational Research and Improvement (OERI), U.S. Department of Education. The findings and opinions expressed in this report do not reflect the position or policies of OERI or the U.S. Department of Education.

IN the half-century after World War II, higher education in the United States triumphed. Few industries grew as fast, gained as much prestige, or affected the lives of so many people. Higher education received remarkable sums of money from federal and state governments; alumni and foundations also gave generously. Families reached into their savings, postponed purchases, and went into debt so that their children could go to college. Higher education came to simultaneously embody both a public good—beneficial to the nation's economy, protective of its national defense, opening up new avenues of knowledge, and able to realize equality of educational opportunity—and a private benefit, so that everyone who possessed it substantially improved their access to higher income, status, and security.

Most remarkably, higher education built upon prewar trends to do what almost no one would have predicted: it achieved a virtual monopoly on middle-class status. It became the licensing agency for Americans who wanted to enter the professions. Every occupation seeking to increase its prestige and income made going to college and beyond the requirement for entry. For countless Americans, college was the route upward; they expected their governments at every level to help facilitate that mobility, through grants and loans to students, as well as establishing branch campuses of state universities and local community colleges. Even when economic returns to higher education plateaued during the 1970s and 1980s and the costs of going to college escalated, families and students—especially older students—dug down into their savings and took out loans in order to attend. Higher education had been converted from a land of opportunity to a necessity for many in order to prevent the loss of status.

Higher education has become a victim of its own successes, however. Able to assume a continuing clientele, to capitalize on the aspirations for upward mobility that so marked American society in the postwar era, and to attract a seemingly unending stream of government funds, higher education charged what the traffic would bear. By the 1980s, those costs would so substantially outpace inflation and the growth rate of median family income that higher education looked like yet another greedy industry.

By the 1990s, higher education had come to look like other monopolies and powerful industries of postwar America. Like the U.S. auto industry in the 1970s, it dominated the market, produced the best products, and paid off for those who invested and worked in it. But also like the auto industry, higher education failed to recognize its hubris and the environmental changes occurring around it. Even the complaints about higher education mirrored those hurled at corporate monopolies: overpriced and poor-quality products, poor service and inattention to customers, inefficient and bureaucratic, unwilling to adapt to new markets, technologically backward, administratively bloated, too concerned with frills rather than the core product. Shocked and confused by criticism and reluctant to change, higher education at the end of the century faced a new world. It was unclear whether it would be routed by the imports and alternatives or made better for the competition.

THE MARKERS OF SUCCESS

By almost any measure, the half-century since 1945 was good for higher education, even with the strains of the 1970s and 1980s. Two kinds of data tell the story: institutional and enrollment growth, and fiscal growth. Between 1950 and 1990, the number of colleges and universities almost doubled, from 1851 to 3535. The number of students increased from 2.66 million in 1949-50 to 8.00 million in 1969-70, and to 13.54 million in 1989-90. In those same years, the percentage of 18- and 19-year-olds in school (overwhelmingly, in postsecondary schools) doubled from 29.7 percent of the age group to 57.2 percent; the proportion of 20- to 24-year-olds in school tripled, from 9.2 percent to 28.6 percent. The most rapid growth occurred during the 1960s, but, after a sluggish decade in the 1970s, the trend was again upward (National Center for Education Statistics [NCES] 1994).

Where students went and who they were also changed. The proportion of students in public colleges—at around 50 percent in 1950—continued to increase, reaching 59 percent in 1960 and a whopping 73 percent in 1970 (Freeland 1992, 88). Women, who composed 30 percent of the student population in 1949-50, were the majority by 1979-80 and rose to 54 percent in 1989-90 (NCES 1994, tabs. 168 and 169). Among African Americans, the proportion of 18- to 24-year-olds in college increased from under

10 percent in 1964 to 20 percent in 1972, and Hispanic Americans showed similar growth in enrollment (Gumport et al. 1997). By 1990, 25 percent of African American youths and 16 percent of Hispanic American youths were enrolled in college (Gumport et al. 1997). The number of nontraditional-age and part-time students also rose after 1970. By 1990, the proportion of students 22 years of age and older were the "new majority" in college, and more than 40 percent of all college students were going part-time (Gumport et al. 1997).

Spending on higher education soared, from $2.66 billion in 1949-50 to $7.14 billion a decade later, to $25.27 billion in 1969-70, to $62.46 billion in 1979-80, and $151.76 billion in 1989-90 (NCES 1994, tab. 32). Higher-education expenditures as a percentage of the gross national product (GNP) rose from 1.7 percent in 1961 to 2.1 percent in 1970; after stabilizing during the 1970s, they rose again to 3.0 percent in 1990 (NCES 1994, tab. 31). Between 1950 and 1970, higher education increased its spending per student by more than double the rate of the GNP. In contrast, between 1930 and 1950, the rate of increase per student rose more slowly than the rate of per capita growth in the GNP. In recent years, the rise in spending on a per-student basis has been enormous, going from $3947 (in 1990-91 constant dollars) in 1949-50 to $7460 in 1969-70, declining over the next decade but rising sharply to $8225 in the 1980s (NCES 1994, tab. 328).

The numbers tell a compelling story: more students, more money, more status. Higher education became one of the most successful industries of postwar America—perhaps the single most successful. It was hard to imagine a world without colleges, without large numbers of people attending them, without higher education's contributions to the resolution of the nation's most complex and important economic, technological, social, and health problems. Its colleges and universities illustrated what made the United States great.

Neither the ride nor the progress was smooth, however. Just as American industry would find itself troubled—by foreign imports and global competition, managerial miscalculations, worker demands for higher wages, and shorter workweeks—so, too, did higher education find itself troubled. The immediate postwar period witnessed the McCarthyism of anti-Communists who were convinced that "Reds" and their fellow travelers had invaded the campuses. The Soviet Union's launch of *Sputnik* in 1957 raised doubts about whether American standards of academic achievement were stringent enough for the Cold War era. Demonstrations, strikes, and violence during the 1960s and early 1970s divided higher education from within and diminished enthusiasm for it among politicians and the public at large as they questioned whether higher education had become yet another mistaken entitlement of the welfare state. A slowdown in income returns to college education during the 1970s combined with the rising costs of going to college.

The industry seemed unable or unwilling to rein in its expenditures, opening higher education to more strident criticism than ever before—this time matched by legislative efforts to reduce federal and state expenditures. During the 1980s, state appropriations, the largest governmental source of funds for higher education, increased only slightly per student but appeared flat when measured in constant dollars. Overall government funding as a percentage of funding for higher education declined during the 1980s. Critics challenged whether colleges and universities were teaching students anything and whether "higher education" was a misnomer as remedial programs proliferated. The media found itself with yet another institution that seemed corrupt, was politically incorrect, and misused funds, leading higher education to become more defensive than at any time in its history.

Nonetheless, before the end of the 1980s, the times of trouble were blips in the trajectory. By turns, they were threatening, annoying, confusing, raising questions, and sometimes lessening the flow of dollars, but they were almost always transitory. Each rocky moment was followed by renewed enthusiasm, more applications for admission, expansiveness, and money. McCarthyism shook some campuses, frightened many faculty, and ruined careers, but it hardly made a dent in the industry's growth or prestige. *Sputnik* produced considerable criticism and a great deal of hand-wringing, but from it came the National Defense Education Act of 1958, which gave unprecedented fiscal support for the sciences, foreign languages, area studies, and campus growth. In the 1960s and 1970s, campus rebellions shocked the nation, leading to angry diatribes directed at overly entitled youths, but the public's shifting attitudes toward the Vietnam war ultimately gave greater legitimacy to the demonstrations. Few, if any, students turned away from attending college because some of their peers had protested. The most obvious direct impact of student demonstrations was to give everyone more freedom. Campus restrictions on student life practically disappeared as "in loco parentis" became a dirty word. The number of required courses declined; the size of the overall curriculum increased. Students and faculty had more choices of what to take and what to teach. Income and status returns to college attendance remained high: even though the rate of growth slowed and may have even tailed off after 1970, attending college, compared to not going beyond secondary school, was still a wise decision, particularly in the 1980s, when the job market for high school graduates collapsed.

Finally, at the start of the 1980s, when it seemed that the declining number of 17- to 21-year-olds in the population would substantially diminish the market for students, higher education discovered the nontraditional student, who, in turn, found that it was never too late to go to college. While it became more and more difficult for families to pay for a college education during the 1980s—

as higher education raised tuition faster than the rise in inflation and the average income of workers—the numbers scrambling to get into college kept going up, as community colleges in particular burst their seams enrolling high school graduates and dropouts, adults seeking job preparation, and others simply wanting a place to learn more about the world and themselves.

For all of the ups and downs, during almost a half-century after World War II, higher education was truly a success story. Build a college and students would come. Expand facilities and resources would arrive. By and large, it was truly a golden age.

DIMENSIONS OF THE PAST

Higher education's postwar success built upon three already established patterns and beliefs, each of which sowed the seeds of conflict: vocationalism, public higher education, and multiple sectors of postsecondary schooling.

Vocationalism—the direct application of schooling to jobs and economic opportunities—had been apparent since the late nineteenth century. Seeking students and public approbation, many nineteenth-century colleges adapted their liberal arts traditions to become multipurpose schools, diversifying their curricula and becoming sensitive to local and regional economic needs and job opportunities (Geiger 1995). For women especially, vocationalism was always central; overwhelmingly, women college students prepared for teaching. At the University of California, Berkeley, early in the twentieth century, 90 percent of the women students expected to become teachers (Gordon 1990).

Between 1880 and the 1930s, vocationalism took full form, with the development of professional schools, the creation of an educational ladder between high school and college, and, increasingly, a reliance by employers on college credentials as a criterion for hiring. Each of these factors was important. The appearance of schools of business, engineering, education, social work, nursing, and dentistry and the growth of law and medical schools defined higher education in terms of its direct application to specific occupations. The creation of an education ladder that went from elementary and secondary schools through college and then to graduate school sharpened the distinction between college and other educational institutions and reduced the undergraduate college's nineteenth-century competitors—academies, high schools, one- and two-year normal schools, private proprietary schools, and apprenticeships—to institutions preparatory to college or to a lesser status. By the 1930s, the high school no longer paralleled the college but had become its subordinate; without a high school degree, there was no entry to college, and more and more professions were requiring graduate training beyond college.

The shift in the criteria for employment, partially due to the growth of white-collar jobs within corporate and public agencies, generated much of the consumer-driven growth in postsecondary enrollments in the first decades of the twentieth century. What David Levine has called "the culture of aspiration," a variation of the Horatio Alger story of rags to riches—or at least, to middle-class respectability—was connected to higher education (Levine 1986). The movement was hardly massive before World War II; too many obstacles still lay in the way of nearly universal higher education, especially the continuing low proportions of youths graduating from high school, but the terms of the postwar expansion had been laid. Going to college meant greater income returns and status than not going.

A second critical ingredient of postwar expansion had also been put in place earlier: the growth of the public sector in higher education. Although we tend to associate public higher education with the post–World War II period, large proportions of young people had always attended publicly supported colleges and universities. Indeed, the perception of a separate private versus public sector was an invention of the nineteenth century. The Morrill Acts of 1862 and 1890 furthered the notion that higher education was a public responsibility. While there was a private gain to the individual from going to college, the primary gain was to the public good. College enrollments strengthened the nation, state, and locality.

This view of higher education as a public good also laid the basis for its politicization. Before postwar expansion, the number of students going to college and the amount of public funds invested in higher education had been small enough to mute political antagonisms. As higher education became a mass system in the postwar decades, however, the politicization inherent in its public character intensified.

The third critical ingredient that fed postwar expansionism comprised the organizational characteristics of decentralization and segmentation. Because higher education was always a decentralized industry, made up of relatively autonomous institutions competing within a deregulated market, it expanded in whatever ways it thought necessary. Often, this meant changing admission requirements to attract more students (or, in a few cases, to become more selective), providing fiscal incentives to students to attend, revising the curriculum to make it more attractive, expanding student life activities, and seeking funding from alumni and philanthropists. Higher education thus established its entrepreneurial orientation in its relationship to students and funders before the mid-twentieth century.

Segmentation was also important. Higher education accepted the equation that access to college could be widespread if the system was segmented. A complex web of different kinds of postsecondary institutions was already formed by the late 1930s, from junior and community colleges through the small number of selective liberal arts colleges and research universities. Providing for gradients of status within a system of increasing access to higher educational opportunity, the web of sectors joined with the ideas of equality of opportunity, meritocracy, the preservation of institutional status, and market sector competition to lay the basis for extraordinary growth.

THE ENTHUSIASMS OF SUCCESS

In a simple fashion, the remarkable expansion of higher education in the first two and a half decades after World War II can be easily stated: large numbers of Americans subsidized higher education because they were convinced that it was a public good that substantially furthered national defense, economic growth, and equality of educational opportunity. Students and their families read the postwar labor market correctly: going to college meant better jobs, more income, higher status, and greater security.

It is hard at the end of the twentieth century to imagine the extraordinary enthusiasm for the postwar growth. Even elite private universities, initially worried that high levels of public investment would diminish their place and would open the doors to unqualified students, soon found themselves caught up in the opportunities of expansion. The Cold War, the ideology of equality of opportunity, state and local pride, the high stature of research, and federal investments all fueled an expansion that was inconceivable a few decades earlier. In particular, by providing direct grants to institutions to be redistributed primarily in student aid, the federal government helped keep the opportunity costs to attending college low, while allowing colleges to increase their charges, a situation in which everyone seemed to win.

Students and their families responded. College going provided opportunities for young people to do better than their parents. In absolute terms, between 1950 and 1970, income returns to college graduation increased in a steady fashion. Each annual cohort of college graduates was likely to earn more money than the previous cohorts, as employers heavily recruited college graduates. Relative to high school graduates and high school dropouts, returns to college graduates during those 20 years grew or remained stable annually, again peaking around 1970. College graduates seemed to have little trouble finding jobs (Gumport et al. 1997; Hecker 1992).

In those 25 years after the war, there was, it seemed, little restraint on the possibilities for higher education. Although student rebellions in the 1960s provoked substantial criticism, the decade ended with the largest growth that higher education had ever seen. Substantial state and federal funding existed; the commitment to civil rights and educational opportunity opened doors for minorities; women were a growing proportion of the college population. Income returns to college graduates were high and had been growing in a seemingly unending progression. There was little reason to think that during the 1970s the surfacing doubts would become more than that, little reason to believe that higher education was about to be seriously challenged.

THE ERA OF DISAPPOINTMENTS

The world of higher education changed after 1970. The preceding rise had been meteoric and substantial. Higher education had become self-confident, assured that it was a public and a private good that strengthened the nation and provided high rates of return to individu-als. The criticisms emerging after 1970 were a surprise; the disenchantment, unsettling; the anger, a shock.

As early as 1971, commentators like Earl Cheit, in *The New Depression in Higher Education*, worried that higher education had lost its capacity to manage itself and suggested that a number of colleges and universities were in serious fiscal trouble. Others criticized the continuing lack of access for minorities despite substantial gains, the neglect of the teaching of undergraduates, the uniformity across institutions, the remoteness of higher education from society, and its excessively close association with government and social concerns. That there were contradictions between the various criticisms was more or less irrelevant. The critics' voices coalesced in the public's mind around the notion that there was something terribly wrong with higher education (Freeland 1992, 97-115).

Initially, the sourest notes were sounded around the behavior of students. The protests of the 1960s and early 1970s, the in-your-face dress and language of that period, and the violence raised questions about whether the entitled were worth the expenditure. President Nixon's urban and domestic affairs adviser, Daniel Patrick Moynihan, may have spoken for countless other Americans when he proclaimed to one of his former graduate students that "even the mathematics students were protesting," and, in the wake of the demonstrations and violence at Columbia University, he was apoplectic because parents were bailing their children out of jail and protesting against undue violence on the part of the police. Why did these parents, he fumed, not let their children take responsibility for their illegal and uncivil actions?

But there was also a deeper malaise affecting higher education after 1970, one that would have an even more substantial impact: the intersection of the costs of college and the income returns to attending. Higher education presumed that its importance allowed it to increase its expenditures substantially faster than the GNP and the rate of inflation. That thinking quickly became an albatross. As the U.S. economy faced soaring inflation, high unemployment, oil crises, wage and price controls, loss of markets to Japanese and German goods, and corporate downsizing in the 1970s and 1980s, the seemingly unconstrained costs of higher education came to look obscene.

Concern about costs coincided with uncertainties about the income returns to higher education. After 1970, depending upon the source, income returns to college graduates either flattened, declined, or increased only modestly over the next two decades (Zemsky 1997; Levy and Murnane 1992).[1] A consensus quickly emerged that going to college was no longer paying off in the ways that it had over the previous decades. Why this was so is the source of intense controversy, with interpretations pointing to an oversupply of college graduates, the deskilling of many managerial and technical jobs, corporate downsizing, the poor quality of elementary and secondary schools, declines in the quality of academic and technical skills possessed by college graduates, lowered college admission standards, the larger proportion of women college graduates entering the labor market, and a mismatch between the skills that college graduates possessed and those required in the advanced labor market.

If enthusiasm waned in the 1970s and 1980s, it also became even more imperative to play the game. Relative to high school graduates, the differential wage increases associated with college graduation declined during the 1970s. In 1971, male college graduates aged 25 to 34 earned 22 percent more, on average, than male high school graduates of the same age. In 1979, the earnings differential had shrunk to 13 percent. For women aged 25 to 34, the changes were similar, with the earnings premium associated with college education declining from 41 percent in 1971 to 23 percent in 1979 (Levy and Murnane 1992, 1354-57). It was thus reasonable to have doubts about going to college in the 1970s.

During the 1980s, the world became even more complicated. The educational premium for male college graduates aged 24 to 35 over high school graduates of the same age jumped from 13 percent in 1979 to 38 percent in 1987. For women in the same categories, the premium rose from 23 percent to 45 percent but with a substantial difference. Whereas the median real earnings of male high school graduates working full-time declined by 12 percent in the 1980s—as did the likelihood of even working full-time—it did not decline for women high school graduates working full-time (Levy and

Murnane 1992, 1356-57). In the case of both women and men, the gap between high school and college earnings was even higher, since the likelihood that high school graduates would hold full-time jobs year-round declined considerably during the 1980s. With women entering new professions and with the income inequality gap between men and women closing, the experiences of college going for the two sexes had shifted. For men, graduating from college after 1970 was considerably less positive than during the golden era between 1945 and 1970; for women, college graduation had become, at least in terms of earnings, much more positive. For both, however, the gap between going to college and not going was huge. It paid to go to college, but it cost more and more to attend.

The psychology of college attendance was also changing. The postwar generation of college students went with great expectations, promises that were fulfilled. From the 1970s on, however, an increasing number of students went to college in order not to suffer the fate of high school graduates. It was a subtle shift in social psychology, from optimism to defensiveness. One went not to get ahead but to avoid falling behind (Zemsky 1997).

The evidence suggests that students and their families agreed that college was, if not a good thing, necessary to getting ahead. The percentage of recent high school graduates enrolled in college, which had climbed from 45 percent in 1960 to a high of 55 percent in 1968, slid down during the 1970s but then began to rise again in the 1980s. While there was a brief drop in full-time undergraduate enrollments in the early 1970s—partly a result of the elimination of the draft deferment for college students—and again around 1977 and between 1983 and 1985, the trajectory was up, sharply so between 1973 and 1975, then more gradually between 1977 and 1983 and again after 1985. The number of part-time undergraduates showed a slightly different profile, but the overall trend between 1971 and 1991 was decidedly up. Among African Americans, participation rates increased in the 1960s, declined in the early 1970s, increased briefly, then flattened or declined until the mid-1980s, and turned upward again. Among African Americans, sharp differences by gender appeared, with the enrollments of women increasing between 1976 and 1985, while the rates for men declined. Between 1986 and 1990, when participation rates went up for both sexes, they did so by almost 16 percent among African American women and by about 9 percent for African American men. Between 1976 and 1990, participation rates for Hispanics and Asian Americans also increased, with the enrollment of women in each group increasing more rapidly than that of men (Hauptman and McLaughlin 1992, 168-78).

Much of this growth came as a surprise. As David Breneman (1994) has pointed out, the 1980s began on a dreary note, punctuated by demographic fears: an anticipated 25 percent decline in the number of 18-year-olds over the next 15 years. Even if larger proportions of high school graduates enrolled in college, the likelihood of actual enrollments dropping by 5 percent to 15 percent was substantial. Combined with high inflation and unemployment, little if any productivity gains, and anticipated drops in real income, the situation did look bleak.

The catastrophic projections at the beginning of the 1980s did not come true, but three things did happen during the decade that would effectively shake higher education's foundations. First, higher education expanded because older, nontraditional students enrolled, many of them attending part-time. Although their participation had been growing since the 1960s, between 1970 and 1975, the number of students aged 22 or older increased by more than 50 percent, while the number of traditional-age students remained relatively constant. Between 1978 and 1989, the number of college students aged 25 and older grew by 44 percent, while the number of 18- to 24-year-olds in college increased by only 7 percent. The number of women college students in that same period grew by 26 percent, accounting for the largest growth among older students.[2] After 1975, students aged 22 or older became the majority of the college-going population; in the late 1980s, those 30 and older were the fastest-growing percentage of matriculants (Gumport et al. 1997). Older students were also much more likely to enroll part-time, accounting for almost all the growth in part-time attendance in the 1980s. In their determination to enroll in college, older students affirmed what was higher

education's greatest triumph: college was the necessary license for middle-class status.

Second, the expansion of enrollment in the 1980s was not matched by a parallel expansion in degree attainment. As Robert Zemsky points out, between 1950 and 1982, the portion of those who started college but left before finishing it dropped from over half to less than 30 percent. Over the next decade, over 40 percent who started college quit before they earned their bachelor's degree. Americans became convinced that it was necessary to go to college—this was an especially striking phenomenon among those over age 30—but they were not receiving the degree they so desperately sought (Zemsky 1997; Gumport et al. 1997).

Third, higher education became caught in a price-income squeeze that was more serious than at any time in the previous half-century. The direct costs of going to college—tuition, fees, room and board—increased dramatically during the 1980s, especially at private universities (the increases hit the public universities in the late 1980s and early 1990s), substantially outpacing inflation and the family incomes of most Americans. At the same time, median income in constant dollars either stayed the same, declined, or increased only slightly for male college graduates aged 25 to 34.

Taken together, these developments revealed both higher education's continuing success and its vulnerability. The proportion of high school graduates aged 18 to 24 going on to college had grown once again, from a low of 30 percent in 1973 to 34 percent in 1986. New populations were attending in record-breaking numbers, signifying how powerful higher education's license to middle-class respectability and status had become. For the selective colleges and universities, which promised entry to the upper class, the fight to get in had all the characteristics of a gold rush. Income returns to college vis-à-vis high school grew dramatically. As David Breneman (1994) has written, "Largely because the bottom fell out of the job market for high school graduates (especially for males), the economic returns to a college education reversed itself, with the wage premium for college graduates increasing between 1979 and 1986 to larger than those found in any earlier period" (31-32).

Yet the promise of success was all too shaky. A greater proportion of those who believed it was necessary to go to college were finding it harder and harder to attain a degree. Those who hoped that higher education would translate into high incomes were finding that just paying for college was harder and harder and, when they got out, worried about finding or holding a job and paying their debts. A person had to go to college, because if he or she did not, the result was to face even bigger financial trouble. At a time when choice was being trumpeted as the new American ideal, higher education's monopoly over access to the middle class—its greatest triumph—was becoming an incitement to condemn it. The public stood ready to unleash a critical onslaught beyond anything higher education had ever witnessed. The disappointments were overshadowing the industry's successes.

Notes

1. The measurement of earnings returns to education is one of the most technically complex areas in the economics of higher education. Zemsky (1997) and Gumport et al. (1997) argue that returns to higher education for men have been declining in constant dollars since the mid-1970s. Levy and Murnane (1992), in contrast, argue that between 1979 and 1987, there was "an eight percent increase in the median earnings of 25-34 year old male college graduates" and a "21 percent increase in the median earnings of 25-34 year old female college graduates," in both cases based on working full-time for the entire year (1355-57). Every analyst agrees that the most significant development of the 1980s was the decimation of the labor market for high school graduates. For a summary of studies on returns to college, see Pascarella and Terenzini 1991.

2. The importance of women in these trends is significant and not well appreciated. Women grew from 40 percent of the student population to a majority during the 1970s and up to 54 percent by 1990. The income returns for women college graduates also rose faster than those for men, so that by the end of the 1980s, while women with comparable education and jobs still earned less than men, the wage inequality gap was closing. Women were thus beginning to get more out of going to college than did men. Most of the scholarly and popular discussion about costs and returns, unfortunately, is based on male income data. The price-income squeeze may be most severe—and generating the most anger—among men, with women having a somewhat different perception of what has been happening.

References

Breneman, David W. 1994. *Liberal Arts Colleges: Thriving or Endangered?* Washington, DC: Brookings Institution.

Cheit, E. F. 1971. *The New Depression in Higher Education*. New York: McGraw-Hill.

Freeland, Richard M. 1992. *Academia's Golden Age: Universities in Massachusetts, 1945-1970*. New York: Oxford University Press.

Geiger, Roger L. 1995. The Era of Multi-Purpose Colleges in American Higher Education, 1850-1890. *History of Higher Education Annual* 15:51-92.

Gordon, Lynn. 1990. *Gender and Higher Education in the Progressive Era*. New Haven, CT: Yale University Press.

Gumport, Patricia, Maria Iannozzi, Susan Shaman, and Robert Zemsky. 1997. The United States Country Report: Trends in Higher Education from Massification to Post-Massification. In *RIHE International Seminar Reports*. No. 10. Hiroshima: Hiroshima University, Research Institute for Higher Education.

Hauptman, Arthur M. and Maureen A. McLaughlin. 1992. Is the Goal of College Access Being Met? In *American Higher Education: Purposes, Problems and Public Perceptions*, ed. Aspen Institute. Queensland, MD: Aspen Institute.

Hecker, Daniel E. 1992. Reconciling Conflicting Data on Jobs for College Graduates. *Monthly Labor Review* (July):3-12.

Levine, David. 1986. *The American College and the Culture of Aspiration, 1915-1940*. Ithaca, NY: Cornell University Press.

Levy, Frank and Richard J. Murnane. 1992. U.S. Earnings Levels and Earnings Inequality: A Review of Recent Trends and Proposed Explanations. *Journal of Economic Literature* 30(Sept.):1333-81.

National Center for Education Statistics (NCES). 1994. *Digest of Education Statistics, 1994*. Washington, DC: Department of Education.

Pascarella, Ernest and Patrick Terenzini. 1991. *How College Affects Students: Findings and Insights from Twenty Years of Research*. San Francisco: Jossey-Bass.

Zemsky, Robert. 1997. Keynote Address: Seminar on Post-Massification. In *RIHE International Seminar Reports*. No. 10. Hiroshima: Hiroshima University, Research Institute for Higher Education.

ANNALS, *AAPSS*, **559**, September 1998

Labor, Markets, and Educational Restructuring

By ROBERT ZEMSKY

ABSTRACT: Using a theoretical framework developed by Professor Akira Arimoto to describe recent changes in the Japanese system of higher education, Robert Zemsky discusses what happens when higher education becomes the norm in a society and when this massification of a higher education system gives way to post-massification. Zemsky demonstrates how, in the current era of post-massification, American higher education is a system under duress, at a time when the economy, shifting demographics, and political lassitude have forced a restructuring of the enterprise. He examines trends such as the price-income squeeze, where the economic returns to college have fallen while the cost has risen; the bifurcation of institutions into outlets and medallions; the reduced demand for young workers; and the dynamics of local labor and education markets. Zemsky concludes that, once the market for college graduates becomes saturated in a locality, the boundary between massification and post-massification is crossed, leading to a restratification of both educational attainment and economic advantage.

Robert Zemsky is professor and director of the Institute for Research on Higher Education and chair of the Higher Education Division of the Graduate School of Education at the University of Pennsylvania. He serves as codirector of the National Center on the Educational Quality of the Workforce and as a senior scholar at the National Center for Postsecondary Improvement.

NOTE: The work reported herein was supported under the Educational Research and Development Center Program, agreement number R117Q00011-91, CFDA 84.117Q, as administered by the Office of Educational Research and Improvement, U.S. Department of Education. The findings and opinions expressed in this article do not reflect the position or policies of the Office of Educational Research and Improvement or the U.S. Department of Education.

IT is an American phenomenon but a Japanese insight. What happens, the Japanese have asked, when higher education becomes the norm instead of the privileged exception—and what happens afterward, when this massification gives way to post-massification? In Japan, this question has been most acutely asked by Akira Arimoto (1997), as part of a larger inquiry into the dynamics of an educational system under duress when the economy, shifting demographics, and political lassitude force restructuring.

At the core of Arimoto's inquiry is the observation that "in every country facing the kind of social change which includes more or less economic retrenchment, some modification and shifting of academic policy may be observed" (1997, 277). According to Arimoto, each country will have its own version of Clark Kerr's "a time of troubles" as the "academic growth model dominant at the massification stage" gives way to the results of "emerging retrenchment" (1997, 277).

Arimoto postulates that, as a national system of higher education moves from massification to post-massification, the following events will occur:

1. Budget retrenchment will force public agencies to focus renewed attention on the social and economic rationalization of university functions. At least one result will be a stronger system of public accountability.

2. The system of higher education will become increasingly privatized, either through greater expansion of the private sector or through increased reliance on student fees to fund public sector institutions—or both.

3. Institutions of higher education will find themselves more responsible for their own management in an era of deregulation.

4. Market forces will increasingly supplant public policy in determining the scale, scope, and price of higher education.

5. With a growing number of institutions on their own, public agencies and public opinion will seek to secure the quality of the system of higher education through new forms of accreditation.

6. As part of that effort to ensure quality, educational outcomes will prove increasingly important for gauging institutional accountability.

7. Inevitably, these changes will result in an increase in the level of psychological stress within the university.

Arimoto also provides a list of the kinds of changes within the university that one is likely to see once the boundary between massification and post-massification has been crossed.

— shifting social priorities that place increased emphasis on general as opposed to specialized education and on teaching as opposed to research;
— changes in the normative structures of the university;
— new demands for academic productivity;
— changes in student populations;

— changes in pedagogy; and

— changes in the professional standing of faculty and the status of students.

Though Arimoto's is an argument derived largely from changes in Japanese higher education, its framework comes remarkably close to describing the current condition of postsecondary education in the United States. The balance between the seven postulated events is different for the United States and Japan; in the former there is greater reliance on market forces (4), more privatization (2), and less emphasis on new forms of accreditation (5). The list of observable phenomena, however, needs little if any alteration to fit the American case. All are apparent in abundance.

There is a special irony to the aptness of an understanding that is inherently Japanese in origin and that provides a general recasting of how we view what has historically been seen as an essentially American enterprise. What Arimoto has proposed is an intriguing, even seductive, schema encompassing a general explanation for the evolution of universities across the developed world and beyond—a sequel to the revolutions of 1968 that propelled Europe and Japan toward massification and that, in the United States, altered the balance of power in many universities.

The critical question becomes, Does the proposed schema provide a general understanding of higher education in a state of post-massification? Is there in fact a link—a causal link—between massification and post-massification? What do we know about the process by which massification gives way to post-massification? Arimoto suggests that the underlying causes for such shifts are primarily economic—changes in the nature, even the robustness, of a nation's economy that then translate into reduced public appropriation for higher education and the telltale signs of institutional reform and stress.

MYTHS AND REALITIES:
THE CONTEXT FOR MASSIFICATION
IN THE UNITED STATES

The first step in answering these questions is to provide a more textured sketch of what massification has meant for American higher education. Here the focus is on two myths—although "exaggerations" might be a more apt term—that have come to characterize how most Americans would describe the importance of higher education. The first exaggeration holds that higher education in the United States is now a truly mass phenomenon: there is now a general expectation that most high school students will go to college; there is a similar assumption that the jobs of the future will require a college education; and there is a growing conviction that lifelong learning will yield ever increasing enrollments for the nation's colleges and universities. The implication is that Americans have confused quantity and quality, suggesting that what the United States has achieved is mass education rather than mass higher education.

In this case, the skeptics have the better of the argument. When one looks at the most standard measure of participation—the percentage of

FIGURE 1
PARTICIPATION VERSUS ATTAINMENT

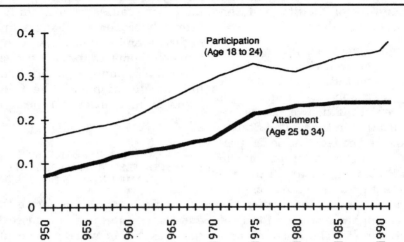

the youth cohort aged 18 to 24 that has matriculated at a college or university—there is an impressive tale to be told. Figure 1 gives the proportion of this cohort from 1950 to 1990 reporting "some college" participation. From this perspective, Americans have achieved a mass system of higher education, in that there is a growing presumption that most citizens will—in fact, should—attend a college or university.

When one turns to a measure of attainment—the percentage of young adults aged 25 to 34 who report having earned a baccalaureate degree—a different picture emerges. From 1950 through 1982, during the final stages of massification, the proportion of those who started, but did not complete, a college education declined from more than half to less than 30 percent. By the 1990s, however, the gap was again widening, as

more than 40 percent of those students who started college quit before receiving a baccalaureate degree. While the proportion of young adults in the United States who have a tertiary educational degree is higher than in any other developed country save Japan and Canada, the gap between American attainment rates and those of other countries continues to narrow.

A second exaggeration of which Americans have grown fond involves the economic advantages that accrue to college graduates. Most Americans take as an article of faith that going to college pays off by providing access to better jobs, better salaries, and brighter futures. This belief has made equal access to a college or university such an important political goal that the federal government has become a major dispenser of student aid. As Sam Stringfield has pointed

FIGURE 2
MEDIAN INCOME OF MALES AGED 25 TO 34 BY LEVEL
OF EDUCATION (In constant dollars)

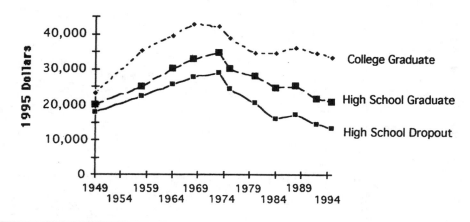

SOURCE: Stringfield 1995, 68.

out, it is a perspective—like the Horatio Alger myth of an earlier time—that contains a kernel of truth that is forgotten when it comes time to draw important lessons about the nature of the numbers. Stringfield (1995) was interested in the average incomes (in constant dollars) of three groups of males aged 25 to 34: college graduates, high school graduates, and high school dropouts. His plotting of these median salaries from 1949 through 1994 is presented in Figure 2.

What Stringfield's analysis makes clear is that, after 1970, while college graduates continued to earn more than those with less education, the economic rewards stopped increasing. Indeed, in constant dollars, the average income of a male college graduate aged 25 to 34 has actually decreased since 1970. What has declined even more precipitously, however, are the incomes of those who are not college graduates. In fact, in 1994, high school dropouts earned substantially less than, and high school graduates without college degrees earned roughly the same as, their grandfathers did almost a half-century earlier with the same level of education. In 1994, college graduates, on the other hand, were still more advantaged than their grandfathers, earning more than college graduates, high school graduates, and high school dropouts did in 1949.

It is the echo of that historic advantage, largely achieved during the heyday of massification (1950 to 1960), which propels the American sense that going to college pays off. A more realistic interpretation would be that college education is a necessary, but not sufficient, condition for achieving economic well-being. We may want to mark the years 1969 to

FIGURE 3
COLLEGE COSTS AND AVERAGE INCOMES, 1976 TO 1994 (In constant dollars)

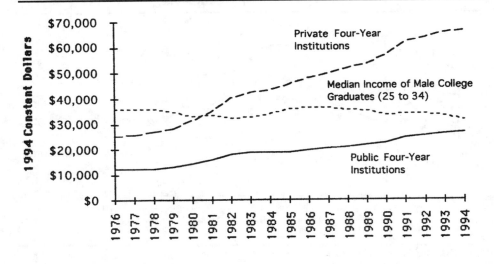

NOTE: College costs include tuition, fees, room and board.

1974 as the last stages of massification, and the years immediately thereafter as the first stages of post-massification.

THE PRICE-INCOME SQUEEZE

We can extend Stringfield's analysis by comparing the average incomes of male college graduates aged 25 to 34 with the average four-year costs associated with earning a baccalaureate degree. Figure 3 presents this analysis as a rough ratio of price to income for American higher education. The stresses on the system are clear. Gone are the days of low cost and high return; they have been replaced with the paradoxical sense that a college education, while increasingly necessary, is also necessarily less rewarding. Figure 3 also provides a ready explanation for the increased focus on cost that has come to dominate the public's scrutiny of American higher education. It is not just that tuition increases have exceeded the rate of inflation; rather, what occasions public anxiety is the sense that it is being asked to pay more for less, in terms of likely income earned by graduates in relation to stated prices for education.

For private higher education, the crisis of cost is long-standing. The first reaction of most institutions in this sector was to rely on federal loan funds to help offset their rising cost of attendance. A second, often parallel, strategy was effectively to reduce the stated price of attendance by offering discounts in the form of student financial aid. This pattern is clearest among liberal arts colleges

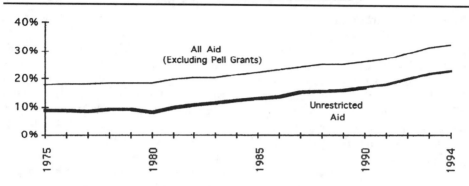

FIGURE 4
STUDENT AID (DISCOUNTS) AS A PROPORTION OF TUITION AND
FEE REVENUE AT LIBERAL ARTS COLLEGES

that do not enroll graduate students. Figure 4 presents two measures of discounting at more than 100 Liberal Arts I Colleges, as defined by the Carnegie Classification. The first plots the ratio of total student aid to tuition and fee income. The second plots the ratio of unrestricted student aid (that is, aid funded largely through tuitions and other fees) to total tuition and fee income.

By 1994, the last year for which data are available, the average liberal arts college was discounting its stated price by one-third—and funding two-thirds of those discounts with recycled tuition dollars. We have every reason to believe similar patterns characterize the pricing practices of private research universities as well. Most commentators believe that such discounting has resulted in diminishing returns, as private institutions begin to lose enrollment simply because they have insufficient revenue to offer the kind of educational experiences the market seems to demand.

For public higher education, the years of greatest challenge lie just ahead. Given current trends, four years of tuition will exceed the average annual income of young adults aged 25 to 34 before the end of the decade, thus erasing the 1-to-4 price-to-income ratio present during the final stages of massification. Unless the downward trend of public appropriation is reversed, public institutions will have to choose between a further ratcheting-up of tuitions and a painful reduction in staff and facilities—a choice that is itself the hallmark of post-massification.

OUTLETS AND MEDALLIONS

Given the extraordinary range of institutions seeking their enrollment, today's students are more likely to see themselves as shoppers buying their higher education one course at a time. They have learned to search for the best price and the most convenient time to take the next set of courses they think they require.

These courses will often be taken at a variety of institutions and, in metropolitan areas, from more than one institution simultaneously. What such purchases collectively form is a growing commodity market for higher education.

The other strategy is to delay entry into the labor market as long as possible by attending a prestigious undergraduate school in preparation for subsequent enrollment in a top graduate or professional school. The structure of this group of students— the most selective part of the market for college and university places—is mirrored in the applicant pools of the nation's most selective law schools. Typically, fewer than 30 undergraduate institutions (of a possible 1800) provide more than half of a top-ten law school's applicants. More than two-thirds of these feeder undergraduate institutions will be either high-priced, highly selective private colleges and universities or public flagship universities. Among a top-ten law school's matriculants, this stratification will be even more pronounced, with less than 20 prestigious undergraduate institutions supplying more than half of the law school's enrollment.

What drives this part of the market, what is responsible for the increasing concentration of top students in relatively few undergraduate institutions in the United States, is middle- and upper-income parents in search of economic security for their children. Unable to will them sufficient wealth or a place in the family business or practice, they instead seek the kind of educational medallion that will give their children an edge, that will boost their changes of getting into a top professional school and later making their way in an increasingly turbulent labor market.

Today, probably fewer than 100 undergraduate institutions can provide that kind of edge, though upward of 250 colleges and universities compete for the students interested in a medallion education. It is a tough market that is getting tougher. It is also the market that *US News and World Report* and its rankings get right: what are important are the "inputs"—size of endowment, size of the budget, selectivity (a school is only as good as the last student it turns down), and reputation. It is a market in which the brand name, not the quality of the education, is what counts—that and the trappings of student life: well-appointed residences, modern athletic and recreational facilities, fraternities and sororities, study-abroad programs, and the plethora of staff that accompanies such programs.

The irony, then, is that, in the transition from massification to postmassification, American higher education is becoming not less but more stratified. Higher education in the United States has always had its pecking order, though once it could be characterized as a relatively flat pyramid where the difference between first-, second-, and third-tier institutions was relatively modest— whether expressed in terms of average SAT scores of entering freshmen, the achievements of each institution's graduates, or the reputation of its faculty. Not so today. The image that most readily comes to mind when describing American higher education's current hierarchy is the Transamerica building that dominates San Francisco's skyline; it is a tall and steep-sided structure, one that is precarious for those colleges and universities perched anywhere but near the top.

A REDUCED DEMAND FOR YOUNG WORKERS

The dynamics of the price-income squeeze (Figure 3) and the concomitant development of a two-tiered market—outlet and medallion—may have their roots in a shift in the market for young workers in the United States since 1981. Perhaps the only advantage enjoyed by young workers today is that there are fewer of them. In 1981, there were more than 27 million young workers aged 16 to 26 in the United States who were not enrolled in school and who either had or were seeking full-time employment. Ten years later, the number of similarly aged young workers was just 22 million, an 18.5 percent decrease. With so many fewer young people competing for jobs, their participation in the labor force actually increased slightly, from 69 percent in 1981 to 70 percent in 1991, while the proportion of those working full-time increased from 75 percent to 79 percent over the same decade.

Offsetting this slight increase in employment, however, were three significant losses that substantially disadvantaged the current generation of young people. In 1981, 19 percent of young workers in the United States were employed in full-time jobs in the manufacturing sector. Ten

years later, only 15 percent of youths worked full-time in the same sector, constituting a net loss of 1.65 million manufacturing jobs for young workers. At the same time, the proportion of full-time manufacturing jobs held by all young workers aged 16 to 26 fell from 23 percent in 1981 to 16 percent in 1991.

Changes in the armed services had a similar impact. In 1987, the armed services enlisted almost 300,000 new recruits, who, for the most part, were young people with high school degrees but little subsequent postsecondary education. By 1993, these annual accessions to the military had been reduced by one-third, or 100,000 fewer recruits each year. This number is expected to drop even further as the military continues to downsize. What will be lost by the end of the decade are almost 1 million good jobs for young people: jobs with good pay, excellent benefits, opportunities to acquire technical skills, and further educational benefits after service.

Not surprisingly, this decline in good jobs for young people was accompanied by a general and persistent decline in the wages paid to them. Compared with their counterparts of a decade ago, young workers in the United States are more likely to have jobs for which they are paid less. When their education, gender, race or ethnicity, and industry of employment are taken into account, young workers today earn, on the average, more than 10 percent less in constant dollars than their counterparts did a decade ago. For young workers without high school credentials, the decline in the real value of their incomes has been even more dramatic (Figure 2).

The causes underlying the declining fortunes of young workers are now the subject of a lively debate in the United States. On one side are arrayed those who argue that the problem lies with the preparation of young people for work—with their schooling and with their antipathy to the discipline of work itself. These scholars and commentators would increase opportunities for young people largely through an aggressive agenda of school reform. Increase the skills and improve the attitudes young people bring with them to the labor market, they have argued, and employment will follow. Within this agenda, probably the most radical proposal would have established a German-style apprenticeship system in the United States.

Those of us who hold the alternative view argue that, whatever the problems inherent in the skills and attitudes of young people, the larger problem is one of demand, not supply. As the American economy has undergone restructuring and its firms have reengineered their enterprises, employers have learned to thrive with fewer of the kind of entry-level positions historically filled by young workers.

Indeed, the youth labor market in the United States has come to provide a contingent labor pool on which employers can draw as needed, without having to make significant investments in either the screening or the training of young workers. The result is an increase in the rate of college attendance, though not necessarily graduation. Except for students at the most prestigious and selective undergraduate institutions, the pattern is increasingly one of work and school, in which time to degree is lengthening and the likelihood of attrition increasing, as older students take on the responsibilities of family or develop the kind of work histories that will allow them to find more permanent places in the labor market.

EDUCATION AND THE CALCULUS OF LOCAL ADVANTAGE

There is also an important, often recursive, relationship between the market for college and university enrollments and the functioning of the youth labor market. As part of my work for the National Center on the Educational Quality of the Workforce, I focused on the interaction of local education and labor markets in five metropolitan areas: Atlanta, Georgia; Cleveland, Ohio; Phoenix, Arizona; Portland, Oregon; and two communities in Pennsylvania's Lehigh Valley—Allentown and Bethlehem. Statistically, these five metropolitan areas can be arrayed along a single continuum, with Atlanta anchoring one end and the Lehigh Valley the other, each exemplifying a contrasting pattern of economic and educational change. The Lehigh Valley is typical of much that is characteristic of an older, more established America. It is a region of settled communities, reflective of a time when one or two manufacturers dominated each local area. Atlanta, on the other hand, is one of America's new go-go cities—an economic engine for a rejuvenated Southern economy. It is big and becoming bigger, and it bustles

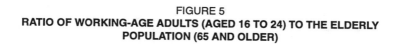

FIGURE 5
**RATIO OF WORKING-AGE ADULTS (AGED 16 TO 24) TO THE ELDERLY
POPULATION (65 AND OLDER)**

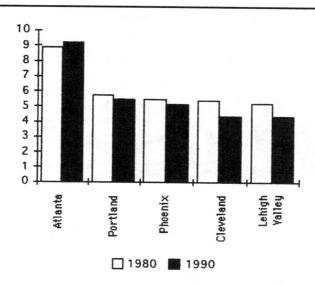

as an exemplar of the modern service-sector metropolis.

The Lehigh Valley has a population that is old and growing older—indeed, growing older substantially faster than three of the four other cities in the study. Here, the key measure is the ratio of residents aged 16 to 64 (the prime working-age population) to residents aged 65 and older. In 1980, that ratio was approximately 5 to 1 for the Lehigh Valley; by 1990, it had dropped to just 4 to 1. Again, it is Atlanta that exemplifies the dynamic of growth. In 1980, it enjoyed 9 residents aged 16 to 64 for every person over the age of 65; by 1990, Atlanta's ratio of working-age to retirement-age citizens had grown to almost 10 to 1, more than twice that of the Lehigh Valley (Figure 5).

Essentially, this is a ratio of producers to nonproducers. A low ratio—in particular, a falling one, such as that found in the Lehigh Valley—suggests an increasing drag on the local economy. A low ratio usually indicates that an area is losing its young population, most likely because the work and educational opportunities are viewed as less attractive than the opportunities available elsewhere. The presumption is that, once young people in substantial numbers move elsewhere for employment, the local economy cannot be sustained.

The changing distribution of workers by industry tells much the same story. Although the Lehigh Valley lost 27.7 percent of its manufacturing jobs over the course of the 1980s, even as late as 1990 one of every

FIGURE 6
SHARE OF EMPLOYMENT BY INDUSTRY, 1994

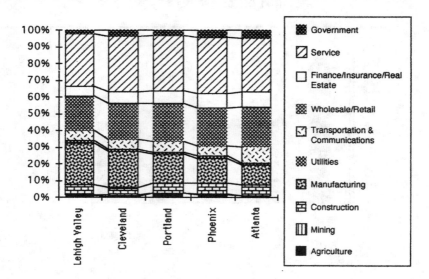

three Lehigh Valley workers was still employed in manufacturing, construction, mining, or agriculture. In Atlanta, less than one in four workers was engaged in primary- or secondary-sector employment (Figure 6).

The distribution of educational attainment completes the story. As measured by the number of years of schooling, the educational attainment of each of the five metropolitan areas improved during the 1980s, although again with noticeable differences. Atlanta had the highest proportion of college graduates in the workforce, one in three; the Lehigh Valley had the lowest, just over one in five. Among the five metropolitan areas in 1990, the Lehigh Valley had the lowest proportion (45 percent) of its workforce reporting at least some postsecondary education. Portland had the highest proportion (64 percent), followed closely by Atlanta with 60 percent reporting some college or a bachelor's degree (Figure 7). In the Lehigh Valley, where the economy is more heavily dependent on traditional primary and secondary enterprises, the high school diploma remains noticeably more important as a credential than in the other four metropolitan areas.

On the other hand, school officials in the Lehigh Valley report that upward of 70 percent of their high school graduates seek college or university enrollment immediately following graduation—a figure not unlike that of the other communities. What happens in the Lehigh Valley, however, is that young people either leave the area to go to school and do not return, or they use the college

FIGURE 7
EDUCATIONAL ATTAINMENT, 1990

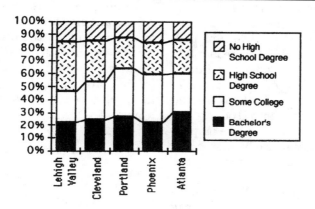

credentials earned at a local institution to qualify for work elsewhere. In either case, massification in conjunction with the changing nature of the Lehigh Valley's economy—and hence the demand for young workers—disperses the best and the brightest of the valley's young people to other locales and more vibrant economies. The same phenomenon works in reverse for cities like Atlanta that have become magnets for young people seeking to escape older communities such as those in the Lehigh Valley.

A CAUSAL NEXUS

It is this nexus of economic opportunity, educational attainment, and community and parental ambitions that underlies the changing context for higher education in the United States. The commitment to access—including, in particular, access to more full-time as well as higher-paying jobs for women—probably came first as a reaffirmation of America's

quest for social and economic mobility. The continuing infusion of college and university graduates during a time of sustained economic growth helped speed the transition to a service economy that paradoxically reduced the proportion of the labor force that could command the higher salaries that a college degree previously conferred.

Once the market for college graduates became saturated—even in booming communities like Atlanta—the boundary between massification and post-massification was crossed, leading to a restratification of both educational attainment and, not so coincidentally, economic advantage. That process is likely to accelerate as the number of young people seeking a college education again increases, while the nation's institutions of higher education are pressed harder to do more with less. Squeezed from above by reductions in higher education's share of public funding, pressed from below by the reluctance of students and their families to pay high tuitions for all but the most prestigious and selective institutions, colleges and universities will find themselves between the proverbial rock and a hard place. What some fear and others eagerly promote is a fundamental recasting of the nature of higher education in the United States—one that is both student- and customer-centered, with less emphasis on the importance of research and with less independence, even respect, for faculty.

There is a powerful case to be made in support of Arimoto's proposition of a general pattern that describes the transition from massification to post-massification—a transition both occasioned and made more difficult by changes in the economy that reduce the resources available to colleges and universities. In the United States, it is the expanding ambitions of middle- and upper-income families in combination with reductions in the demand for young workers that is leading to the restratification of American higher education on the one hand and, on the other, the formation of an outlet market for students who combine work with learning and are more likely to purchase their college educations one course at a time.

References

Arimoto, Akira. 1997. Massification of Higher Education and Academic Reforms in Japan. *Academic Reforms in the World: Situation and Perspective in the Massification Stage of Higher Education*. RIHE International Seminar Reports, no. 10. Hiroshima, Japan: Hiroshima University, Research Institute for Higher Education.

Stringfield, Sam. 1995. Attempting to Enhance Students' Learning Through Innovative Programs. *School Effectiveness and School Improvement* 6:62-96.

ANNALS, *AAPSS*, **559**, September 1998

Adult Enrollment and Educational Attainment

By JERRY A. JACOBS and SCOTT STONER-EBY

ABSTRACT: This article examines the growth of adult enrollment in recent decades in the United States and its impact on the educational attainment of the population. First, in order to better understand the growth of adult enrollment, the change between 1970 and 1990 is decomposed into its demographic elements. Next, the projected growth of enrollment over the next decade is analyzed. Finally, the article examines the cumulative impact of adult enrollment on educational levels, as well as on race and sex differentials in educational attainment. The study draws on data from the Integrated Postsecondary Education Data Systems, the U.S. decennial censuses, and the School Enrollment Supplements of the October 1970, 1980, and 1990 Current Population Surveys. The results highlight the role of the baby-boom generation in spurring the growth of adult enrollment. They also show that adult enrollment contributes significantly to the educational attainment of the U.S. population.

Jerry A. Jacobs is professor of sociology at the University of Pennsylvania. He has studied topics related to women's careers, including authority, earnings, working conditions, and entry into male-dominated occupations. He is currently conducting a study of women in higher education, funded by the Mellon and Spencer foundations.

Scott Stoner-Eby is a doctoral candidate in sociology and demography at the University of Pennsylvania. His research interests center on educational attainment, social stratification, and urban poverty.

NOTE: This project was partially supported by a research grant from the Spencer Foundation. The work reported herein was also supported under the Educational Research and Development Center Program, agreement number R309A60001, CFDA 84.309A, as administered by the Office of Educational Research and Improvement (OERI), U.S. Department of Education. The findings and opinions presented in this report do not reflect the position or policies of OERI or the U.S. Department of Education.

LIFE-course transitions have become a focal point for demographic and other social science research. Many contemporary social concerns can be viewed as problems encountered en route to stable adulthood: out-of-wedlock pregnancy, dropping out of high school, unemployment and underemployment, and marriages that end in divorce. Only a minority of the population experiences the still-normative sequence of completing school first, starting full-time employment next, getting married third, and only then having children (Rindfuss 1991; Rindfuss, Swicegood, and Rosenfeld 1987).

Here we focus on one out-of-sequence life-course transition—namely, delayed school enrollment. Older students who return to school remain an understudied population. For example, in Pascarella and Terenzini's 691-page review of the literature on the effect of college on students (1991), older students are mentioned on only 9 pages.

Research on adult students inevitably divides along disciplinary lines. Psychologists have examined the role of personality and social support in predisposing some individuals to return to school (Kasworm 1990; Spannard 1990; Clayton and Smith 1987; Tittle and Denker 1977), although the growing size and changing composition of the population of returning students suggests that more research is needed on this issue. Psychologists have also found evidence of an increase in independence and marital conflict among women who return to school (Ballmer and Cozby 1981), but more research is needed on larger samples and especially on returning students who do not succeed in completing a degree.

Sociologists have studied the marital, family, and job factors that are associated with returning to school (Bradburn, Moen, and Dempster-McClain 1995; Felmlee 1988; Suitor 1988). Here again, there is much room to expand on the research that has been completed, since the population of older students continues to change.

Economists and sociologists have studied the career consequences of returning to school, and the evidence suggests modest increases in earnings and occupational status (Felmlee 1988; Kanter 1989). Studies are mixed on whether older students receive a smaller return on their educational investment than those who complete their degrees earlier in life (Leigh and Gill 1997; Light 1995; Marcus 1984; Griliches 1980). Again, more research is needed that compares returns at different ages, different degree levels (for example, associate's versus bachelor's degrees), different types of institutions, and in different fields of study.

Large gaps remain in this research literature. While many studies have noted the growth in the enrollment of older students, few have tried to explain why this enrollment increased. Most studies in this area focus on women (except Light 1995 and Griliches 1980). Few include men or compare men and women, and fewer still have considered race and ethnic differences among older students. In this article, we focus on three aspects of the education of older students: the growth in enrollment; its effects on educational attainment; and its effects on race and gender disparities.

It is well known that the proportion of traditional college-age students has declined, while the proportion of older people returning to school has grown steadily. What is less appreciated is the role that the baby boom has played in these changes. When the large baby-boom cohort passed through the traditional college-age years into adulthood, older cohorts grew in size relative to their younger counterparts. We examine how much of the growth of the enrollment of older students is simply the result of this shift in the age structure—and how much is due to increases in age-specific enrollment rates. We further explore the impact of the age structure on enrollment by examining the age pattern of projected enrollment over the next decade.

After exploring the growth of enrollment, we turn to the effect of adult education on the educational levels of the population. Many of those who return to school do so part-time, and they are often faced with many competing demands for their time and attention. Are those who return to school completing additional years of schooling and completing their degrees? We document the cumulative effect of returning to school on high school graduation, college graduation, and average number of years of school completed. Finally, we assess the effect of delayed enrollment on race and gender differentials in educational attainment. What impact does delayed enrollment have on the gender differential in educational attainment? Do African Americans narrow the attainment gap vis-à-vis

whites by acquiring more education later in life?

We examine both college enrollment and the cumulative educational attainment of white and African American men and women in the United States between 1970 and 1990, drawing on fall enrollment data from the Integrated Postsecondary Education Data Systems (IPEDS), as reported in the *Digest of Educational Statistics* (National Center for Education Statistics [NCES] 1996), and Census Bureau estimates of the size of the population in specific age and sex groups, as measured in the Current Population Survey (CPS) (U.S. Bureau of the Census 1978, 1990, and 1992b). We present the results of analyses of enrollment and attainment using data from the October School Enrollment Supplement of the Current Population Survey for 1970, 1980, and 1990. We also draw on published reports of educational attainment by age (U.S. Bureau of the Census 1970, 1976, 1984, 1987, 1992a, 1996).

THE GROWTH IN ADULT ENROLLMENT

Table 1 documents the growth in the enrollment of students in institutions of higher education by age group.[1] Figures 1 and 2 draw on IPEDS data on enrollment in higher education (NCES 1996, tab. 171). The percentage change in enrollment between 1970 and 1990 is presented for all students, full-time and part-time. We refer to those aged 24 and younger as traditional-age students, and those 25 and older as adult students.

TABLE 1
ENROLLMENT BY AGE, SEX, AND FULL-TIME AND PART-TIME STATUS, 1970-90

	Percentage Change 1970-90 Actual	Percentage Change 1970-90 Imputed at 1970 Rates	Projected Percentage Change 1990-2006
All students			
Total			
Age 14-24	25.1	9.3	27.5
Age 25+	154.5	56.1	7.2
Men			
Age 14-24	8.6	14.6	21.8
Age 25+	61.9	59.7	10.4
Women			
Age 14-24	47.1	4.4	33.2
Age 25+	312.5	52.1	5.1
Full-time			
Total			
Age 14-24	18.4	8.6	27.7
Age 25+	164.0	57.4	25.2
Men			
Age 14-24	1.7	13.9	22.5
Age 25+	53.8	61.2	44.3
Women			
Age 14-24	42.1	3.5	32.8
Age 25+	477.2	71.3	10.6
Part-time			
Total			
Age 14-24	59.2	12.9	27.0
Age 25+	150.7	55.8	0.3
Men			
Age 14-24	50.6	18.5	18.4
Age 25+	65.9	59.2	−4.1
Women			
Age 14-24	67.6	7.6	34.6
Age 25+	274.2	52.1	3.0

SOURCES: NCES 1996, tab. 171; Census Bureau population estimates.

The growth in enrollment has clearly been faster among adult students than among traditional-age college students. The total enrollment for students aged 24 or younger grew 25.1 percent between 1970 and 1990, compared with 154.5 percent for students 25 and older. As Table 1 reveals, this is not simply a reflection of growing part-time enrollment among older students. The faster growth in the enrollment of older students is most evident among full-time students, because there has been very little growth among traditional-age full-time students. What has occurred instead is that many traditional-age students are now enrolled part-time. Indeed, part-time enrollment has been the fastest growing segment of traditional-age college students.

FIGURE 1
MALE UNDERGRADUATE ENROLLMENT RATES, 1970 AND 1990

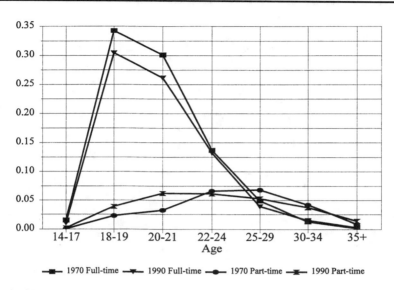

—■— 1970 Full-time —▼— 1990 Full-time —●— 1970 Part-time —✕— 1990 Part-time

SOURCES: IPEDS enrollment data and Census Bureau population estimates.

The enrollment of women grew faster than that of men during this period—but, for both men and women, the enrollment of older students grew faster than that of younger students. The largest percentage gain occurred among older women enrolled full-time (up 477.2 percent), but this group was starting from a small base.

As a result of these trends, older students now constitute a larger fraction of higher education enrollment than ever before. In 1970, students aged 25 and over composed just over one-quarter of all enrolled students (27.8 percent) and just over one-tenth (11.0 percent) of full-time students. By 1990, these figures had grown to 43.9 percent of all students and 21.6 percent of full-time students.

Yet this sharp growth was not entirely due to a growth in enrollment rates for specific groups of men and women. Instead, an upward shift in the age distribution accounts for much of this change. As the baby-boom generation aged, the size of the adult population grew more quickly than did that of the traditional college-age population. In 1970, the ratio of the population aged 25-39 to the standard college-age population (aged 18-24) was 1.22. By 1990, this ratio had increased to 2.33. In other words, the age group most likely to return to school grew sharply in size relative to that of the traditional college-age population.

These figures suggest that the number of older students returning to school would have grown even if

FIGURE 2
FEMALE UNDERGRADUATE ENROLLMENT RATES, 1970 AND 1990

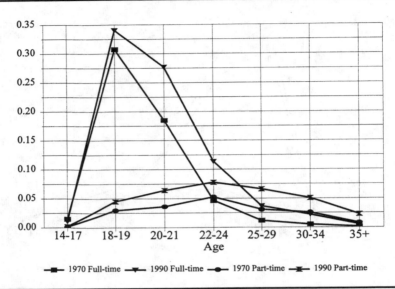

SOURCES: IPEDS enrollment data and Census Bureau population estimates.

the age-specific rate of returning had remained constant at its 1970 level. We calculated just how much of this growth would have occurred when holding age-specific enrollment rates constant at their 1970 level and allowing only the age distribution of the population to vary.[2] The results are presented in the second column of Table 1. For men, changes in age structure and the size of the underlying population account for the vast majority of the growth in enrollment at older ages. In other words, we can predict most of the trends in the enrollment of men by holding the 1970 age-specific enrollment rates constant and simply substituting the 1990 age structure. For example, holding age-specific rates constant at their 1970 level, we would have ex-

pected an increase of 59.7 percent in the total enrollment of men aged 25 and up between 1970 and 1990. The actual increase in enrollment for this group was 61.9 percent. Thus, for men, the actual outcome supports the assumption that age-specific rates did not change; in fact, the only change during this period was a growth in the size of the pool of older students from which to draw. Indeed, in a number of cases, the changes predicted for men are greater than those observed. As we will see, this is consistent with a decline in age-specific enrollment rates for men.

For women, changes in enrollment rates, as well as changes in age structure, are needed to account for the observed trends in enrollments. For no group does the assumption of static age-specific enrollment rates adequately predict the sharp enrollment growth experienced by women during this period. Total enrollment of women aged 25 and older grew 312.5 percent between 1970 and 1990, while the growth of population of students aged 25 or more would have predicted a growth rate of only 52.1 percent. Changes in the age structure account for only a small proportion of enrollment growth for women enrolled both full-time and part-time.

These results are not just an interesting window into the recent past. They also hold important implications for the future, because changes in the age structure will have the opposite effect over the next decade. The last column of Table 1 compares enrollment projections for 2006 with actual enrollments in 1990, by age.[3] For both men and women, the growth of enrollment among students aged 25 and older is, for the most part, projected to be smaller than the enrollment growth among younger students. Enrollments of older students will, on the whole, not decline, but this group will no longer grow as fast as the pool of younger students, unless age-specific enrollment rates increase. Colleges and universities that are just now seeking to tap the pool of older students may have waited too long, for this population is no longer the growth market that it was during the 1970s and 1980s.

Figures 1 and 2 display age-specific enrollment rates in institutions of higher education for men and women. We calculated these rates by comparing IPEDS enrollment data (numerator) with Census Bureau population data (denominator) for the same age and sex groups in 1970 and 1990. Figure 1 shows a slight drop from 1970 to 1990 in the age-specific enrollment rates of male full-time students. For men enrolled as part-time students, there was an increase in enrollment for those under age 25, and a decline for those 25 and older. Thus there was a shift from full-time to part-time enrollment among traditional-age male students. In contrast, Figure 2 shows a marked increase in enrollment rates for women at all age levels for both part-time and full-time students.

Figures 3, 4, 5, and 6 corroborate this picture. In these figures we present an original analysis of data from the 1970, 1980, and 1990 October Current Population Surveys. In these figures, we focus on undergraduate enrollment in order to avoid conflating the growth of older undergraduates with the growth of graduate education. To estimate college enrollment rates, we restricted our measure of enrollment to include only those who had enrolled in their thirteenth through sixteenth year of school. In this way, we were able to target college enrollment rather than those enrolled in high school or graduate school. The 1970 curve ends at ages 30 to 34 because the questions on educational enrollment were not asked of those aged 35 and older.[4]

Figure 3 shows that the enrollment rates of white women over age 25 did indeed increase over time, and increases are evident during both the 1970s and 1980s. For African American women (Figure 4), the 1970-1980 comparison shows a sharp increase in undergraduate enrollments be-

FIGURE 3
WHITE FEMALE UNDERGRADUATE ENROLLMENT RATES

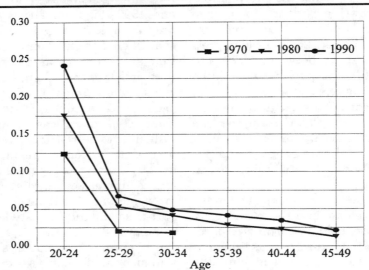

SOURCES: CPS Oct. 1970, 1980, 1990.

tween 1970 and 1980. During the 1980s, African American women's enrollments continued to increase among traditional-age college students but declined among those aged 25 and older.

Figure 5, which presents similar results for white men, shows remarkably little upward secular trend in undergraduate enrollments. Enrollment rates dropped between 1970 and 1980 for traditional-age white men but had rebounded by 1990. There was very little change for older white men over the same period. For African American men (see Figure 6), there was an increase in undergraduate enrollment rates at older ages between 1970 and 1980, followed by a decline between 1980 and 1990. On the bright side, the undergraduate enrollment rate of traditional-age Af-

rican American men jumped sharply between 1980 and 1990. For both white and African American men, undergraduate enrollment rates of adult students had roughly returned to their 1970 levels by 1990.

For men, then, it is clear that an increase in the enrollment of older college students between 1970 and 1990 was due to changes in the age structure of the population, rather than changes in age-specific enrollment rates. For women, the aging of the baby boomers reinforced the effect of increasing age-specific undergraduate enrollment rates.

The levels as well as the trends are worth noting. CPS data suggest that, by 1990, 4.9 percent of white women aged 30 to 34 were enrolled in college. Even for white women between the ages of 40 and 44, 3.5 percent were

FIGURE 4
BLACK FEMALE UNDERGRADUATE ENROLLMENT RATES

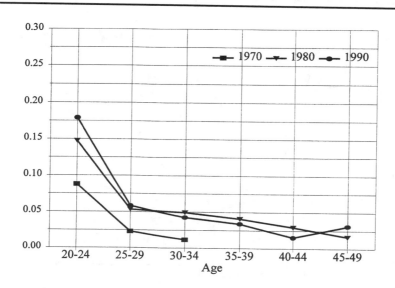

SOURCES: CPS Oct. 1970, 1980, 1990.

enrolled in college. Similar rates are evident for African American women for 1990, although there is greater variability in these rates due to smaller sample sizes. For white men, enrollment rates exceed 2.7 percent at ages 30 to 34 and 2.1 percent at ages 35 to 39. The comparable figures for African American men are 1.4 percent at ages 30 to 34 and 1.8 percent at ages 35 to 39.

It should be noted that full-time enrollment drops more sharply with age than does total enrollment. As a result, a much larger fraction of 40-year-olds are enrolled part-time than are 30-year-olds. This pattern is evident in Figure 7, which presents the proportion of students enrolled full-time in 1990 for each race and sex group, by age. The decline in the proportion of full-time students is broadly similar for the different race and sex groups, once the greater sampling variability for data on African American students is taken into account. At ages 20 to 24, roughly three-quarters of students are enrolled full-time; by ages 40 to 44, only about one-quarter of students are enrolled full-time.

CUMULATIVE EDUCATIONAL
ATTAINMENT AND RACE
AND GENDER DISPARITIES

Figures 1 through 6 show that a small proportion of the population continues to be enrolled in higher education through at least age 45. However, what appear to be low enrollment rates are in fact potentially quite significant because they extend over so many years. The cumulative

FIGURE 5
WHITE MALE UNDERGRADUATE ENROLLMENT RATES

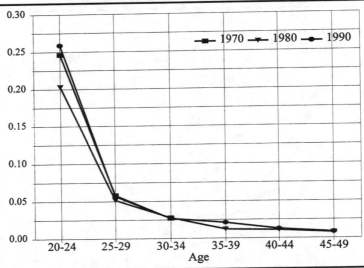

SOURCES: CPS Oct. 1970, 1980, 1990.

impact of schooling between ages 25 and 45 may indeed be much greater than one might guess from a quick glance at these enrollment rates. We now turn to the question, What impact does this extended enrollment have on the educational attainment of the population? In other words, how much of this extensive enrollment translates into eventual completed years of schooling and degree attainment? We examine the data by race and sex, considering the issue of the impact of later-life education on different groups, along with the issue of cumulative attainment patterns.

Figure 8 presents the number of cumulative years of schooling completed by a cohort of men and women, based on successive samples of CPS respondents.[5] In this and subsequent analyses, we broaden our focus from college enrollment to all formal school enrollment, including high school equivalency programs and graduate school programs. The data clearly indicate that the mean number of years of schooling completed by the cohort continues to rise as the group passes through its thirties and even forties. The cohort of white men aged 20 to 24 in 1970 had completed an average of 12.8 years of schooling; by the time they were 30 to 34 in 1980, they had completed 13.4 years of schooling. They continued to acquire additional schooling even as they entered their early forties and, by 1990, had completed 13.7 years of schooling. Thus approximately 7 percent of the years of schooling completed by this cohort was acquired at the ages of 25 and older.[6]

The average number of years of schooling completed trends upward with age for all of the race and sex

FIGURE 6
BLACK MALE UNDERGRADUATE ENROLLMENT RATES

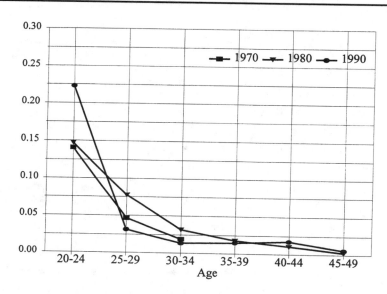

SOURCES: CPS Oct. 1970, 1980, 1990.

groups examined, with the exception of African American males aged 40 and over (undoubtedly reflecting some sampling variability). The gap between the four race-sex groups remains of roughly similar size for this cohort as it ages. In other words, in this cohort women and minorities did not catch up to white males in average educational attainment at later ages. Note that Figure 8 (as well as Figures 9 and 10) reflects the experiences of the cohort that was aged 20 to 24 in 1970. Recall from Figures 4 and 5 that the enrollment of women at all ages has jumped sharply since 1970. As a result, the gender gap in educational attainment has been much smaller in recent years, and the experience of adult enrollment will enable women to catch up with men—and perhaps surpass them—in educational attainment.[7]

Figure 9 focuses on completion of high school, rather than the average number of years of schooling presented in Figure 8.[8] Here, again, we see that later-life enrollment in education continues to have an impact on the levels of educational attainment. For white men and women, the proportion completing high school increased from just over 80 percent (82.6 percent for white men, 82.7 percent for white women) at ages 20 to 24 to about 90 percent (89.5 percent for white men, 90.1 percent for white women) by ages 45 to 49. It is notable that the graph continues to slope upward, even when white men and women are in their thirties and forties, indicating not only continued

FIGURE 7
PROPORTIONS ENROLLED IN COLLEGE FULL-TIME, 1990

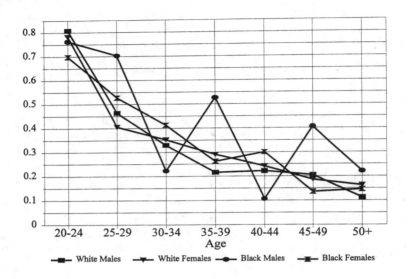

SOURCES: CPS Oct. 1970, 1980, 1990.

enrollment but the completion of additional years of schooling.

In the case of high school completion, African Americans narrowed the attainment gap vis-à-vis white Americans. The race differential in high school completion narrowed from 15 to 20 percentage points at ages 20 to 24 (20.2 percentage point gap for men, 15.2 for women) to less than 10 percentage points (8.9 percentage points for men, 8.0 for women) at ages 40 to 44.[9] The sex differential within races was quite small in terms of high school completion.

While, each year, few individuals complete high school after age 25, the cumulative impact of low rates of high school completion are nonethe-less quite significant. The data indicate that the proportion of this cohort completing high school after age 25 increased by 8.4 percent for white men, 8.9 percent for white women, 22.6 percent for African American men, and 16.0 percent for African American women.

We must take into account that the data on educational attainment are self-reported and may reflect some degree of exaggeration on the part of respondents. As noted in note 4, CPS self-reported enrollment data are higher than IPEDS enrollment figures for the corresponding age and sex groups. Nonetheless, even assuming the tendency of some respondents to inflate their educational credentials as they become older, these

FIGURE 8
MEAN NUMBER OF YEARS OF SCHOOL COMPLETED

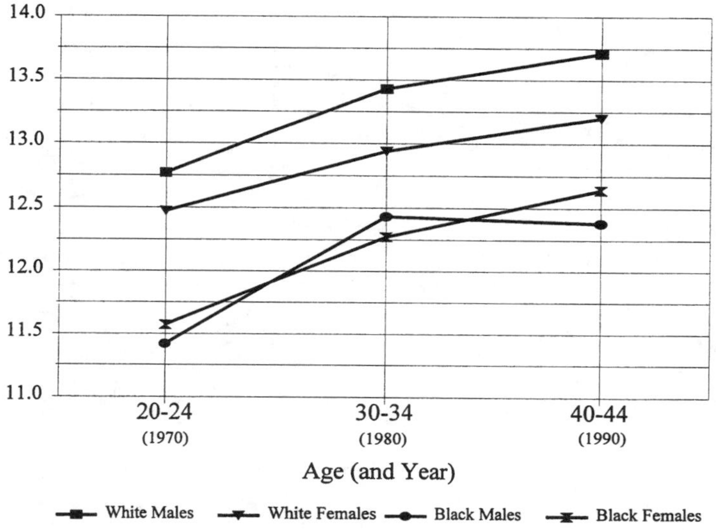

SOURCES: CPS Oct. 1970, 1980, 1990.

data do suggest the importance of adult enrollment in the attainment of additional years of schooling.

Figure 10 focuses on college completion. Here, again, there are continued increases in attainment as the cohort ages. The proportion of white men that had completed college climbed from about 26.3 percent at ages 25 to 29 to nearly 37.0 percent by ages 45 to 49.[10] In terms of college completion, white men increased their lead on other race and sex groups. The racial disparity in college completion also increased as this cohort aged.

As with the case of high school completion, the cumulative effect of later-life degree completion is quite impressive. For white men, the proportion who reported having com-pleted 16 or more years of schooling increased by 40.7 percent after age 30. The comparable figures are 38.7 percent for white women, 34.2 for African American men, and 45.5 for African American women. In other words, for each of these race and sex groups, more than one-third of those who completed their college degrees did so at age 30 or older.

DISCUSSION

In this brief report, we advance several ideas about the growth and impact of adult enrollment in higher education. First, we show that the aging of the baby-boom generation into their thirties and forties has had a profound impact on the growth of adult enrollment. Nearly all of the

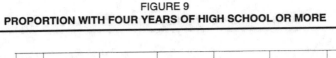

FIGURE 9
PROPORTION WITH FOUR YEARS OF HIGH SCHOOL OR MORE

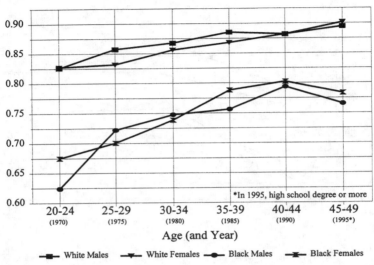

SOURCES: U.S. Bureau of the Census 1970, 1976, 1984, 1987, 1992a, 1996.

growth in adult enrollment for men, and a modest fraction of the growth for women, is due to the aging of this generation. This result is important, because future growth will not follow this trend. Through the year 2006, the growth in enrollment of traditional-age college students will surpass that of older students.

Trachtenberg (1997) suggests that, as the baby boomers continue to age, there will be enrollment growth at ever older ages. While this is, of course, a possibility, the historical pattern of low enrollment rates among those in their forties and fifties suggests that the baby boomers are unlikely to make as much of a mark in future years as they have in the past. The more likely consequence of the changing age structure is a return to the importance of the traditional-age college student.

A second important conclusion we document is that adult enrollment does indeed have a significant cumulative effect on the educational attainment of the population. When an age cohort is followed through their thirties and forties, educational levels do advance. This pattern is evident in the average number of years of schooling completed, in the proportion of the population that has completed high school, and in the proportion that has completed college. This brief report suggests that adult education leads to the completion of additional years of schooling and even degree completion.

A third conclusion we reach is that adult education does not rectify im-

FIGURE 10
PROPORTION WITH FOUR YEARS OF COLLEGE OR MORE

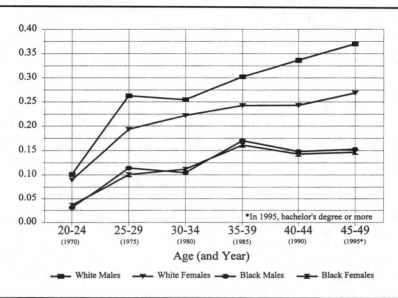

Age (and Year)

—■— White Males   —▼— White Females   —●— Black Males   —✕— Black Females

SOURCES: U.S. Bureau of the Census 1970, 1976, 1984, 1992a, 1996.

portant differentials in educational attainment. The extent of the gap between race and sex groups depends on the particular measure of education employed. For both African Americans and whites, men and women differ little in the level of high school completion, and this similarity changes little with age. As they grow older, African Americans narrow the gap with whites in the level of high school completion. The race differential in college completion persists, however, and may even grow slightly with age, as does the gender gap in college completion among whites. It should be noted, however, that in recent years, more women than men graduated from college, and adult education may well enable women to surpass men in the acquisition of overall educational credentials.

Should we promote the acquisition of education among older students? On the one hand, one could argue that investments in schooling should be made early in life, because younger graduates can benefit from these investments for a longer period of time than older graduates. For example, a college degree earned at age 22 can enhance earnings over a career spanning five decades, whereas a degree earned at age 40 can be expected to pay off for perhaps three decades. Even if the increases in hourly wages that result from these two degrees are comparable (a point that remains in dispute), the longer payback period argues in favor of promoting earlier rather than later investments.

On the other hand, we maintain that adult education has become just too important a source of educational investment to ignore. High school completion after age 25 constitutes a significant fraction of high school completion, especially for African Americans, and college completion after age 30 represents an even more significant fraction of college completion. If increasing the educational levels of the population is a national goal, evidence from the recent past suggests that adult education is an important source for training and skill development.

Policies designed to promote the acquisition of schooling by the population should include adult students as one of the target populations, but not at the expense of investments in schooling focused on younger groups. Changes in social policies, such as welfare reform, should be designed to facilitate rather than inhibit the life-long acquisition of additional education. If steps were taken to improve persistence and completion rates, the impact of adult education might well be even greater than is documented here.

The findings sketched here clearly call for further research. The growth of enrollment rates of older women especially call for more careful investigation. In particular, light needs to be shed on how women's changing labor force participation, changing fertility patterns, and changing occupational patterns are related to this increasing tendency to return to school.

Notes

1. We focus on formal enrollment in institutions of higher education, rather than on-the-job training or seminars sponsored by employers. As a result, we understate the extent of adult educational investments.

2. We calculated age-specific population rates for men and women by dividing IPEDS enrollment data by age-specific population data for each sex from the same year. The IPEDS enrollment data were obtained from the *Digest of Educational Statistics*, and the population estimates were obtained from *Current Population Reports*, ser. P-25. We then applied the 1970 age-specific enrollment rates to the 1990 population base. This calculation provides an estimate of the rate of change in enrollments among specific age groups due to changing population size rather than changing enrollment rates.

3. We rely here on NCES projections for the year 2006. See NCES 1996, tab. 171.

4. Estimates of age-specific enrollment rates are slightly higher when using CPS self-reports compared with IPEDS enrollment data. However, the age patterns obtained from the two data sources match each other quite closely.

5. These calculations were based on the comparison of age-specific groups, by race and sex, in successive CPS cross-sections. For example, we obtained educational attainment data for white men aged 20 to 24 in 1970. We then plotted this result against the attainment of those aged 30 to 34 in 1980 and 40 to 44 in 1990. In this way, we followed the experiences of a cohort via the analysis of repeated cross-sectional surveys.

6. The growth of education at age 25 and older was 0.9 years (13.7–12.8), which, divided by 12.8, equals 7 percent.

7. We displayed the experience of the cohort aged 20 to 24 in 1970, rather than more recent cohorts, in order to display the full educational trajectory of the group. More recent cohorts have not yet completed their attainment of schooling.

8. In 1990, the data reflect high school completion; for earlier years, the data represent the completion of 12 years of schooling.

9. In principle, schooling levels should remain the same or increase as a cohort ages, and they should never decline. However, the procedure of following a cohort through repeated cross-sectional surveys allows for the possibility of decline due to altered responses to survey questions or sampling variability.

10. It should be noted that the 1995 data points refer to the completion of a bachelor's degree, while the earlier surveys reflect the completion of 16 years of schooling.

References

Ballmer, H. and P. C. Cozby. 1981. Family Environments of Women Who Return to College. *Sex Roles* 7(10):1019-26.

Bradburn, Ellen M., Phyllis Moen, and Donna Dempster-McClain. 1995. Women's Return to School Following the Transition to Motherhood. *Social Forces* 73(4):1517-51.

Clayton, Diane E. and Margaret M. Smith. 1987. Motivational Typology of Reentry Women. *Adult Education Quarterly* 37(2):90-104.

Felmlee, Diane. 1988. Returning to School and Women's Occupational Attainment. *Sociology of Education* 61:29-41.

Griliches, Zvi. 1980. Schooling Interruptions, Work While in School and the Returns from Schooling. *Scandinavian Journal of Economics* 82(2):291-303.

Kanter, Sandra. 1989. The Value of the College Degree for Older Women Graduates. *Innovative Higher Education* 13(2):90-105.

Kasworm, Carol E. 1990. Adult Undergraduates in Higher Education: A Review of Past Research Perspectives. *Review of Educational Research* 60(3):345-72.

Leigh, Duane E. and Andrew M. Gill. 1997. Labor Market Returns to Community Colleges: Evidence for Returning Adults. *Journal of Human Resources* 32(2):334-53.

Light, Audrey. 1995. The Effects of Interrupted Schooling on Wages. *Journal of Human Resources* 30(3):472-502.

Marcus, Richard D. 1984. Measuring the Rate of Return to Interrupted Schooling. *Journal of Educational Statistics* 9(4):295-310.

National Center for Education Statistics (NCES). 1996. *Digest of Educational Statistics*. Washington, DC: Department of Education.

Pascarella, Ernest T. and Patrick T. Terenzini. 1991. *How College Affects Students*. San Francisco: Jossey-Bass.

Rindfuss, Ronald R. 1991. The Young Adult Years: Diversity, Structural Change and Fertility. *Demography* 28(4):493-533.

Rindfuss, Ronald R., C. Gray Swicegood, and Rachel A. Rosenfeld. 1987. Disorder in the Life Course: How Common and Does It Matter? *American Sociological Review* 52:785-801.

Spannard, Jan-Marie A. 1990. Beyond Intent: Reentering College to Complete the Degree. *Review of Educational Research* 60(3):309-44.

Suitor, J. Jill. 1988. Husband's Educational Attainment and Support for Wives' Return to School. *Gender & Society* 2(4):482-95.

Tittle, Carol K. and Elenor R. Denker. 1977. Re-Entry Women: A Selective Review of the Educational Process, Career Choice and Interest Measurement. *Review of Educational Research* 47(4):531-84.

Trachtenberg, Stephen J. 1997. Preparing for "Baby Boomers": Older Students Will Bring New Opportunities to Colleges. *Chronicle of Higher Education*, 21 Mar., p. B-7.

U.S. Bureau of the Census. 1970. Educational Attainment in the United States. *Current Population Reports*, ser. P-20, no. 207.

———. 1976. Educational Attainment in the United States. *Current Population Reports*, ser. P-20, no. 295.

———. 1978. U.S. Population Estimates, by Age, Sex, Race and Hispanic Origin. *Current Population Reports*, ser. P-25, no. 721.

————. 1984. Educational Attainment in the United States. *Current Population Reports*, ser. P-20, no. 390.

————. 1987. Educational Attainment in the United States. *Current Population Reports*, ser. P-20, no. 415.

————. 1990. U.S. Population Estimates, by Age, Sex, Race and Hispanic Origin. *Current Population Reports*, ser. P-25, no. 1045.

————. 1992a. Educational Attainment in the United States. *Current Population Reports*, ser. P-20, no. 462.

————. 1992b. U.S. Population Estimates, by Age, Sex, Race and Hispanic Origin. *Current Population Reports*, ser. P-25, no. 1095.

————. 1996. Educational Attainment in the United States. *Current Population Reports*, ser. P-20, no. 489.

Employer Participation in School-to-Work Programs

By PETER CAPPELLI, DANIEL SHAPIRO,
and NICHOLE SHUMANIS

ABSTRACT: This article assesses the extent to which employers participate in school-to-work partnerships and work-based learning, using data from the National Employer Survey (NES). It opens with a brief discussion of the history of the school-to-work movement and the development of the School-to-Work Opportunities Act, which seeks to improve the preparation of college- and non-college-bound students for the workforce. The authors then present a review of the literature that focuses on incentives for employer participation in these programs and obstacles to implementing the programs on a national scale. The authors then report on previous attempts to measure the number of participating employers and compare these estimates with a recent analysis of data from the NES. They find that, while 25 percent of U.S. companies participate in a school-to-work partnership and another 40 percent provide a work-based learning experience, it is not clear how substantive such involvement and experiences are.

Peter Cappelli is professor and chair of the Management Department at the Wharton School of the University of Pennsylvania; director of Wharton's Center for Human Resources; and codirector of the National Center on the Educational Quality of the Workforce.

Daniel Shapiro is director of research at the Institute for Research on Higher Education at the University of Pennsylvania.

Nichole Shumanis is a doctoral student at the University of Pennsylvania's Graduate School of Education, Higher Education Division.

NOTE: The work reported herein was supported under the Educational Research and Development Center Program, through the National Center for Postsecondary Improvement (NCPI), agreement number R309A60001, CFDA 84.309A, as administered by the National Institute on Postsecondary Education, Libraries, and Lifelong Learning, and the Consortium for Policy Research in Education (CPRE), agreement number R308A60003, CFDA 84.308A, as

RECENT interest in improving the quality of the U.S. education system has been driven by many factors, but arguably the most important in recent years has been concerns about the economic consequences of poor education. Most of these concerns have been focused on non-college-bound students, a group that has over time experienced significant difficulties in the labor market and has also increased significantly in size.

According to Current Population Survey data, as reported by the U.S. Department of Education (1997), the proportion of the population aged 25 to 29 that completed high school rose from 78 percent in 1971 to 87 percent in 1996. The increase in the percentage of high school graduates in that cohort that completed at least some college was even larger—a rate that rose from 44 to 65 percent over the same period. However, less than half of those college matriculants—only 31 percent of the 25- to 29-year-old high school graduates in 1996—ever received a four-year degree. As a result, high school curricula have largely been geared toward the college-bound student, particularly those aiming for a bachelor's degree. Students who go directly into the workforce have received less attention.

This "forgotten half" (W. T. Grant Foundation 1985) of American society has been the target of a series of proposals for reform over the past decade, many of which have made use of the mechanism of bringing school and the workplace closer together. Reports such as *America's Choice: High Skills or Low Wages!* (National Center on Education and the Economy 1990) warned that the ability of the U.S. economy to compete in the future would be tied to the success of current education reform efforts that were needed to raise the skills of the production workforce. The apparent failure of various vocational education programs to address the problems of this group of students also contributed to a rethinking of how the workplace and the education system should relate to each other.

At the same time, a convergence of research was pointing toward a new model that might simultaneously raise academic performance and help students who were not headed for college to make the transition to successful careers. Part of this research included comparative studies of national economic performance, particularly in Germany, which has a model of economic success that also produced high wages—at least through the early 1990s. These studies focused on the role that youth apprenticeship and programs like it that combined classroom studies with workplace experience played in producing skilled workers and competitive enterprises. Their authors argued that similar efforts could

administered by the National Institute on Educational Governance, Finance, Policy-Making and Management, Office of Educational Research and Improvement (OERI), U.S. Department of Education. The data analysis for this article was conducted at the U.S. Bureau of the Census's Center for Economic Studies. The findings and opinions expressed by NCPI and CPRE do not reflect the position or policies of the Bureau of the Census, OERI, or the U.S. Department of Education.

work in the United States (Hamilton 1990; Lehrman and Pouncy 1990). The remaining segment of research came from cognitive psychology and documented the learning advantages of placing academic content in the context of real problems (Resnick 1987).

These arguments began to coalesce in public policy around a model that became known as school-to-work.[1] At its center was an effort to provide experiences in work-based settings that could be integrated with material in high schools to provide three elements. The first was a real context for learning academic material. The academic concepts were illustrated in real work-based problems that provided a practical use for those concepts, a reason for learning them, as well as clearer demonstrations of how they work.

The second element was the teaching of work-based skills via experience in the workplace. The skills taught—such as how to use various pieces of equipment or work with real materials—would be related directly to work. The skills were difficult to duplicate in the classroom and included some of the vocational skills that would help students secure jobs.

The third element was a context for supporting the social development of students, particularly students who might otherwise be at risk. The attention of adult role models in the context of a constructive work atmosphere helped develop social skills such as the ability to work with others, to be punctual, and to monitor one's own behavior.

The School-to-Work Opportunities Act (STWOA) of 1994 was designed to support the development of programs to pursue these goals by bringing schools and employers together in partnerships and advancing programs of work-based learning. The main difficulty, many anticipated, was getting employers to participate.

Assessments of the amount of employer involvement in secondary education programs produced for the National Assessment of Vocational Education suggested that, with the exception of co-op programs, employer involvement was essentially trivial. Youth apprenticeship programs that integrated classroom lessons and workplace experience were the closest in spirit to the school-to-work model. The largest of these programs, in Wisconsin, had no more than about 100 participants in the entire state. Estimates suggested that only about 1000 students were participating in youth apprenticeship programs across the entire country, while as many as 3 million places would be needed to provide experiences to all of the relevant population (Osterman 1995). What would make enough employers participate to move the school-to-work agenda from a novel educational experiment to a mainstream program?

INCENTIVES TO PARTICIPATE

Employer participation is a necessary condition for school-to-work programs. Perhaps because the promise of these programs for students appeared to be so great, less attention was given to thinking about what was in it for employers—what would get them to participate? In European countries, apprenticeships had been backed by legislation and an infrastructure that effectively compelled many employers to participate or provided strong economic subsidies for participating. In the United States, however, apprenticeship programs had been introduced in a decentralized way without the supporting infrastructure of the European models, such as collective bargaining agreements or legislative mandates that created explicit incentives for employers to participate.

President Bill Clinton had encouraged business leaders to become involved in school-to-work partnerships, and leading companies interested in advancing these programs created the National Education Leadership Council. The civic-mindedness that encouraged many companies to participate in these programs was an important resource. Early studies of school-to-work pilot programs found that employers cited their desire to improve their communities as one of the most significant reasons for their participation (Bailey 1995). Another study of more general employer involvement in work-based learning programs found the same interest in civic-mindedness as the primary motivation for participating (Lynn and Wills 1995). But most observers doubted that this motive would be enough to get the school-to-work movement off the ground.

A second, and arguably more sustaining, motive behind employers' participation in school-to-work programs is the practical, economic benefits. Bailey (1995) outlines some aspects of these benefits. Employers who participate may enjoy positive public relations as a result of employing high school students, which helps promote their businesses. These companies may also use high school students as a cheap source of labor, particularly when needed on a short-term basis only. In a study conducted by the Institute on Education and the Economy, the most common impetus for a company's involvement in school-to-work programs was its need for low-cost, short-term labor (Hughes 1996). Companies recognize that student labor is less expensive than hiring adults on a temporary basis, because student interns often work for free or for a low hourly wage and receive no benefits (Hughes 1996).[2]

Another potential advantage of school-to-work programs for employers is that companies might use them to help meet their recruitment goals. These programs essentially give employers information about the job performance of a pool of workers while in their own establishment— workers who are about to look for permanent jobs, and information that is crucial for improving the success of employee selection efforts. Nearly 50 percent of the companies surveyed by Lynn and Wills (1995) had hired students as regular employees upon completion of their school-to-work programs. Similarly, the Office of Technology Assessment found that nearly two-thirds of employers surveyed considered recruitment goals the most important reason for their involvement in work-based learning programs (Hughes 1996). By employing students, then, corporations are potentially making an investment in their firm and, at the same time, reducing their recruitment expenditures.

Bailey (1995) argues that "collective motivation" may also be a reason that employers participate in school-to-work programs. The underlying concept here is that, by working together and by participating in programs such as school-to-work projects, corporations will help create a skilled labor force for the region or the broader economy. In other words, their self-interest might be advanced by acting collectively to raise skill levels in the economy as a whole. A 1991 Louis Harris poll found that, of corporations familiar with youth apprenticeship programs, 48 percent believed their company's involvement could help in producing a skilled labor force (Osterman 1995). Another outcome of collective motivation is the marketing of an industry to young people, changing their perceptions of it. Hughes (1996), a senior researcher at the Institute on Education and the Economy, describes an employer in the construction industry who feels his participation in the school-to-work program enables his company to tear down negative stereotypes associated with his industry.

The same study also found that some employers experienced an improvement in employee morale as a result of having work-based learning programs in their facilities. The argument is that employees enjoy working with students, take pride in their work when they see students interested in it, and may better understand their tasks when they must explain and teach them to a novice (Hughes 1996). This last factor may not be, in and of itself, reason enough to justify an employer's involvement in school-to-work programs, but, taken in conjunction with other motivating factors, this variable may prove to be a welcome fringe benefit.

In addition to these motivating factors, there was a financial incentive in some parts of the country for employers to participate in school-to-work programs. The STWOA empowered states to facilitate the development of school-to-work programs, and by 1996 the federal government had granted $643 million to 29 states to help make that possible. Some states, including Michigan, Oregon, and Wisconsin, offer incentives in the form of tax credits or wage subsidies for those companies that hire youth apprentices (Hershey et al. 1997).

OBSTACLES TO PARTICIPATION

Even after the act was implemented, however, most observers doubted that school-to-work programs would have more than a token representation across the country; it was thought that employers felt there was not enough self-interest to participate and the obstacles to participating were considerable (Bailey 1995; Osterman 1995; Stern 1995). For example, participation typically requires a substantial financial commitment up front. ProTech in Boston, one of the most successful school-to-work programs, placed high school students in part-time jobs in Boston-area hospitals. A representative hospital, which placed 28 students in its program, calculated that it spent

$5678 per student on the program in addition to wages paid to the students (Osterman 1995).

The important element of cost begins with training. Even in Germany, known for its extensive apprenticeship programming, which reaches two-thirds of all youths, larger companies are finding the expense of apprenticeship training difficult to support. Dietmar Harhoff and Thomas Kane found that German employers lost $9381 (in 1990 dollars) for every student trainee (Osterman 1995). In the United States, many companies do not offer systematic training, even for their regular employees. Lynch (1992) reports, for example, that only 4.0 percent of 16- to 24-year-old workers received more than four weeks of formal training over a three-year period on the job. Only 1.5 percent of 21- to 29-year-olds were in apprenticeship programs in 1993 (Bishop 1996). Employers that do not currently offer formal training would have to develop such programs in order to be involved in school-to-work efforts, and the obstacles that prevent them from training, such as severe lack of resources, are also likely to be obstacles to participation.

In fact, the burden of developing a school-to-work program is likely to be even greater than the burden of developing a training program because the former requires mentoring, coordination with the school curriculum, and broader instruction in aspects of the industry as a whole as well as in specific skills (Stern 1995). Moreover, the costs of supervising young students may be significantly greater than for full-time workers. Many companies surveyed by the Youth Entitlement Demonstration program in the 1970s, for example, believed that students could not contribute enough to justify the effort needed to supervise them (Bailey 1995).

Furthermore, many employers have a bias against hiring high school students. Fewer than a third of American employers in 1991 believed that recent high school graduates were capable of holding jobs in their companies (U.S. Department of Education and Department of Labor 1993). Employers may believe that recent high school graduates lack the basic skills and work habits required to become valued employees. Consequently, employers tend to hire older applicants over recent high school graduates, even when the older candidates are less qualified (Gregson 1995). The focus groups of employers conducted by Zemsky (1993) suggested that hiring was not a problem for them—and when they did hire, they saw no reason to pursue recent high school graduates when older, more "reliable" applicants were available.

Exacerbating the general bias against high school students is the perception that the quality of students in these school-to-work programs would be lower, that is, that the programs would be targeted to students with less ability. During the 1980s, the Targeted Job Tax Credit perpetuated this stigma by providing tax credits only for those students who were on welfare or who suffered from some other legitimate disadvantage (Ascher 1994). Finally, employers may be reluctant to place students in some positions due to concerns about safety and liability (Hershey et al. 1997).

MEASURING THE INCIDENCE OF EMPLOYER PARTICIPATION

In summary, the key obstacle for the school-to-work movement appears to be the lack of participation by employers, particularly in providing sites for work-based learning. The explanation for that lack of participation has been the apparent lack of economic incentives for providing work-based sites. The evidence before the STWOA of 1994 was introduced suggested that there was very little employer involvement in existing work-based programs at school and little employer training of recent school leavers. Given all of the costs and drawbacks to employer participation noted earlier and the low level of initial involvement, most observers were skeptical that the school-to-work programs would expand.

There was some evidence, however, that once programs were in place, it might be easier for them to expand. Lynn and Wills (1995) found, for example, that while most employers initially agreed to provide work-based learning places for students out of general civic-mindedness, they were, on average, pleasantly surprised by how well the students performed in their jobs. Similar findings came from studies of youth apprenticeship programs in the United Kingdom (Cappelli 1996). These findings suggest that, once these programs have a foothold in the business community, they might generate support from within each company to expand them.

Another crucial factor determining the potential amount of employer involvement in these programs has been the state of the labor market. The importance of most of the incentives for employers to participate in these programs turns on how difficult it is to find qualified employees in the regular labor market. The value of student work or of recruiting qualified students into regular jobs is judged relative to the alternatives. We know, for example, that the amount of training that employers provide rises when it is more difficult to hire workers; employers are more willing to make these investments when they cannot easily find qualified workers on the outside market (Bishop 1996). The two decades before the passing of the STWOA in 1994 were a period of relatively high unemployment, especially for youths, and the estimates of low employer involvement in work-based learning and training were generated in these periods.

A set of case studies of employers who participated in school-to-work programs found that the benefits to the employers often did exceed the costs. Perhaps the main feature that distinguished the programs that paid off was that they were located in areas with tight labor markets (Bassi et al. 1997).

An initial study of employer participation in school-to-work programs prepared in 1995, one year after the STWOA was passed, found 59,239 employer-provided sites for work-based learning, offering a total of 119,047 positions. A study in the following year of 11 states receiving school-to-work grants from the federal government reported 39,000 work-based learning sites provided by employers (U.S. Department of Education and Department of Labor 1996). These numbers are dramatically higher than the estimate of 1000 students in youth apprenticeship programs, and the 1996 study suggests that they might be increasing rapidly. But the numbers still seemed far short of anything like a large-scale program for the country as a whole. Furthermore, some observers wonder privately what these estimates include—whether they are, for example, only reporting the traditional vocational education and co-op programs as part of new school-to-work initiatives, substantially understating the true extent of employer involvement.

THE EQW NATIONAL EMPLOYER SURVEY

Against this background, the National Center on the Educational Quality of the Workforce implemented the National Employer Survey (NES) to measure employer attitudes toward and participation in programs associated with developing worker skills, including programs targeted at youths. The survey was administered by the U.S. Bureau of the Census by telephone in August and September of 1994. Public sector employers, nonprofit institutions, and corporate headquarters were excluded from the sample. Establishments in the manufacturing sector and establishments with more than 100 employees were oversampled. The sampling frame represents

establishments that employ about three-quarters of all workers. The target respondent in the manufacturing sector was the plant manager; in the nonmanufacturing sector, it was the local manager of the business site. In addition, the survey was designed to allow for multiple respondents so that information could be obtained in cases where the plant manager, or business site manager, did not have ready access to all information. Of the 4633 eligible establishments contacted by the Census Bureau, 1275 refused to participate in the survey, yielding a 72 percent response rate.

A supplement to the NES was administered in March and April of 1996, again by the U.S. Bureau of the Census as a telephone survey. Those establishments that completed the original NES were resurveyed. In addition to creating some short-term longitudinal data elements, the supplement explored areas that were not addressed by the original NES. Several items that focused on employers' participation in work-based learning projects, the extent to which employers hired young workers, and employers' evaluations of working students were included. With the data from the NES and its supplement, one can directly address questions concerning the nature of establishments that participate in work-based learning programs.

Seventy-five percent of the establishments that participated in the initial NES were retained in the supplement. There was some selection bias in the retained establishments across industry characteristics because of different response rates, but this bias is not severe. The retention rate for the smallest establishments (those hiring fewer than 50 employees) was less than 70 percent, for example, as it was for establishments in the transportation, communications, wholesale trade, and retail trade industries. Slightly more than 80 percent of the establishments in the chemical and petrochemical, lumber and paper, primary metals, and metal products industries ended up in both surveys.

The supplement to the NES posed several questions to establishments concerning their participation in work-based learning activities. Establishments were asked if they participated in

— job shadowing, where a student follows an employee for one or more days to learn about a particular occupation or industry;
— mentoring, where a student and an employee are paired for an extended period of time during which the employee helps the student learn certain skills and knowledge that the employee possesses; models workplace behavior; challenges the student to perform well; and assesses the student's performance;
— internships, where for a specified period of time students work for an employer to learn about a particular occupation or industry and which may or may not include financial compensation;
— cooperative education, a method of instruction whereby students alternate or parallel their academic and vocational studies with a paid or unpaid job in a related field;
— registered apprenticeships, which are formal programs registered with the U.S. Department of Labor or with an approved state apprenticeship agency and which are typically paid work experiences; and
— youth apprenticeships, which are multiyear programs combining school and work-based learning in an occupational area; are designed to lead directly into a related post-secondary program, entry-level job, or registered apprenticeship program; and may or may not include financial compensation.[3]

A composite measure was developed to indicate if a given establishment participated in any type of work-based learning, whether or not its programs were under the aegis of the STWOA. Thus the NES supplementary data measure participation in both government-sponsored programs and any programs developed on an autonomous basis by individual establishments. Since the STWOA was quite new when the NES supplement was administered, it is safe to assume that most of the work-based learning activity measured was not a result of the legislation.

Table 1 shows the reported participation rates in various forms of work-based learning. An estimated 19 percent of establishments were involved in some form of work-based learning activities in the spring of 1996. The

TABLE 1

PARTICIPATION IN WORK-BASED LEARNING ACTIVITIES, 1996

Type of Work-Based Learning	Percentage of Establishments
Internship	17
Mentoring	12
Cooperative education	11
Job shadowing	11
Registered apprenticeships	3
Youth apprenticeships	2

TABLE 2

PARTICIPATION IN WORK-BASED LEARNING ACTIVITIES BY SIZE OF ESTABLISHMENT, 1996

Establishment Size	Percentage of Establishments of a Particular Size Doing Any Work-Based Learning Activities	Establishments of a Particular Size as a Percentage of All Employers Doing Work-Based Learning Activities
20-49 employees	15	40
50-99 employees	17	21
100-250 employees	23	20
251-1000 employees	38	14
1000+ employees	45	6

universe from which the first NES sample (NES-I) was drawn consisted of about 650,000 establishments. A 19 percent participation rate would translate into about 124,000 workplaces engaged in some form of work-based learning. Tables 2 and 3 show participation rates in work-based learning by establishment size and industry, respectively. While small establishments (those hiring fewer than 100 employees) accounted for over 60 percent of the establishments participating in work-based learning, this is an artifact of the large number of such establishments. These establishments actually participated less than larger ones. Indeed, the propensity to engage in work-based learning is directly related to establishment size.

In the summer of 1997, a new NES was conducted by the Census Bureau, with funding from the National Center for Postsecondary Improvement and the Consortium for Policy Research in Education. The Census Bureau was again retained to administer the survey via telephone, and the sampling frame was identical to that of the initial NES. Of the 6971 establishments that the bureau approached to participate in the survey, only 1506 (22 percent) refused, for a participation rate of 78 percent.[4]

The sample of the National Employer Survey, Phase II (NES-II), consisted of three components:

— a state component of about 2000 completed interviews representing establishments in five states (California, Kentucky, Michigan, Maryland, and Pennsylvania); these interviews included questions on statewide education reforms that would enable researchers to document the effects of reform;

— approximately 2500 completed interviews that composed a representative sample of the rest of the United States (45 states plus the District of Columbia);

— a longitudinal component of about 900 completed interviews with business establishments

TABLE 3

PARTICIPATION IN WORK-BASED LEARNING ACTIVITIES BY INDUSTRY OF ESTABLISHMENT, 1996

	Percentage of Establishments of a Particular Industry Doing Any Work-Based Learning Industry	Establishments of a Particular Industry as a Percentage of All Employers Doing Work-Based Learning Activities
Communications	57	5
Health services	35	15
Machinery or instrumentation	31	6
Finance	26	6
Transportation equipment	25	1
Hotels	25	3
Utilities	24	1
Insurance	24	2
Chemicals and petroleum	23	2
Printing and publishing	22	3
Business services	22	8
Primary metals	19	1
Freight	18	2
Textiles and apparel	17	1
Retail trade	16	28
Food and tobacco	14	1
Lumber and paper	13	1
Miscellaneous manufacturing	12	2
Construction	11	5
Wholesale trade	11	6
Metal products	8	1

that had participated in the initial NES.

The NES-II explicitly asked establishments about their participation in formal school-to-work programs. The wording of the query was "School-to-work partnerships consist of joint activity between schools and employers to build connections between school-based learning and work-based learning. Is your establishment participating in such a school-to-work partnership?"

An estimated 26 percent of those establishments employing 20 or more people reported involvement in a school-to-work partnership (see Tables 4 and 5). As did the NES-I, the NES-II asked employers about their participation in work-based learning activities. Overall, 39 percent of NES-II establishments reported participating in some form of work-based learning. In 1997, there were about 670,000 private establishments in the United States employing more than 20 people. The NES-II data would indicate that more than 170,000 of these were participating in a school-to-work partnership and that over 250,000 were engaged in some type of work-based learning for high school and/or community college students (Table 6). Ninety-one percent of those establishments that reported participating in a school-to-work partnership also reported participating in some form of work-based learning activity, as compared with 21 percent of other establishments.

The incidence of both participation in school-to-work partnerships and the sponsoring of work-based learning activities is substantial, much higher than indicated by earlier surveys. What explains these relatively high participation rates by private establishments? Some of the work-based learning activity we observe is likely attributable to the implementation of the STWOA of 1994. The participation in work-based learning by establishments that do not iden-

TABLE 4

PARTICIPATION IN SCHOOL-TO-WORK (STW) PARTNERSHIPS BY SIZE OF ESTABLISHMENT, 1997

Establishment Size	Percentage of Establishments of a Particular Size Participating in STW	Establishments of a Particular Size as a Percentage of All Employers Participating in STW
20-49 employees	24	56
50-99 employees	24	20
100-250 employees	33	16
251-1000 employees	42	7
1000+ employees	60	2

tify themselves as school-to-work participants in the summer of 1997 is similar to the overall reported rate in the spring of 1996, suggesting that any growth in that period could be tied to efforts associated with the STWOA. It seems reasonable to argue that full implementation of the STWOA was just beginning in early 1996, and what the NES-I supplement measures is really a baseline level of activity. As dollars became available and acquired by localities under the auspices of the STWOA, more establishments would be encouraged to participate in school-to-work partnerships and, consequently, in work-based learning activities.

A second factor, more likely contributing to the acceptance of work-based learning programs by private establishments, is the current era of economic growth and its associated tight labor markets. The need for a qualified labor force is real and pressing. In the past, an expanding enterprise could hope to fill its labor needs

with experienced workers in their mid-twenties who already had work experience, possibly having been downsized out of a responsible position. Indeed, employers seemed readily able to find the "twenty-six-year-old with three previous employers" whom Zemsky (1993) reports one manager holding up as the preferred new hire for entry-level jobs. As labor markets became tighter, such applicants became scarce indeed. Employers had to begin turning instead to recent school leavers and therefore have become more interested in whether graduates of the secondary school system have the skills to meet, and exceed, job requirements. Being active in a school-to-work partnership and sponsoring work-based learning experiences may be a way to address a current need.

In North Carolina, for example, the state commerce secretary has complained about a shortage of qualified employees available for sophisticated manufacturing jobs and in response has set up a program in the Commerce Department to help schools work with employers in developing workplace preparation programs like school-to-work (Catanoso 1997). No doubt, similar reactions in tight labor markets around the United States are contributing to the expansion of such programs. One can legitimately ask, however, whether we have truly built a new infrastructure that will develop work-based skills and facilitate the transition from the world of school to that of work, an infrastructure that will continue to work even when labor markets slacken. Will these initiatives wither with the next economic

TABLE 5
PARTICIPATION IN SCHOOL-TO-WORK (STW) PARTNERSHIPS BY INDUSTRY OF ESTABLISHMENT, 1997

Industry	Percentage of Establishments of a Particular Industry Participating in STW	Establishments of a Particular Industry as a Percentage of All Employers Participating in STW
Communications	44	3
Health services	44	13
Utilities	37	1
Finance	35	5
Transportation equipment	35	1
Hotels	32	2
Primary metals	30	1
Retail trade	28	38
Printing and publishing	27	2
Machinery or instrumentation	25	4
Metal products	25	2
Chemicals and petroleum	24	1
Textiles and apparel	24	1
Miscellaneous manufacturing	22	3
Wholesale trade	21	8
Insurance	19	2
Business services	18	5
Food and tobacco	16	1
Freight	15	2
Construction	15	4
Lumber and paper	12	1

downturn and the labor surplus it produces?

CONCLUSION

In general, there seems to be greater consensus regarding the factors that may encourage a company's participation in school-to-work pro-

grams and less consensus regarding the factors that may dissuade a company from participating. Most observers believe, as we have argued here, that the most important incentives for employer participation in these programs are economic and center on the need to fill job vacancies. However, even when the economy provides such incentives, other obstacles remain, and observers disagree as to their importance. According to the U.S. General Accounting Office, the major obstacle to employers' participation lies in educating employers about school-to-work programs and their benefits (Ascher 1994). Still others have suggested that employers and schools do not trust each other and that this accounts for employer resistance (Barton and Frazer 1980). Along the same lines, the National Center on the Educational Quality of the Workforce recommends that interactions between schools and companies be more "direct, substantive, and business-like" as a way to overcome resistance (National Center 1995).

Another issue concerns the extent and depth of employer participation in these programs. Though the National Center on the Educational Quality of the Workforce has found that more than 20 percent of American companies participate in some type of internship program, schools nationwide have experienced difficulty in recruiting large numbers of employers who are willing to devote the time and resources to developing worthwhile internships for high school students (National Center 1995). Presumably, this suggests that

TABLE 6

**ASSOCIATION BETWEEN PARTICIPATION IN SCHOOL-TO-WORK (STW)
PARTNERSHIPS AND WORK-BASED LEARNING PROGRAMS, 1997**

Type of Work-Based Learning Activity	Participation Rate for STW-Identified	Participation Rate If Not STW-Identified	Overall Participation Rate	Average Number of Slots
Internship	44	12	20	4.10
Cooperative education	42	5	16	3.76
Job shadowing	41	6	16	6.32
Mentoring	33	1	10	8.86
Registered apprenticeship	13	6	8	6.80
Youth apprenticeship	9	2	4	3.98

employers who do participate are not providing nearly enough places for students in their programs.

Similarly, while 25 percent of U.S. companies report participating in a school-to-work partnership and another 40 percent report providing some sort of work-based learning experience, it is not clear how substantive such involvement and experiences are. The relatively low rates of formal apprenticeship opportunities could indicate that the current work-based learning activities are less far-reaching than the school-to-work community might hope. It is possible that the relatively high overall participation rates we are witnessing could be near the maximum we can reasonably expect from employers, short of coercive federal and state regulations along the European model. Even with tight labor markets, not all employers will find it cost effective or useful to engage in school-to-work partnerships or provide work-based learning.

As Osterman (1995) suggests, an alternative approach to expanding these opportunities may lie in expanding less intensive programs, such as unpaid job shadowing, mentoring, and field trips, that make fewer demands on employers. Whether we can construct a useful system for moving students from the world of school to the world of work using such less intensive programs, or whether we can more aggressively promulgate the use of more formal programs, seems to be the policy question of the moment.

Notes

1. A good guide to the rise of the school-to-work movement, as well as to its content, is provided in Olson 1997.

2. In fact, unpaid student interns are prohibited from doing work of value for an employer under the Fair Labor Standards Act, although remarkably few participants seem aware of this requirement.

3. These activities, and their definitions, were taken from National School-to-Work Office 1996.

4. The 6971 establishments exclude those that were unavailable, closed, or otherwise unreachable.

References

Ascher, Carol. 1994. Cooperative Education as a Strategy for School-to-Work Transition. *CenterFocus* (National

Center for Research in Vocational Education, Berkeley, CA), no. 3.

Bailey, Thomas R. 1995. Incentives for Employer Participation in School-to-Work Programs. In *Learning to Work: Employer Involvement in School-to-Work Transition Programs*. Washington, DC: Brookings Institution.

Barton, Paul E. and Bryna Shore Frazer. 1980. *Between Two Worlds: Youth Transition from School to Work*. Vol. 2, *Program from Experimentation*. Washington, DC: U.S. Department of Labor, Employment and Training Administration, Office of Youth Programs.

Bassi, Laurie J., Theresa Seeley, John Hillmeyer, and Jens Ludwig. 1997. Learning and Earning: An Employer's Look at School-to-Work Investments. American Society for Training and Development, Alexandria, VA. Report for the National Education Leadership Council.

Bishop, John H. 1996. What We Know About Employer-Provided Training: A Review of the Literature. Working Paper #96-09, Center for Advanced Human Resource Studies, Cornell University, Ithaca, NY.

Cappelli, Peter. 1996. Youth Apprenticeship in Britain: Lessons for the United States. *Industrial Relations* 35(1).

Catanoso, Justin. 1997. Worker Training Key, Official Says. *News and Record* (Greensboro, NC), 20 Aug.

Gregson, J. A. 1995. The School-to-Work Movement and Youth Apprenticeship in the US: Educational Reform and Democratic Renewal? *Journal of Industrial Teacher Education* 32(3):7-29.

Hamilton, Stephen F. 1990. *Apprenticeship for Adulthood: Preparing Youth for the Future*. New York: Free Press.

Hershey, Alan M., Paula Hudis, Marsha Silverberg, and Joshua Haimson. 1997. Partners in Progress: Early Steps in Creating School-to-Work Systems. Mathematica Policy Research, Inc., Princeton, NJ. Executive summary.

Hughes, Katherine L. 1996. Employer Motivations for Providing Work-Based Learning Placements to Students: Preliminary Results from Research in Progress. Transcript of lecture presented at a symposium of the American Psychological Association, Toronto, Ontario, Canada.

Lehrman, R. and H. Pouncy. 1990. The Compelling Case for Youth Apprenticeships. *Public Interest* (Fall):62-77.

Lynch, Lisa. 1992. Private Sector Training and the Earnings of Young Workers. *American Economic Review* 82:299-312.

Lynn, Irene and Joan Wills. 1995. School Lessons, Work Lessons: Recruiting and Sustaining Employer Involvement in School-to-Work Programs. EQW Working Paper #WP28. National Center on the Educational Quality of the Workforce, University of Pennsylvania, Philadelphia.

National Center on Education and the Economy. 1990. *America's Choice: High Skills or Low Wages!* Rochester, NY: National Center on Education and the Economy.

National Center on the Educational Quality of the Workforce. 1995. *The Other Shoe: Education's Contribution to the Productivity of Establishments*. EQW Results, #RE02. Philadelphia: University of Pennsylvania, National Center on the Educational Quality of the Workforce.

National School-to-Work Office. 1996. *School-to-Work Glossary of Terms*. Washington, DC: National School-to-Work Office.

Olson, Lynn. 1997. *The School to Work Revolution: How Employers and Educators Are Joining Forces to Prepare Tomorrow's Skilled Workforce*. Reading, MA: Addison-Wesley.

Osterman, Paul. 1995. Involving Employers in School-to-Work Programs.

In *Learning to Work: Employer Involvement in School-to-Work Transition Programs*, ed. Tom Bailey. Washington, DC: Brookings Institution.

Resnick, Lauren B. 1987. *Education and Learning to Think*. Washington, DC: National Academy Press.

Stern, David. 1995. Employer Options for Participation in School-to-Work Programs. In *Learning to Work: Employer Involvement in School-to-Work Transition Programs*, ed. Tom Bailey. Washington, DC: Brookings Institution.

U.S. Department of Education. 1997. *The Condition of Education: 1997*. Washington, DC: Department of Education, National Center for Education Statistics.

U.S. Department of Education and U.S. Department of Labor. 1993. School-to-Work Transition. U.S. Department of Education and U.S. Department of Labor, Washington, DC. Background paper.

———. 1996. Implementation of the School-to-Work Opportunities Act of 1994. National School-to-Work Office, Washington, DC. Report to Congress.

W. T. Grant Foundation. Commission on Work, Family, and Citizenship. 1985. *The Forgotten Half*. Washington, DC: William T. Grant Foundation.

Zemsky, Robert. 1993. What Employers Want: Employer Perspectives on Youth, the Youth Labor Market, and Prospects for a National System of Youth Apprenticeships. EQW Working Paper #WP22, National Center on the Educational Quality of the Workforce, University of Pennsylvania, Philadelphia.

Restructuring and Skill Needs: Will Firms Train?

By HAROLD SALZMAN

ABSTRACT: In this article, Harold Salzman presents an analysis of corporate restructuring and resulting organizational outcomes to provide a framework for analyzing the role of the firm in workforce skill development. Salzman bases his analysis on case studies of firms in two industries, insurance and medical imaging equipment, supplemented by case studies of other firms engaged in significant levels of workforce skill development. The study addresses the extent to which restructuring firms are unstable in terms of organizational form—losing the capacity to provide skill development for their workforces—and the extent to which job changes, restructuring, and/or technology increases skill levels and therefore the demand for upgrading the skills of incumbent and new workers. His findings show that, although demand for skills has increased, a number of countervailing factors within firms and in the market inhibit firms' active engagement in skill development.

Harold Salzman is a sociologist and senior research scientist and program director at the Center for Industrial Competitiveness at the University of Massachusetts–Lowell. His research interests include changes in workplace organization, skills, work, and technology. His previous publications include Software by Design: Shaping Technology and the Workplace.

NOTE: This study is supported by grants from the U.S. Department of Education's Office of Educational Research and Improvement (OERI), the Alfred P. Sloan Foundation, and the GE Fund as part of two projects on corporate restructuring and workforce skill development. The analysis of training is supported by OERI through the National Center for Postsecondary Improvement, Stanford University. The Sloan and GE Fund project is being conducted in collaboration with Philip Moss and Chris Tilly of the University of Massachusetts–Lowell; the findings on the nature of corporate restructuring in the insurance and medical equipment industries are based on that collaborative study. This article has benefited immensely from the comments of Chris Tilly and Philip Moss. Katrina Buchau has supported this project throughout with superb research assistance and editing.

DRAMATIC changes in the economy and consequent corporate restructuring are significantly changing the structure of jobs, skill requirements, and the labor-management social contract developed in the postwar period. A central dilemma in these events is the need for a more highly skilled workforce at the same time that firms are restructuring in ways that reduce their capacity and/or willingness to provide workforce skill development.

Two key policy issues are emerging: the extent to which there is a need for workforce skill development and the extent to which firms will engage in training and education for youths and incumbent workers. The extent to which firms engage in workforce skill development is dependent upon an interaction of economic and organizational factors. Thus an analysis of corporate restructuring and the resulting organizational outcomes and job structures provide a framework for analyzing the role of the firm in workforce skill development.

The economy of the 1990s is generally characterized as one of intense global competition, rapid technological advances, and significant transformation in work practices and firm structure, requiring greater levels of workforce skill. It is thought that the best way for both firms and workers to develop a competitive global advantage is to improve the level of workforce skills (Murnane and Levy 1997). Skill demands grew from the 1960s through the 1980s, though there is no clear evidence of a significant skill shift in the 1990s, with the exception of requirements for the lowest-level jobs (Moss 1997). Although a better-skilled workforce is thought to be beneficial to the economy and certainly to individuals in terms of increased earnings (Murnane and Levy 1997; Lerman 1997), less clear is the extent to which firms are experiencing recent, acute shortages of skill (again, with the exception of the very lowest level jobs and specific technical occupations).[1]

Whether or not there has been a dramatic shift recently toward increased skill, long-term trends certainly are for increased workforce skill. Many researchers and policymakers, however, find a fundamental weakening in the commitment and/or capacity of core institutions to provide that skill. Core firms in the U.S. economy traditionally had strong internal labor markets providing opportunities for skill development and advancement, training, and/or prospects for long-term employment that allowed for on-the-job training and returns to investment in education. Ongoing economic flux leads many firms to believe that they can no longer keep a relatively stable workforce in terms of size and skill composition but will need to turn to the market—they believe that they will need to fire those without requisite skills and hire those with needed skills. In a comprehensive analysis of corporate restructuring, Cappelli et al. find that with the breakdown of "traditional methods of managing employees and developing skilled workers inside companies," a new employment relationship, "where pressures from product and labor markets are brought inside the organization," establishes market-mediated employment relationships (1997, 4). Thus many corporate executives, researchers, and policymakers are declaring an end to the role of core institutions (firms and governments) in providing workforce skill development.

Accompanying—or perhaps causing—this change is what some (Davis, Diekmann, and Tinsley 1994) view as widespread "deinstitutionalization" of the traditional organizational form of the firm, implying that firms as single entities will no longer be the central economic institutions (and will be replaced by networks, virtual corporations, and so on). One consequence is the deintegration of the firm. Segments of the workforce that were formerly considered part of the organization are now either located in other, supplier firms—often smaller, with less capacity and fewer resources to train—or, in the case of contingent workers, not considered eligible for training and skill development opportunities.

We may be entering an era in which workers' skill development is no longer being provided by their firms, where workers may be unable to obtain new skills on the job and advance internally. Instead, it is said, individuals will be responsible for their own skill development in order to remain employable, thus facilitating frequent job changes as firms continually readjust the size and skill composition of their workforces. These changes in the economy and within the corporation are thought to increase the need for skill, but, at the same time, diminish the institutional capacity to develop it.

The issues addressed in the study reported here are the trends in corporate restructuring—particularly, how unstable these firms become in terms of organizational form—and the dynamics of corporate restructuring and job changes that influence the demand for skill by firms. These two factors are important for assessing the extent to which firms are likely to engage in skill development, to address the question posed by Lisa Lynch: "If there is an emerging consensus in the United States that training is necessary for competitiveness, why isn't everyone doing more training?" (1994, 65).

This study involves case studies of large firms that have undergone, or are undergoing, restructuring that encompasses changes in organizational structure and changes in job structure. The focus of the study is how structural changes in firms and jobs affect the skills needed and the involvement of firms in skill development efforts. The focus is broader than job training because it includes how changes may affect formal and informal opportunities for on-the-job learning; linkages with, and the use of, education providers; and approaches to workforce development.[2] The study adopts an organizational, as well as economic, perspective, seeking to understand firms' training and workforce development decisions by building on the work of Scott and Meyer (1991).[3] Little research has been done from an organizational perspective on the dynamics of skill demand—on how restructuring firms obtain needed workforce skills; how they develop plans for skill development; and how the internal dynamics of firms, the market environment, and other firm-level factors influence workforce development.

CASE STUDIES OF RESTRUCTURING FIRMS

This research is primarily of two industries—insurance and medical imaging equipment—supplemented by case studies of several other firms that are engaged in significant levels of workforce skill development (such as apprenticeship programs or linkages with community colleges).

The insurance industry is a service industry employing workers with a broad range of skill levels; it traditionally has had a highly developed internal labor market in which on-the-job learning, supplemented in some functional areas with externally obtained education, offered the potential for significant mobility. It is an industry that has only within the past five years been sharply exposed to economic pressure and is now undergoing significant restructuring both in terms of internal organizational structure and industry structure. In the life insurance market, the product itself is undergoing change as it becomes a financial planning product, putting insurance companies into competition with financial product companies.

The medical imaging equipment industry is part of the manufacturing sector. Medical imaging equipment includes five basic types, known as "modalities": X-ray (both conventional and digital radiography), computed tomography (CT), magnetic resonance imaging (MRI), ultrasonic, and nuclear medical instruments.

This industry is representative of new, high-technology-based manufacturing and is of interest as a knowledge-intensive industry that is crossing the boundary between hardware and software, manufacturing and services, involving highly skilled work combined with high-quality demands for assembly and basic parts manufacturing. It is a global industry with about $8 billion in sales per year.

Within the past five years, the industry has experienced significant market pressure as a result of increased health care cost containment. The industry changed from being almost a cost-plus business into one that is significantly cost constrained. In many countries, the medical industry is subject to increased scrutiny and regulation, further increasing the pressure to improve quality performance (see Tilly and Handel 1997 for an analysis of this industry and recent changes).

The case studies reported here are of three companies, including smaller specialty equipment companies. To better understand the factors that motivate firms to engage in skill development and, in particular, use community colleges, these cases are supplemented by case studies of firms that have actively engaged in significant skill development efforts. This has allowed us to explore cases in which there is a strong initiative to provide training and education through linkages with community colleges. One company is a large firm that manufactured electronic and mechanical devices, and the other produced computer hardware.

FINDINGS

This study addresses the extent to which restructuring firms are unstable in terms of organizational form— losing the capacity to provide skill development for their workforces— and the extent to which job changes, restructuring, and/or technology increases skill levels and therefore increases demand for upgrading the skills of incumbent and new workers. The findings first discussed are the macro-level structural changes in firms, followed by discussion of internal job structure changes. The implications for training and skill development are then discussed.

The dynamics of corporate restructuring

The study's findings suggest that corporate restructuring actually involves three distinct types of change in corporate organization and strategy. What is notable about this period of restructuring is that it appears to reverse a historical pattern of growth that involved the acquisition of other companies and internalization of ever more functions and steps in the production process. The companies in the study were highly vertically integrated firms. The insurance companies had developed multiple lines of insurance to foster growth and market position (to be so-called full-service companies). They did not integrate various product lines in terms of organizational structure, however; thus they resembled in some ways an insurance conglomerate rather than an integrated single-product company.

Each industry, for different reasons, developed intense cost pressures that made existing approaches to business less viable. For the medical industry in the early 1990s, cost containment, changes in reimbursement practices, and other factors led to drops in sales and significant profit declines following a decade of nearly constant double-digit growth (Tilly and Handel 1997). In insurance, deregulation, which allowed more companies to offer a range of financial products, coupled with large investment and underwriting losses—for example, the collapse of real estate markets and a series of casualty losses from hurricanes and earthquakes (Salzman and Buchau 1997)—and changes in health care all threatened the viability of the multiline organization of insurance, as well as profitability.[4]

The first stage of corporate restructuring involves the overall reorganization or sale of unrelated businesses or lines to achieve organizational focus. This ranged from the breakup of diversified conglomerates to the narrowing of product focus (for example, reducing the number of lines in a multiline insurance company). The second stage involves improving operational efficiency through downsizing, delayering, outsourcing, and changing jobs in ways such as broad banding, forming work groups, and increasing work loads, but generally not significantly changing the nature of the job activities.

The first two phases of restructuring—organizational focus and operational efficiency—are consistent with the common characterizations of restructuring. It is the attributes of these phases that have led to predictions of constant turmoil in labor markets, with the end of long-term employment and the rise of market-mediated employment relationships. Some of these changes result in initial cost savings and increases in stock values, though not uniformly (Moss, Salzman, and Tilly 1998; American Management Association 1996). Whether or not these strategies reduce costs and increase stock values, they do lead to a number of problems as companies try to innovate and grow.

To innovate and grow, firms developed a third restructuring stage (cf. Porter 1996). This stage of restructuring, for innovation and growth, is one that is developing and only in its early stages in the case study companies. It is too early to have a clear description of the characteristics that will define companies in this stage; the exact forms are still quite varied; and a dominant form is probably not yet established. It is possible, however, to postulate that the dynamic in this stage will be toward reconstituting organizational integration and recognition of organizational boundaries as important. The importance of firms as organizational entities implies that internal labor markets—and the firm-workforce commitments that are necessary to support these structures—will also be developed, albeit in new forms.[5] This trend can be illustrated by patterns found in the insurance industry. Each company experienced problems after the initial stages of restructuring to varying degrees, but all were experiencing a distinct shift in organizational restructuring from

focus and efficiency to innovation and growth.

In one insurance company, the changes were in organization, product, and customer focus. The firm was redefining the organization from being a product-defined to a market-defined financial services company, viewing its competition not as other insurance companies but as financial service companies. The product was being redefined from a set of individual products to an integrated and comprehensive set of financial services and instruments; the customer was shifting from institutions to end buyers. This involved yet another organizational restructuring, following the downsizing and delayering of the first two stages.

To support its new focus on offering a portfolio of financial products to customers, this insurance company integrated strategic business units and product lines that had been traditionally separate or were separated as part of the initial restructuring (such as annuities and life insurance). This integration created a larger organizational entity and pushed the cost and efficiency evaluation (individual profit-loss accounting) to a higher level (to the combined division, rather than the level of product line, as in the previous restructuring). This, the company felt, allowed it to focus on product- and customer-based strategies without being hampered by focusing on the microefficiencies of single products or operations, as it had been during the efficiency stage of restructuring.

To support the new organizational structure, the insurance company began a series of significant changes in the job structure. The effort in this company is to transform one side of the business from an insurance company into a financial services company, involving a set of changes not just in products and business practices but also in organizational culture. Some of the requirements for, and initiatives toward, innovation in products and selling strategies, however, were hampered by several of the previous efforts to achieve greater efficiency and now required new measures to stabilize the organization.

In other companies, similar effects of the first two stages of restructuring were observed. After a transitional phase of downsizing, selling off business units, and delayering to achieve operational efficiency, the firms began to focus on growth and innovation strategies. This effort is leading to reestablishing stability and reintegrating many of the functions that were externalized. Notable are the changes in outsourcing, jobs, and job structure.

Outsourcing and
contingent workers

A central change in internal organizational structure during the late 1980s and early 1990s was the increased use of outsourcing and contingent workers. The use of both types of workers represents different dimensions of firms' changing their organizational boundaries. The shift to suppliers often represents a shift in the type of workforce used for a function formerly internal to the firm, as does the use of contingent workers. In the initial stages of corporate restructuring, firms in this study focused almost exclusively on cost reduction through outsourcing and the use of contingent workers. The magnitude of outsourcing and contingent workers varied widely across the firms. At one extreme, a firm outsourced 12,000 parts over 18 months after deciding to restructure. In doing so, it eliminated most of its production workforce. Another manufacturer went to contingent workers for about 25 percent of its production workforce. Because these shifts were cost- and focus-driven, there was little assessment of the impact on production, service delivery, quality, or the remaining workforce.

Examining the impact of outsourcing revealed a number of shortcomings that suggest that these strategies may be reaching their limits. In the initial stages of restructuring, the focus was on externalizing formerly internal functions, often for use of the market to improve cost and efficiency. That was generally accomplished by using suppliers who provided significantly lower-quality jobs (in terms of both skills and wages) to their workforces and had minimal internal infrastructures (to track processes and procedures). When outsourcing non-commodity components and larger subsystems, firms found quality suffered because of low workforce skills and a lack of infrastructure and procedures to ensure quality in the supplier firms.

As the problems of the initial wave of outsourcing became recognized, companies began to require their suppliers to increase quality through implementing quality processes and technology. The firms also had to increase their staff to test incoming products from suppliers and therefore increased their monitoring costs. The increased demands on suppliers led to many either giving up the contracts or building an infrastructure resembling that of the outsourcing firm. In some ways, what core firms gained by not having to focus on production issues they lost in having to focus on supplier management and, not uncommonly, involvement in developing or managing the supplier's infrastructure and workforce.

The outcome of this third restructuring stage is the rebuilding of stable organizations. These new organizational forms tend to be more occupationally—or at least functionally—homogeneous as a result of the outsourcing and deintegration of noncore functions.[6] There is also a move back to organizational integration through "in-sourcing," reducing the number of suppliers and expanding the permanent workforce. The in-sourcing observed tends to be the reintegration of areas that were considered strategic and/or fit with other maintained functions, such as an engineering function but not production. In the third restructuring stage, growth strategies of firms usually involve organizational growth and often the shrinking of extra-organizational linkages (such as suppliers).

The use of contingent workers is also being reconsidered in some of these companies. In nearly all instances, managers found that using contingent workers hindered some aspect of efficiency, skill development, and overall workplace climate. Contingent workers had higher turnover, fewer skills, and less organizationally specific knowledge. Moreover, the firms were less likely to invest in training for contingent workers while having to provide more basic orientation because of higher turnover. Production and service quality were considered lower, requiring more supervision and more rework. In other companies, the use of contingent workers created a second-class workforce, which, it was often felt, created divisions between workers, lowered morale, and/or hampered integration of contingent workers as equal participants (for example, in the assignment of work tasks and learning opportunities). Contingent workers were useful in conducting narrowly defined tasks but not in contributing to the broader scope of organizational performance that firms in the third stage were trying to make part of all jobs.[7]

In both outsourcing and the use of contingent workers, there are areas where externalizing the activity was done with little change and/or was easily divisible and not strategic (such as security, custodial, and cafeteria services), but often once outsourcing or the use of contingent workers became a strategy, it expanded throughout the firm. These findings suggest that, as firms move toward innovation and growth, significant outsourcing and use of contingent workers become inhibiting factors.

Job structure and skills

In the first two stages of restructuring, job changes tend to focus on ways of increasing productivity without deep structural change in the organization of work. Job expansion tends to be horizontal, expanding the number of tasks in a given job at the same level. Other changes often streamline processes to increase output and reduce labor requirements without changing job structures. To develop competitive strategies in the third stage, firms find that conceptually new job structures are necessary. The resulting redesign of jobs into broad functional categories and elimination of a finely graded hierarchy presents new opportunities and new barriers: the skill barriers to entry are greater and the gaps between job functions are greater, but skill development and responsibilities as well as wage progression are also much greater within each broad functional area.

One company, for example, eliminated specific job descriptions and instead defined broad functional area responsibilities (such as "customer associate," which encompasses the responsibility of six former discrete jobs), going from 7000 separate job descriptions or classifications to 2000. Workers no longer enter a narrowly defined job that is part of a vertical career ladder but enter a broadly defined job that encompasses a number of functions. Advancement involves increased mastery of competencies rather than specific task learning. Hiring criteria are no longer based on the assessment of a person's ability to perform a particular function or set of task skills but, rather, on the assessment of his or her ability to master a host of skills and responsibilities. To the extent that this type of restructuring occurs

throughout an industry, it suggests not only an increase in the entry-level skills required at even the lowest level (or a shift to hiring applicants at a different level, such as four-year-college graduates instead of high school graduates) but potentially greater skill and wage development within formerly low-level jobs.

Work content

An important consequence of eliminating task-defined jobs is that organization-specific knowledge becomes more important. Thus one finding is that workforce retention and longer tenure become more, not less, important in these firms. Firms try to develop mechanisms to increase job attachment rather than provide for high turnover; downsizing and workforce reductions may have been a consequence of a transitional phase in a firm's restructuring, but they do not appear sustainable as a permanent feature of its future functioning.

Job structure and skill requirements change as companies move their focus from only operational efficiency to innovation and growth. The commonly discussed increase in skills due to a broadening job structure and increased levels of performance has occurred. What we find is that much of the change is organizationally driven—by use of teams, cross-selling, and multiple service responsibilities—with technology as a supporting, but not driving, factor. The major skill needs or selection criteria identified in our interviews are for soft skills in lower-level employees and for leadership and managerial skills in professional or managerial employees.

Most of the technology-related changes in insurance and medical equipment production require basic computer literacy rather than high-level computer skills. These technology-related skills were not viewed as significant barriers to hiring and brought generally marginal changes for incumbent workers. On the other hand, eliminating highly divided tasks in insurance meant in some cases that high school–level jobs were reduced or eliminated, with an expansion of college-level jobs. This compositional shift of occupations led to hiring from a different pool of applicants, often defined by formal educational credentials.

RESTRUCTURING AND THE DYNAMICS OF SKILL DEVELOPMENT

The case studies identify the ongoing dynamics of corporate restructuring leading to new stages of development. These new stages create pressures for firms to develop in a direction different from that of the earlier restructuring stages. First, the expectation that firms are becoming fundamentally unstable as organizations—in terms of functions, size, form, and technology—is the central premise underlying expectations of high labor market mobility, short tenure, and constant changes in skill needs by firms. Our findings suggest instead that instability associated with restructuring represents a transitional stage and that firms "reinstitutionalize" as more stable organizations and seek to build stable, albeit changed, employment relationships.

Second, as firms change organizational form, they also change job structures to support new competitive strategies. The changes in job structure are fundamentally organizational changes to deliver services or produce goods differently; although they often require new technology in a supportive role, technology tends not to be the driver of job structure change or the most important factor defining the changes. Thus, often there is not a dramatic change in the hard technical skills needed but in what is assessed as the capacity for learning (for example, for acquiring multiple job skills through training and/or on-the-job learning), as well as soft and character skills.

These findings, along with those of many other studies, would suggest that firms should be very concerned about improved skill development. Our findings about restabilizing, innovation, and growth strategies of firms should also indicate that firms are interested in, and have the capacity to engage in, greater skill development. Yet we find that, although firms report a shift to higher workforce skill composition, they are not engaging in significantly greater skill development than in the past. This poses an apparent contradiction between the genesis of much recent U.S. policy—which is based on the contention that American employees are underskilled and that U.S. firms need to upgrade their skill levels—and the behavior of firms that are not investing in skill development or significantly greater training.

This apparent contradiction can be explained at least in part by two broad areas: the organizational context of the skill shift and the dynamics of skill development. First, as noted, the significant skill change tends to be compositional—through outsourcing, job restructuring, and/or work process restructuring, lower-level jobs within the core firm are eliminated so that the remaining skill mix shifts upward (although those lower-skilled jobs may still be part of the overall value chain, just located in another organization). Workforce shifts are often accomplished through retention of higher-skilled workers and by hiring higher-skilled workers during periods of higher unemployment (often as a result of industrywide downsizing). Additionally, the new skill needs reflect a change that may make some of the incumbent workforce skills deficient, but they may not necessarily reflect a skill shortage in the labor market (for example, skill deficits reflecting both previous hiring from a different pool of workers and inadequacies in education and training from previous decades).

Thus examining the organizational context of the skill shifts suggests three factors influencing the actual impact of the observed increase in skill requirements:

1. Firms have, by and large, been able to find workers at the level needed, both within their existing workforce (reduced in the restructuring) and in the labor market, though they may be recruiting from a pool of workers different from the previous pool.

2. The compositional shift in the workforce establishes hiring criteria at a level where skill development is at least adequate and often more than adequate for the tasks (for example, the idea of finding qualifications at a subbaccalaureate level is abandoned because of the wide variability of both hard and soft skills at that level and the difficulty of selection, leading to targeting an applicant pool that, on average, has higher technical skills than required and that has a higher probability of having the soft skills needed). Thus firms may be interested in increasing rates of postsecondary attendance and completion but less interested in the content of the specific education and skill development at the postsecondary level.[8] For example, one insurance company said it hires only new entrants with four-year college degrees because "if they get through four years of college, they must have some persistence and learning ability." That is, they could be expected to have good work habits, to have some minimal levels of basic skills, and to be able to learn on the job, but employers were not concerned with the content of their education.

3. Skill shifts are often very gradual, involving only a few hires at a time. Thus the magnitude of the problem tends to be seen as minimal, even if chronic. When there is a significant shift or change that requires a large number of new hires, it is viewed as—and usually is—an episodic event. A sudden expansion of capacity, the opening of a new plant, or relocation are generally not ongoing events and often occur with relatively short notice. Thus a long-term investment for skill development is not viewed as meeting the immediate and short-lived problem. When hir-

ing is constant, it is often viewed as a problem of turnover and thus the focus is on retention rather than development of the hiring pool.

The second explanation involves the dynamics of skill development within the firm and the countervailing factors to investing in skill development, even if skill deficits are recognized. From the perspective of human resource managers, skill development represents a competitive strategy that reflects their functional focus. For line managers, however, workforce skill is but one factor in a portfolio of competitive strategies and production or service delivery deficits. Operations-level factors may include quality systems, inventory management, scheduling, or a host of other factors, of which workforce skill is only one and, often from the line manager's perspective, one that has the less predictable and less immediate payback. Although some of these processes require training, the training required is often minimal and can be done on the job, and overall the barriers to learning new methods are not seen as consequential.

From the perspective of others in the firm, workforce skill at the front line is only one competitive strategy. Improvements in marketing, finance, and other areas can provide the basis for highly successful competitive strategies. Although some would say that not investing in frontline workforce skill development is a shortsighted competitive strategy, the evidence supporting this position is mixed at best. In the medical equipment industry, our study finds that superior product quality, engi-

neering, and performance often lead to second-best market sales, behind firms that have superior financing and marketing.

Finally, when evaluating a firm's competitive strategy, it is important to recognize the influence of Wall Street in valuing the company. Production or frontline-level returns to investment in human resource development are often not part of Wall Street performance measures, which pose constraints on expenditures for longer-term investment in human resources. For example, one firm that had used a minimum of 45 contingent workers for the previous five years found contingent workers to be less productive than permanent employees and would not invest in their skill development, yet it would not increase its employment of permanent workers. One measure of the firm's performance was sales per employee, and contingent workers were not counted in the equation. Thus whatever losses in production efficiency and quality it suffered on the shop floor, it made up in its stock price on Wall Street. External pressures such as these can encourage firms to cut their workforces beyond operational requirements and inhibit investment in workforce skill development.

In summary, our findings show a mixed picture in terms of investment in frontline worker skill development. Some firms are starting to rethink the initial employment strategies of low job tenure or high turnover, of using temporary workers, and even skill development strategies to buy skill, but some firms are also focusing on competitive strategies that depend less on frontline workers, developing competitive strategies around marketing and finance, and responding to short-term pressures to maintain and improve stock prices. Although the latter strategies may not be successful—or at least may be limited if pursued to the exclusion of job and skill development strategies that lead to innovation, quality, and timeliness in their product and service—the evidence on this point is not unequivocal. Thus it is not clear the extent to which firms will sustain long-term or deep skill development once an initial workforce skill upgrade or shift in occupational composition is complete. Our findings suggest that although the demand for skills has increased, a number of countervailing factors within firms and in the market inhibit firms' active engagement in skill development.

Notes

1. This perception of an increased need for skills is seen as supported by findings of increasing wage returns to education (for example, Murnane and Levy 1997; Lerman 1997; Berman, Bound, and Grilches 1994), but overall increases in skill and wage inequality appear to have occurred in the early to mid-1980s (Lerman 1997); Howell (1997) finds that recent changes have been very small. Moss (1997), in a comprehensive review of the research, concludes that basic skill requirements have increased (for example, inventory requires numeracy; janitorial work requires literacy to understand hazardous-material handling instructions), but, in terms of advanced skill, "there is no evidence of any really noticeable increase in skills or training needed to get a job and no evidence of any sizeable increase in training obtained while on the job" (25). Moreover, because "training is concentrated among the top professions, the most educated, and most experienced workers . . . one might argue that, on average, less training was pro-

vided to most workers" (Moss 1997, 25; see also Holzer 1996). Useem (1993) reviews the research and finds that training was focused on more experienced and educated employees and that it declined for less experienced, less educated workers. The extent to which factors such as technology and job complexity explain the increase in wage premiums versus the changes in institutional factors that lowered the wages for less skilled workers has been questioned (Howell 1997; Moss 1997). Moss (1997) argues, "Taken as a whole, the studies that attempt to look directly at skill changes indicate that skill demands appear to be increasing, but not at the pace suggested by the statistical literature that infers skill changes, not at a pace commensurate with the importance placed upon it by economists explaining the worsening earnings distribution, and not in a way that is so concentrated on computer use as the technological change argument would require" (15). Although the demand for more educated workers has increased, Moss argues that analysis of changes "in the strategy, behavior, and organization *inside of firms*" is necessary to fully understand changes in skill demand and job quality (23).

2. There has been some discussion in the United States about "skill development" and education as differentiated from "training." Carnevale and Desrochers (1997), for example, note that employer-based training "has less durability than broader educational preparation" and that it "tends to lose its economic value and transferability over time" (8). King (1996) discussed the long-term implications of skill development versus more narrowly targeted training, and the value of the former for building workforce skill that can provide longer-term competitive advantage to firms and provide the skill base for workers to adapt to technology and other changes without extensive retraining. Other studies also show that education has a higher payoff over the long term and that return-on-investment studies tend to focus only on short-term returns (for example, Lynch 1994). Support for these positions is suggested by observations that Germany is able to maintain one of the world's most highly skilled workforces with the highest training rates for workers aged 20 to 24 but the lowest rate of training for incumbent workers in the industrialized countries (Lynch 1994). Further, Lynch's findings suggest that training expen-

ditures for incumbent workers in countries such as the United States, where there is a comparatively weak underlying base of skills and education, do not achieve the same levels of skill quality as countries that spend less on training but have better initial skill development.

3. Factors explaining the training behavior of firms were explored by Scott and Meyer (1991) from an organizational or institutionalist perspective, and they discuss the reasons why firms do train. They argue that training programs serve organizational functions beyond direct skill development, as part of an overall trend for firms to expand "membership rights." These rights include training as a way of career mobility or as a means of having employees internalize the norms of the organization, particularly as job structures move away from direct supervising or control mechanisms and as a result of training professionals in expanding their profession. Thus training has multiple determinants in addition to its technical function of increasing efficiency, and this may explain why there is an expansion of training to a broader focus on skills that may not contribute directly to efficiency or productivity and that are more transferable (which economic theory would predict not to occur).

4. Employment growth for employees of insurance carriers declined from 2.7 percent annual growth between 1982 and 1987, to 1.1 percent from 1987 to 1992, down to 0.2 percent from 1992 to 1996. Average annual growth is projected to be 1.2 percent in this sector between 1996 and 2006. For the wage and salary category of insurance agents and brokers (which excludes the self-employed and unpaid family), employment growth declined from 4.7 percent annual growth between 1982 and 1987, to 1.4 percent between 1987 and 1992 and increased to 1.9 percent from 1992 to 1996. Average annual growth is projected to be 0.9 percent in this sector between 1996 and 2006 (U.S. Department of Labor 1997). Related to these changes, merger and acquisition activity doubled from $12.5 billion in 1994 to $27 billion in 1995 (Standard & Poor's 1996).

5. The consequences and emerging developments in the firms studied may or may not represent the situation for large numbers of firms; generalizability is always a question in evaluating case studies. Since the companies we studied are large and influential in their industries, however, what they do will be noted and likely imitated if they are successful or, if they are not, will become practices not to follow.

6. They may not be more homogeneous in skill levels because, for example, the elimination of manufacturing could be accompanied by an increase in support staff for engineering, of clerical workers to track contingent workers, and of suppliers.

7. Although contingent workers reduced permanent headcount (a performance measure in some firms and on Wall Street) and made layoffs easier, managers seldom seemed to think that overall costs were reduced. Although the direct wage bill might be less for using contingent workers than using permanent workers, managers identified other costs that were higher but not accounted for in formal assessments of contingent-worker cost savings (cf. Doeringer et al. 1991). For example, contingent workers required more orientation training and still required indirect personnel costs to administer contracts with the employment agency, which required maintaining the support capacity of permanent workers (for example, supervisor capacity to provide training and oversight; administrative capacity to administer the contracts; and so forth). The firm used contingent workers as its disposable workforce, which it could easily hire or fire, and the contingent workers reciprocated in attitude and behavior.

8. This change in hiring level would imply an increase in labor costs given higher premiums for college-educated workers. The companies interviewed, however, said they were not paying significantly more in labor costs than in the past. Two potential explanations are that the existing non-college-educated workforce was more senior and thus earning pay comparable to that of new college-educated entrants, and that, although the wage differential has increased, this increase is due to a decline in real wages of non-college-educated entrants while college-level entrant wages have remained flat. Thus current college-educated entrants are earning wages comparable to the real wages of non-college-educated workers of previous cohorts.

References

American Management Association. 1996. 1996 AMA Survey on Downsizing, Job Elimination, and Job Creation. Research report.

Berman, Eli, John Bound, and Zvi Grilches. 1994. Changes in the Demand for Skilled Labor Within U.S. Manufacturing: Evidence from the Annual Survey of Manufacturers. *Quarterly Journal of Economics* 109(2):367-97.

Cappelli, Peter, Laurie Bassi, Harry Katz, David Knoke, Paul Osterman, and Michael Useem. 1997. *Change at Work*. New York: Oxford University Press.

Carnevale, Anthony P. and Donna M. Desrochers. 1997. Employer Training: The High Road, the Low Road, and the Muddy Middle Path. Paper presented at the Conference on Restoring Broadly Shared Prosperity, Economic Policy Institute and Lyndon B. Johnson School of Public Affairs, University of Texas–Austin.

Davis, Gerald F., Kristina A. Diekmann, and Catherine H. Tinsley. 1994. The Decline and Fall of the Conglomeration Firm in the 1980s: Deinstitutionalization of an Organizational Form. *American Sociological Review* 59(4):547-70.

Doeringer, Peter B., Kathleen Christensen, Patricia M. Flynn, Douglas T. Hall, Harry C. Katz, Jeffery H. Keefe, Christopher J. Ruhm, Andrew M. Sum, and Michael Useem. 1991. *Turbulence in the American Workplace*. New York: Oxford University Press.

Holzer, Harry J. 1996. *What Employers Want: Job Prospects for Less Educated Workers*. New York: Russell Sage Foundation.

Howell, David R. 1997. *Institutional Failure and the American Worker: The Collapse of Low-Skill Wages*. Public Policy Brief No. 29. Annandale-on-Hudson, NY: Jerome Levy Economics Institute.

King, Jeffrey. 1996. Post-Taylorization or Re-Taylorization: Outsourcing Skills in the World Knowledge Economy. Paper presented at the symposium "The Future of Training and Vocational Education in the Global Economy," Hannover, Germany.

Lerman, Robert I. 1997. Reassessing Trends in Earnings Inequality in the US. *Monthly Labor Review*, Dec.

Lynch, Lisa M. 1994. Payoffs to Alternative Training Strategies at Work. In *Working Under Different Rules*, ed. Richard B. Freeman. New York: Russell Sage Foundation.

Moss, Philip. 1997. Earnings Inequality and the Quality of Jobs: The Status of Current Research, and Proposals for an Expanded Research Agenda. Working paper no. 198, Jerome Levy Economics Institute, Annandale-on-Hudson, New York.

Moss, Philip, Harold Salzman, and Chris Tilly. 1998. Corporate Restructuring, Job Structure, and Inequality: Implications for Human Resource Strategies, Skill Development, and Training. Working paper, Department of Regional Economic and Social Development, University of Massachusetts, Lowell.

Murnane, Richard J. and Frank Levy. 1997. *Teaching the New Basic Skills*. New York: Free Press.

Porter, Michael E. 1996. What Is Strategy? *Harvard Business Review* 74(6):61-78.

Salzman, Harold and Katrina Buchau. 1997. An Overview of the Insurance Industry. Jobs for the Future, Boston. Draft paper.

Scott, W. Richard and John W. Meyer. 1991. The Rise of Training Programs in Firms and Agencies: An Institutional Perspective. *Research in Organizational Behavior* 13:297-326.

Standard & Poor's. 1996. Property-Casualty Insurance Survey. 24 Oct.

Tilly, Chris and Michael Handel. 1997. The Diagnostic Imaging Equipment Industry: What Prognosis for Good Jobs? Center for Industrial Competi-

tiveness, University of Massachusetts, Lowell. Draft paper.

U.S. Department of Labor. Bureau of
Labor Statistics. 1997. Unpublished
tables. Office of Employment Projections, Washington, DC.

Useem, Michael. 1993. *Executive Defense:
Shareholder Power and Corporate Re-*
organization. Cambridge, MA: Harvard University Press.

———. 1996. Corporate Education and
Training. In *The American Corpora-*
tion Today, ed. Carl Kaysen. New
York: Oxford University Press.

Military Downsizing and the Career Prospects of Youths

By STEPHEN R. BARLEY

ABSTRACT: In this article, Stephen Barley examines the extent to which the U.S. military serves as a provider of skills in the civilian economy. His investigation centers around the following questions: Do training and education in the military transfer into the civilian workforce? If the military does prepare individuals for civilian jobs, will reductions in accessions constrict the availability of trained personnel, just as firms are realizing that they require a workforce more highly skilled than in the recent past? Barley presents a review of studies focusing on the economic returns to military service, which fall into one of three categories: the effect of military service on earnings potential; the effects of military training and occupational specialty; and the effects of military service on employment. Barley concludes by offering a series of recommendations for policy, highlighting the fact that returns to service are primarily due to access to further education.

Stephen R. Barley is professor of industrial engineering and engineering management and codirector of the Center for Work, Technology, and Organization at Stanford University's School of Engineering. His research focuses on the contract labor force, the impact of new technologies on work systems, and the social organization of technical work. Barley recently edited (with Julian Orr) Between Craft and Science: Technical Work in the United States *(1997).*

NOTE: The work reported herein was supported under the Educational Research and Development Center Program agreement number R117Q00011-91, CFDA 84.117Q, as administered by the Office of Educational Research and Improvement, U.S. Department of Education. The findings and opinions expressed in this article do not reflect the position or policies of the Office of Educational Research and Improvement or the U.S. Department of Education.

ALTHOUGH the military does not serve society primarily as an educational institution, many Americans now view military service as a springboard to careers in the civilian economy. The perception is most likely rooted in the legendary economic success of the veterans of World War II. Not only were many returning veterans trained in lines of work valuable to the economic expansion that followed (Fredland and Little 1980) but the GI bill enabled many others to acquire a postsecondary education that further enhanced their economic prospects. In recent decades, the armed forces have consciously promoted enlistment as a way to invest in training relevant for later life. The fact that a sizable percentage of recruits cite career benefits as a reason for joining the military (Richardson 1967) testifies to the effectiveness of the campaign, which highlights what may be the most unique aspect of military training: unlike schools, the military not only trains young people; it also provides "students" with a salary and subsidizes additional training after "graduation."

With the end of the Cold War has come the decision to downsize the military. The American economy and the military are deeply entwined; therefore a reduction in military spending promises to create serious social and economic difficulties. The closing of military bases imperils the livelihood not only of the communities surrounding the bases but, in some cases, entire regions and states. Cutbacks in military procurement may bankrupt firms and even cripple entire industries for whom the Pentagon has been a primary customer. Reductions in force also imply fewer opportunities for 18- to 24-year-olds. Finally, if military training does prepare individuals for civilian jobs, then reductions in force may constrict the availability of trained personnel—just as firms have begun to realize that they require a workforce more skilled than in the recent past (Parnell 1985; Johnston and Packer 1987; Aerospace Education Foundation 1989).

Three questions must be answered before one can determine how to offset the potential loss of training opportunities for young people and the consequent shortage of skilled personnel that may be caused by military reductions. Of initial concern is whether veterans actually fare better in the civilian economy than they would have had they not served and, if so, why?

If evidence supports the claim that veterans enjoy economic returns to military service, one must then ask, Which veterans benefit most? Conceivably, all veterans may enjoy returns from military service, although this seems unlikely, since no other form of education confers benefits equally. A more plausible scenario is that some veterans benefit more than others. At issue, then, is the identity of the groups that benefit and their relative numbers. Only after policymakers have verified the existence of returns to military service, understood the causes of such returns, and identified the groups that benefit can they formulate reasonable strategies for addressing the deleterious consequences of military cutbacks for the labor force.

This article seeks to inform the debate on military reductions by examining the evidence for returns to military service in the civilian economy. The objective is to identify the dynamics that enable veterans to do better in the civilian economy and the groups of veterans that benefit most. The article concludes by considering policy options that are consistent with the evidence on the civilian effects of military service.

EVIDENCE OF CIVILIAN RETURNS TO MILITARY SERVICE

Most studies of economic returns to military service fall into one of three categories defined by the outcomes that researchers have examined. The largest category consists of studies that compare the civilian earnings of matched samples of veterans and nonveterans. Most of these studies have sought to confirm or disconfirm the existence of returns to military service, although they also offer insights into the mechanisms that underwrite returns. The second category consists of studies that assume that technical training is the primary source of a veteran's edge in the civilian economy. One line of research asks whether differences in the earnings of veterans and nonveterans can be attributed to military training rather than to military service per se. Another concerns the probability that a veteran will continue in the occupation for which he or she received military training and, if so, whether continuing affects earnings. Finally, a handful of studies have asked whether military service affects the probability of being employed.

The effect of military service on earnings potential

Studies of the earnings of veterans and nonveterans usually employ regression models to predict whether military service raises or lowers hourly wages or annual salaries after controlling for other factors correlated with income. The dominant finding that emerges from this stream of research is that returns to military service have declined since World War II. A systematic examination of the literature suggests, however, that to describe the trend as a decline may be an understatement: earnings differences may have become negligible, if not negative.

Table 1 summarizes by war and race the results of 14 studies conducted since the mid-1970s on returns to military service.[1] A plus sign in a table cell indicates that the study found that veterans earn more than nonveterans. A minus sign indicates the reverse. Findings of no difference are denoted by an entry of a zero. When a study does not assess the earnings of veterans of a particular war or racial group, the corresponding cells remain empty.

A casual glance at the pattern of entries reveals that most of the evidence for positive returns to military service comes from research on veterans of World War II and Korea. Studies of veterans who served during or after Vietnam almost universally report that veterans earn the same or less than their civilian counterparts. Of 17 positive findings, only 2 involve veterans who served during or after Vietnam. Conversely, all but 3 of the 15 findings of negative returns have involved veterans of Vietnam or the

TABLE 1

**SUMMARY OF EMPIRICAL ASSESSMENTS OF THE EFFECT OF
MILITARY SERVICE ON CIVILIAN EARNINGS BY WAR AND RACE**

Article	Date	World War II			Korean War			Vietnam War			Post-Vietnam		
		A	W	M	A	W	M	A	W	M	A	W	M
Villemez and Kasarda	1976		+	+		+	+		−	−			
Martindale and Poston	1979		+	+		+	+		−	+			
DeTray*	1982		+	+		+	+		−	0			
Rosen and Taubman	1982	+			+			−					
Fredland and Little†	1980	0											
Angrist and Krueger	1989	−	−	−									
Knapp‡	1976				+								
Schwartz	1986				0	0	0	−	0	0			
Berger and Hirsch	1983							−	0	0			
Angrist	1990							−		0			
Cohany	1992							0	0	+			
Crane and Wise	1987										−	−	−
Mangum and Ball	1989											0	
Bryant and Wilhite	1990										−		

Key: A = all veterans, W = white veterans, M = minority veterans, + = veterans earn more than nonveterans, − = nonveterans earn more than veterans, 0 = no difference between veterans and nonveterans.

NOTE: Unless otherwise noted, effects reported are those estimated before controlling for education or military occupational specialty.

*Although DeTray did not control for war, he calculated coefficients for returns to military service for a number of birth cohorts. Therefore it is possible to assign effects to wars from DeTray's data.

†Return to military service calculated after controlling for military occupational specialty.

‡Although Knapp does not explicitly control for the war in which veterans served, because he sampled veterans who were aged 18-32 in 1964, most would have served either in the Korean War or the period between Korea and the very early years of Vietnam. Hence I have treated Knapp's study as a study of Korean War vets.

post-Vietnam era. Evidence that military service has no effect on civilian earnings is also found predominantly (69 percent) in studies of recent cohorts.

Thus the pattern in Table 1 strongly suggests that civilian returns to military service since Vietnam have been, at best, negligible and possibly negative. Estimates of the cost of military service to a newly discharged veteran range from an 11 percent (Crane and Wise 1987) to a 19 percent (Rosen and Taubman 1982) reduction in earnings. Bryant and Wilhite (1990) estimated that military service costs the average veteran approximately 85 cents per hour. Table 1 indicates that the loss of returns may have been less severe for minorities, however; they were the only group to experience positive returns to service in Vietnam.

The patterns in Table 1 raise two questions: why have returns to military service dwindled since Korea, and why has the decline been less severe for minorities? Two explanations seem plausible.[2] First, the demise of positive returns may reflect the dynamics of selection. Veterans of World War II and Korea may have possessed attributes that would have made them more attractive to employers regardless of their service. A similar distinction may continue to be true of minorities in the military. Alternatively, the pattern of declining returns may reflect the presence of moderating variables. Trends in society associated with, but distinct from, military service may conceivably explain positive returns before Vietnam, negative returns after Vietnam, and the greater severity of the change for whites. Shifting patterns of educational attainment are a primary candidate for such a moderating variable. As a group, the studies in Table 1 enable us to evaluate these explanations, while also assessing the mechanisms that may underwrite returns to military service in general.

Selection dynamics. In an influential study, DeTray (1982) discovered that returns to military service before Vietnam were directly proportional to the percentage of veterans in an age cohort. He interpreted this result as evidence for a screening dynamic based on selection differences. DeTray argued that the larger the proportion of a cohort who served in the military, the more employers would assume that nonveterans were somehow inferior because they were more likely to have been rejected by the military.

Angrist and Krueger's study of World War II veterans (1989) offers stronger support for the thesis that selection dynamics are responsible for different patterns of economic returns before and after Vietnam. After controlling for the risk of being drafted, Angrist and Krueger found that "veterans earn no more than comparable non-veterans and may well earn less" (1). Angrist and Krueger attributed their discovery of negative returns to military service among World War II veterans to the fact that draftees did not benefit from the continuous civilian employment enjoyed by those who did not serve. Angrist and Krueger concluded that veterans of World War II and Vietnam probably experienced similar economic returns to military service—both negative.

The foregoing studies provide relatively direct evidence for the possibility that declining returns to military service are by-products of selection dynamics associated with period effects and draft procedures. In contrast, no direct evidence is available that would allow one to conclude that selection differences also explain why returns have declined less severely for minorities. Indirect evidence is available, however. A number of studies have shown that even when returns to military service are negative, veterans without a high school education earn more than nonveterans who have not completed high school (Villemez and Kasarda 1976; DeTray 1982; Rosen and Taubman 1982; Berger and Hirsch 1983; Cohany 1992). Berger and Hirsch (1983) suggest that high school dropouts who enter the military may have an advantage over other dropouts, because the military is particularly careful when screening applicants from this population: they induct only the most capable. If Berger and Hirsch's conjecture is accurate, then minority veterans may experience an advantage relative to nonveterans not only because they are more able than their peers but because their veteran status signals their ability to employers.

Education as a moderating variable. To the degree that selection dynamics account for the pattern in Table 1, returns to military service are best viewed as the product of attributes possessed by veterans prior to enlistment or conscription. Military service adds no human capital. In contrast, the argument that education moderates returns to military service draws attention to increments in human capital that are usually acquired after military service. In this case, military service may indirectly enhance human capital. The hypothesis that declining returns to military service can be explained by an association between military service and educational attainment rests on three entwined propositions: (1) that earnings increase with increasing education; (2) that veterans, on average, acquire more education than nonveterans; and (3) that differences in the educational attainment of veterans and nonveterans have diminished over time. The first proposition is so well established that it requires no further documentation. The argument therefore pivots on the viability of the second and third propositions.

There can be little doubt that large numbers of veterans of World War II eventually profited by taking advantage of the educational benefits associated with the GI bill. O'Neill, Ross, and Warner (1976) report that 51 percent of all World War II veterans eventually used the GI bill to obtain some form of training. They also show that the use of GI bill benefits has increased since World War II: by the Vietnam era, 59 percent of U.S. veterans were using their educational benefits.

In recent years, minorities have apparently taken greater advantage of the military's educational benefits than have whites. After controlling for ability (using the Armed Forces Qualification Test) and level of education pursued, O'Neill, Ross, and Warner (1976) found that African American Vietnam veterans were between 4.5 percent and 9.9 percent more likely than whites to make use of the GI bill. Moreover, African Americans were more likely to use their benefits for college and vocational and technical schools, whereas whites were more likely to use their benefits for on-the-job training. Cohany (1992) also found that minority veterans were more likely than white veterans to avail themselves of educational benefits and that both African American and Hispanic veterans were more likely than comparable nonveterans to pursue some form of postsecondary education (51.6 percent versus 26.5 percent for African American, and 60.6 percent versus 20.8 percent for Hispanic veterans and nonveterans, respectively).

Thus data generally confirm the proposition that veterans acquire more education than comparable nonveterans and that the acquisition generally occurs after discharge. This suggests the possibility that differential educational attainment largely explains economic returns to military service. Villemez and Kasarda (1976) explicitly put this hypothesis to test. In a path analysis designed to predict income, Villemez and Kasarda (1976, 416-17) found that the direct effect of military service on earnings was small and that the indirect effect through occupation was "practically nonexistent." Military service was, however, a strong predictor of educational attainment, and educational attainment was an even stronger predictor of income. Hence Villemez and Kasarda concluded that returns to military service were almost entirely explained by the fact that veterans pursued more education. Moreover, these researchers found that the indirect effect of military status on earnings through education was stronger for African Americans than for whites.

If veterans have always become more educated than comparable nonveterans, then why have returns to military service diminished over time? The paradox appears to be explained by the fact that, since World War II, levels of education have increased throughout American society, thereby reducing the competitive edge that veterans once acquired from the GI bill (Villemez and Kasarda 1976).

Thus it appears that differences in educational attainment and educational trends in society may account both for the pattern of declining returns to military service for most of the observed differences in earnings among veterans and nonveterans and for the fact that African American veterans have been less severely affected than whites.

The effects of military training and occupational specialty

Because earnings are so strongly tied to education, it seems plausible that military service should most enhance civilian wages when veterans acquire skills in the military that are of direct value in the civilian economy. For this reason, a number of researchers have attempted to distinguish payoffs to military training from payoffs to military service itself. Using data on World War II veterans, Fredland and Little (1980) reported that military training brought a 12 percent premium in earnings if a veteran used his or her training in the civilian economy. Using data on Vietnam veterans, Norrblom (1976) arrived at an identical estimate of the payoff for a year of military training. Norrblom also found that military service was unrelated to earnings after controlling for whether veterans had received training in the military.

In a study of veterans who served after Vietnam, Bryant and Wilhite (1990) reached less optimistic conclusions than Fredland and Little (1980) or Norrblom (1976). Bryant and Wilhite regressed hourly wages on the time veterans spent in the military as well as on the number of months of military training they received. The regressions indicated that each month of military service reduced a veteran's civilian wages by 4 cents per hour. Since the typical veteran served 31 months, a tour of duty reduced civilian wages by a total of $1.24 per hour. In contrast, a month of military training enhanced civilian wages by 20 cents per hour. Because the armed forces provided the average veteran with 1.78 months of training, Bryant and Wilhite's estimates imply that even those who received training experienced no payoff in later earnings. The weakness of such results is that simple measures of time spent in training ignore differences in occupation. It is unlikely that a person trained as a cook can expect the same career boost as a person trained in computer technology, even if both are trained for identical periods of time. Consequently, returns to military training are likely to vary widely by occupational specialty.

Following this line of reasoning, a number of researchers have estimated the payoff to veterans who entered civilian jobs that matched their military occupational specialty (MOS) and have sought to identify those specialties where matches are most likely to occur (Norrblom 1976; O'Neill, Ross, and Warner 1976; Fredland and Little 1980; Mangum and Ball 1987, 1989; Bryant and Wilhite 1990). Three findings repeatedly surface. First, after controlling for matches between military and civilian occupation, all returns to military service and training disappear. Thus civilian payoffs to military service are largely a function of the MOS in which a veteran is trained. Second, only veterans trained as technicians consistently appear to profit from their military training. Military personnel trained in electronics, the repair of electrical and mechanical equipment, and the crafts are most likely to find their training useful.

Those who specialize in combat, communications, or intelligence are least likely to find related civilian employment. Finally, a number of studies indicate that only training in the Air Force consistently yields positive returns (O'Neill, Ross, and Warner 1976; Mangum and Ball 1987; Bryant and Wilhite 1990).

One measure of the value of an MOS is the proportion of veterans who find civilian jobs in related lines of work. Norrblom (1976) and Mangum and Ball (1989) reported that approximately 50 percent of the veterans in their samples landed civilian jobs related to their MOS. Proportions were even higher for particular specialties. For instance, Mangum and Ball (1987) estimated that 61 percent of male military personnel trained in electronic equipment repair and in the crafts found similar jobs after being discharged.

In an appendix to an article on sources of training, Carey and Eck (1984) reported that only 2 percent of the working population thought their military experience was valuable training; the percentage rose to 5 percent for both "technicians and related support occupations" and "precision production, craft, and repair occupations." All other broad occupational groups reported less reliance on military training. That the military was most important in these occupational clusters concurs with the results of the studies of transfer of training discussed earlier. However, as Table 2 indicates, even for the relatively technical occupational clusters, military training was among the least important sources of training.

TABLE 2

**PERCENTAGE OF MEMBERS OF VARIOUS OCCUPATIONAL GROUPS
WHO REPORT THAT VARIOUS SOURCES OF TRAINING WERE USEFUL
IN OBTAINING THEIR CURRENT JOB**

Occupational Group	Sources of Training								
	High School	Vocational Education	Junior or technical College	College	Company Training	On the Job	Military	Correspondence School	Friends
Executive, administrative, managerial	3 (6)	4 (5)	5 (4)	34 (2)	12 (3)	39 (1)	3 (6)	1 (7)	3 (6)
Professional specialties	2 (7)	5 (5)	7 (4)	70 (1)	9 (3)	22 (2)	2 (7)	1 (8)	3 (6)
Technicians and related support	5 (6)	11 (5)	20 (3)	24 (2)	14 (4)	32 (1)	5 (6)	2 (7)	2 (7)
Sales	2 (5)	2 (5)	3 (4)	8 (3)	12 (2)	23 (1)	1 (6)	1 (6)	3 (4)
Administrative support	16 (2)	5 (6)	8 (3)	6 (5)	7 (4)	31 (1)	1 (7)	1 (7)	1 (7)
Private household	1 (4)	0	0	0	1 (3)	4 (2)	0	0	5 (1)
Service workers	2 (6)	6 (3)	4 (4)	3 (5)	9 (2)	18 (1)	1 (8)	0	2 (7)
Farming, forestry, and fishing	2 (4)	1 (5)	2 (4)	4 (3)	1 (5)	16 (1)	0	0	11 (2)
Precision production, craft, and repair	5 (4)	4 (5)	5 (4)	2 (6)	17 (2)	40 (1)	5 (4)	2 (6)	8 (3)
Operators, assemblers, and inspectors	3 (3)	2 (4)	2 (4)	1 (5)	6 (2)	26 (1)	1 (5)	0	3 (3)
Transportation and materials moving	1 (5)	1 (5)	0	0	8 (2)	26 (1)	2 (4)	0	5 (3)
Handlers, helpers, and laborers	1 (3)	0	1 (3)	0	2 (2)	13 (1)	1 (3)	0	1 (3)
Total	5 (4)	4 (5)	5 (4)	17 (2)	10 (3)	28 (1)	2 (7)	1 (8)	3 (6)

SOURCE: Data are based on Carey and Eck 1984, tab. 1.

NOTE: Row percentages do not sum to 100 because respondents could indicate more than one source of training. In parentheses is the rank of the source's importance to the occupational category.

The pattern is similar even when one examines less aggregated data. In only 34 of the 284 detailed occupations mentioned in Carey and Eck's tables (1984) did more than 5 percent of the respondents claim that military training was useful "for qualifying for their current job." These 34 occupations are listed in Table 3, ordered according to the percentage of

TABLE 3

**OCCUPATIONS WITH MORE THAN
5 PERCENT OF MEMBERS REPORTING MILITARY TRAINING IS IMPORTANT**

Occupation	Percentage	Source Rank
Aircraft engine mechanics	45	1
Data processing equipment repairers	22	4
Electronic repairers, commercial and industrial equipment	21	2
Miscellaneous electrical and electronic equipment repairers	19	3
Electrical and electronic technicians	17	4
Aerospace engineers	14	4
Construction inspectors	12	3
Electricians	12	3
Water transportation occupations	12	3
Supervisors, mechanics, and repairers	11	3
Office machine repairers	11	4
Telephone line installers and repairers	10	3
Electrical and electronic engineers	9	4
Bus, truck, and stationary engine mechanics	9	3
Inspectors and compliance officers, except construction	8	4
Industrial engineers	8	4
Engineering and related technologists and technicians	8	6
Mechanics and repairers, except supervisors	8	4
Vehicle and mobile equipment mechanics and repairers	8	4
Electrical power installers and repairers	8	3
Sheet-metal workers	8	3
Plant and systems operators	8	3
Engineers (not elsewhere classified)	7	5
Operations and systems researchers and analysts	7	5
Heating, air conditioning, and refrigeration mechanics	7	6
Millwrights	7	4
Personnel and labor relations managers	6	4
Management analysts	6	5
Purchasing agents and buyers	6	5
Dentists	6	2
Firefighting and fire prevention occupations	6	4
Police and detectives	6	5
Guards	6	3
Automobile mechanics	6	5

SOURCE: Data are from tables in Carey and Eck 1984.

respondents who reported that military training was important. Table 3 also reports the rank order of military service as a source of training for

TABLE 4

RELATIVE IMPORTANCE OF MILITARY TRAINING BY OCCUPATION

Occupation	Importance Relative to First Source
Aircraft engine mechanics	1.00
Electronic repairers, commercial and industrial equipment	0.75
Data processing equipment repairers	0.71
Miscellaneous electrical and electronic equipment repairers	0.63
Electrical and electronic technicians	0.44
Guards	0.30
Electricians	0.27
Telephone line installers and repairers	0.27
Supervisors, mechanics, and repairers	0.26
Construction inspectors	0.26
Inspectors and compliance officers, except construction	0.25
Office machine repairers	0.24
Electrical power installers and repairers	0.24
Plant and systems operators	0.23
Water transportation occupations	0.23
Engineering and related technologists and technicians	0.21
Mechanics and repairers, except supervisors	0.21
Bus, truck, and stationary engine mechanics	0.21
Vehicle and mobile equipment mechanics and repairers	0.20
Aerospace engineers	0.19
Millwrights	0.19
Sheet-metal workers	0.19
Heating, air conditioning, and refrigeration mechanics	0.18
Purchasing agents and buyers	0.16
Industrial engineers	0.16
Operations and systems researchers and analysts	0.16
Automobile mechanics	0.16
Personnel and labor relations managers	0.15
Firefighting and fire prevention occupations	0.15
Electrical and electronic engineers	0.14
Management analysts	0.14
Police and detectives	0.14
Engineers (not elsewhere classified)	0.10
Dentists	0.06

SOURCE: Data are based on tables in Carey and Eck 1984.

each occupation. In only one case—aircraft engine mechanics—was military training the most important source of training. In only two occupations was military training the second most important source of training: dentistry and "electronic repairers, commercial and industrial equipment."

A measure of the relative standing of military training for an occupation can be derived from Carey and Eck's data by calculating the ratio P_m/P_f, where P_m is the percentage of respondents who report that military training is an important source of training, and P_f is the percentage of respondents who cite the occupation's most common source of training, whatever it might be. When the military is the most important source of training, the ratio attains a value of 1. When no members of an occupation claim that military training is important, the ratio assumes a value of 0. Table 4 lists the 34 occupations in Table 3 according to this ratio, which falls off rapidly. By the time one accounts for the top 34 occupations, the ratio has fallen to 0.06. The list indicates that military training seems most important for aircraft mechanics and for those who operate or repair electronic or computational devices. In general, then, it would appear that military training is relatively unimportant outside of a handful of occupations and, even in most of these, the military is neither a primary nor a secondary source of training.

Several studies have attempted to assess how people who obtain occupational training in the military fare relative to those who receive training elsewhere. Fredland and Little (1980) estimated that military training brought World War II veterans a 12 percent premium in wages but that comparable civilian training brought a premium of 16 to 17 percent. Veterans trained by the military in the skilled trades apparently enjoyed no premium for their training. Persons trained in the skilled trades in the civilian economy, however, received a return of 18 to 21 percent. Norrblom (1976) found that a year of

military training brought a 12 percent return on wages. However, preservice civilian training yielded a 16 percent return and preservice work experience in an occupation yielded another 7 percent. Thus Norrblom's data indicate that civilian training may be worth at least 25 percent more than comparable training in the military.

The effects of military service on employment

Different sources of training may be unequally available (or even viable) for different groups of young people. For instance, there is reason to believe that the military may be a much more accessible source of training for the less privileged and for minorities, in particular. Although Crane and Wise (1987) found no difference between the ability of high school graduates who enlisted and those who attended two-year colleges or entered the labor force, they reported that enlistees were more likely to come from poorer families and to be minorities. African Americans currently represent 16 percent of all enlistees but only 10 percent of the civilian labor force (Crane and Wise 1987). From 1969 to 1978 the percentage of white 18- to 24-year-olds in the military fell from 20 percent to 7 percent, whereas the percentage of African Americans in the military from the same age bracket remained constant at 14 percent (Ellwood and Wise 1987). Thus the military appears to be twice as important as an employer (and, one would assume, a trainer) of young African Americans as it is for young whites.

In fact, it appears that military service may significantly lower aggregate unemployment among African American, but not white, youths. Ellwood and Wise (1987) estimated the effect of enlistment on civilian employment rates for young white and young African American males. Although their estimate was statistically insignificant, they found that when a white male enlists in the military, civilian employment among young white males falls by 0.29 of an individual. When a young African American male enlists, employment of African American youths increases by 1.00 individuals. Thus, even if the military does not serve as an important source of training for black youths, it does represent a significant source of employment. Reductions in the armed forces may well increase the rate of unemployment among minority youths.

WHAT RESEARCH TELLS US: CONCLUSIONS AND RECOMMENDATIONS

Although returns to military service may have been positive prior to Vietnam, since Vietnam the average veteran has, at best, neither benefited nor suffered economically from military service. In fact, returns to military service, whether positive or negative, have probably never been related to military service itself. Conceivably, selection dynamics created an illusion that military service enabled World War II veterans to earn more than comparable nonveterans. It is more likely, however, that educational attainment is the primary reason veterans have earned more than

nonveterans in some eras and less in others. As a result of the GI bill and its later incarnations, veterans were simply more likely to pursue postsecondary education than nonveterans were. In recent years, the edge conferred by educational benefits has diminished because the population as a whole has become more educated. Having an associate's or a bachelor's degree no longer sets the average veteran apart from comparable nonveterans. Thus military service does not seem to carry much of an economic advantage for the average veteran.

This generalization, however, must be tempered for three groups of veterans. First, military service continues to be economically advantageous for minorities. Minorities benefit from military service for two reasons. Because minorities take considerable advantage of the military's educational benefits and because the levels of education remain lower among minorities than among whites, minority veterans profit from military service because they eventually become more highly educated than nonveteran peers. Minorities also benefit because military service seems to reduce unemployment among African American youths. Thus the military functions as a highly effective job and scholarship program for minority youths.

The second group that may benefit from military service comprises high school dropouts. Evidence consistently shows that veterans with less than a high school degree do better than dropouts who do not enlist. Why this occurs is unclear. Perhaps because the armed forces screen dropouts closely, military service may serve as a credential for veterans without a high school degree. Alternately, because of the availability of educational benefits, dropouts who enter the military may be more likely to finish school than their civilian counterparts. Finally, dropouts who enter the military may be more likely to receive occupational training. Ultimately, however, the issue of why military service benefits veterans without a high school diploma is rapidly becoming moot: the proportion of enlistees without high school degrees has declined precipitously since Vietnam (Schwartz 1986). In 1992, only 2 percent of all enlisted military personnel had less than a high school degree (U.S. Department of Defense 1992).

Veterans trained in technical specialties related to computers, electronics, and the repair of electrical and mechanical equipment constitute a third group that benefits from military service because their skills transfer readily to the civilian economy. The armed forces train approximately 5 percent of the persons who pursue such occupations in the civilian economy. If 50 percent of all veterans make use of their military training as Norrblom (1976) and Mangum and Ball (1989) report, and if one also assumes that most veterans who use their training have had a technical MOS, then in 1991 the military may have trained as many as 53,000 new entrants to the civilian labor force.[3] This number is roughly equivalent to 8 percent of all students who graduate annually from institutions of postsecondary education that offer less-than-four-year degrees. Nevertheless, the military may not be the optimal source of training even for people in these occupations. Civilians trained by other institutions are just as likely to secure work related to their training, and their earnings are likely to be greater, at least during the early years of their career.

Policy considerations

On the basis of existing research, there seems to be little reason to anticipate broad shortages of trained labor because of reductions in military force. Yet military reductions may exacerbate shortages of trained technicians and craftspersons, since technical jobs are growing more rapidly than any other occupational sector and since shortages already exist in numerous technical specialties (Barley 1991). Whether policies are required to offset such shortages depends on the vulnerability of technical MOSs. Given the increasingly technological nature of warfare, it would seem unwise for the military to target technical specialties for heavy reductions. All else being equal, reductions are more likely to come from nontechnical specialties that impart skills that transfer less well to the civilian economy. Nevertheless, if policymakers wish to minimize the effect of military cutbacks on shortages of trained personnel in the civilian economy, they should consider placing the burden of reductions in force on nontechnical occupational specialties.

Although the military may not be as important a source of training as is sometimes intimated, one should not conclude that the military has no broad effects on civilian labor markets. The educational benefits that the military provides to veterans after discharge appear to matter a great deal. Because of these benefits, African American veterans, in particular, have attained levels of education that they otherwise might not have been able to afford. Thus military cutbacks may indirectly cause a shortage of trained civilians by reducing educational opportunities for those segments of the population least likely to have alternative means of financing an education.

Given that the military functions effectively as a job and scholarship program for minorities and the poor, the primary policy issue facing those concerned with the labor implications of military reductions is how to ensure educational benefits to those who would be unable to acquire further education without military service. Policymakers might consider programs for inducing minorities to complete high school and to pursue some form of postsecondary education. Postsecondary education should not, however, be construed solely as attendance at an established educational institution. Research shows that many veterans use their benefits to pursue on-the-job training (O'Neill, Ross, and Warner 1976) and that such forms of training are potentially the most effective even in technical occupations (Barley 1993). In fact, it may be the hands-on knowledge obtained by technical specialists in the military that makes them attractive to employers.

Subsidies for postsecondary education might cost less per person than the cost of supporting a serviceman or -woman for an entire tour of duty. Such an approach, however, is likely to encounter several difficulties. First, some political factions will undoubtedly frame such a program as an entitlement and hence oppose any government effort to support the education of minorities in lieu of some form of service. Second, and perhaps even more troubling, such programs may be unattractive to those who would benefit most. Research by Portes and Stepick (1993) indicates that educational attainment may be less highly valued than military service in some minority youth cultures.

Policymakers may have several options for circumventing such difficulties. One approach would be to create a job corps or a community service program for which volunteers would be repaid, in part, by a civilian equivalent of the GI bill. A second approach would be to reemphasize the importance of the National Guard as a standing militia. High school graduates might enlist for service in the National Guard rather than the armed forces, be asked to participate for a reasonably long period of time, and then be repaid immediately by stipends and access to scholarships. Finally, if advanced education is as critical for employment today as recent studies suggest (Parnell 1985; Johnston and Packer 1987; Aerospace Education Foundation 1989), then it may be time for policymakers to consider some approximation of compulsory postsecondary education. In this regard, apprenticeship programs that link high school students to community college programs seem to have considerable promise. Whatever steps are taken, policymakers must formulate their decisions in light of the realization that reductions in military personnel are likely to increase the unemployment rate among minorities. Policies ought to be fashioned to create alternative forms of employment as well as alternative sources of training.

Notes

1. Most studies prior to those summarized in Table 1 focused on the earnings of men and women who retired from military careers, rather than on servicemen and -women who served shorter tours of duty. Given that the policy debate does not concern those who pursue full-term careers in the military, I have restricted my attention to studies relevant to the average recruit.

2. A third explanation may be changes in culture, in particular the declining prestige of military service in American society. Several researchers have suggested that Vietnam veterans were disadvantaged in the civilian economy due to the war's unpopularity. Patterns of earnings for recent veterans are similar to those of Vietnam vets, however, so a cultural explanation for dwindling returns is not particularly compelling.

3. This figure represents half the number of servicemen and -women discharged in 1991.

References

Aerospace Education Foundation. 1989. *America's Next Crisis: The Shortfall of Technical Manpower.* Arlington, VA: Aerospace Education Foundation.

Angrist, Joshua. 1990. Lifetime Earnings and the Vietnam Draft Lottery: Evidence from Social Security Administrative Records. *American Economic Review* 80:313-36.

Angrist, Joshua and Alan B. Krueger. 1989. Why Do World War II Veterans Earn More Than Nonveterans? Working paper #254, Industrial Relations Section, Princeton University, Princeton, NJ.

Barley, Stephen R. 1991. The New Crafts: On the Technization of the Workforce and the Occupationalization of Firms. Working paper, National Center on the Educational Quality of the Workforce, University of Pennsylvania, Philadelphia.

———. 1993. What Do Technicians Do? Working paper, National Center on the Educational Quality of the Workforce, University of Pennsylvania, Philadelphia.

Berger, Mark C. and Barry T. Hirsch. 1983. The Civilian Earnings Experience of Vietnam-Era Veterans. *Journal of Human Resources* 18:455-79.

Bryant, Richard and Al Wilhite. 1990. Military Experience and Training Effects on Civilian Wages. *Applied Economics* 22:69-81.

Carey, Max and Alan Eck. 1984. How Workers Get Their Training. *Occupational Outlook Quarterly* (Winter):3-21.

Cohany, Sharon R. 1992. The Vietnam-Era Cohort: Employment and Earnings. *Monthly Labor Review* (June):3-15.

Crane, Jon R. and David A. Wise. 1987. Military Service and Civilian Earnings of Youths. In *Public Sector Payrolls*, ed. David A. Wise. Chicago: University of Chicago Press.

DeTray, Dennis. 1982. Veteran Status as a Screening Device. *American Economic Review* 72:133-42.

Ellwood, David T. and David A. Wise. 1987. Military Hiring and Youth Employment. In *Public Sector Payrolls*, ed. David A. Wise. Chicago: University of Chicago Press.

Fredland, John Eric and Roger D. Little. 1980. Long Term Returns to Vocational Training: Evidence from Military Sources. *Journal of Human Resources* 15:49-66.

Johnston, William B. and Arnold Packer. 1987. *Workforce 2000: Work and Workers for the 21st Century*. Indianapolis, IN: Hudson Institute.

Knapp, Charles B. 1976. The Effect of Military Experience on Postservice Earnings Without the Draft. In *Defense Manpower Policy*, ed. Richard V. C. Cooper. Santa Monica, CA: RAND.

Mangum, Stephen L. and David E. Ball. 1987. Military Skill Training: Some Evidence of Transferability. *Armed Forces and Society* 13:425-41.

———. 1989. The Transferability of Military Provided Occupational Training in the Post-Draft Era. *Industrial and Labor Relations Review* 42:230-45.

Martindale, Melanie and Dudley L. Poston. 1979. Variations in Veteran/ Nonveteran Earnings Patterns Among World War II, Korea and Vietnam War Cohorts. *Armed Forces and Society* 5:219-43.

Norrblom, Eva M. 1976. *The Returns to Military and Civilian Training*. Santa Monica, CA: RAND.

O'Neill, Dave M., Sue Goetz Ross, and John T. Warner. 1976. Military Occupation, GI Bill Training, and Human Capital. In *Defense Manpower Policy*, ed. Richard V. C. Cooper. Santa Monica, CA: RAND.

Parnell, Dale. 1985. *The Neglected Majority*. Washington, DC: Community College Press.

Portes, Alejandro and Alex Stepick. 1993. *City on the Edge: The Transformation of Miami*. Berkeley: University of California Press.

Richardson, Robert Brooks. 1967. An Examination of the Transferability of Certain Military Skills and Experience to Civilian Occupations. Ph.D. diss., Cornell University.

Rosen, Sherwin and Paul Taubman. 1982. Changes in Life Cycle Earnings: What Do Social Security Data Show. *Journal of Human Resources* 17:321-38.

Schwartz, Saul. 1986. The Relative Earnings of Vietnam and Korean-Era Veterans. *Industrial and Labor Relations Review* 39:564-71.

U.S. Department of Defense. 1992. *Selected Manpower Statistics: Fiscal Year 1992*. Washington, DC: Government Printing Office.

Villemez, Wayne J. and John D. Kasarda. 1976. Veteran Status and Socioeconomic Attainment. *Armed Forces and Society* 2:407-21.

ANNALS, *AAPSS*, 559, September 1998

The Benefits to Bridging Work and School

By DANIEL SHAPIRO and MARIA IANNOZZI

ABSTRACT: In this article, the authors use the 1997 National Employer Survey to examine the benefits that result from an improved articulation between the nation's economic and educational systems. Specifically, they demonstrate that there are real and substantial benefits to be gained by individual employers that participate in activities related to school reform and the educational process. While the realization of such rewards does not seem to mitigate the current disconnect between employers and schools, those establishments that do engage in school-relevant activities assess more positively the ability of local secondary schools to prepare students for the world of work.

Daniel Shapiro is director of research for the Institute for Research on Higher Education at the University of Pennsylvania and project manager for the National Employer Survey.

Maria Iannozzi is a writer and editor who focuses on education and labor issues.

NOTE: The work reported herein was supported under the Educational Research and Development Center Program, through the National Center for Postsecondary Improvement (NCPI), agreement number R309A60001, CFDA 84.309A, as administered by the National Institute on Postsecondary Education, Libraries, and Lifelong Learning, and the Consortium for Policy Research in Education (CPRE), agreement number R308A60003, CFDA 84.308A, as administered by the National Institute on Educational Governance, Finance, Policy-Making and Management, Office of Educational Research and Improvement (OERI), U.S. Department of Education. The data analysis for this article was conducted at the U.S. Bureau of the Census's Center for Economic Studies. The findings and opinions expressed by NCPI and CPRE do not reflect the position or policies of the Bureau of the Census, OERI, or the U.S. Department of Education.

TO a remarkable extent, the re-form of K-12 education in the United States has focused on the capacity of that system to adequately prepare students to become productive young workers. As Cappelli, Shapiro, and Shumanis point out elsewhere in this issue, a predominant strategy that developed in the United States during the 1990s was to exploit the educational experiences already occurring at places of work in order to retain and motivate students who were not responsive to traditional pedagogical techniques. This strategy was given both official sanction and administrative reality with the passage of the 1994 School-to-Work Opportunities Act.

While these and related activities that ease the transition between school and work may be beneficial overall and in the long run, it is still not clear what role work itself can play in transforming education or whether engagement in such activities is in the immediate interests of any particular employer. Cappelli, Shapiro, and Shumanis lay out a summary of those factors that would both encourage and discourage employers from participating in work-based learning activities. A similar set of factors could be generated for other types of activities that engage employers, ranging from sponsoring before- or after-school programs, to working on curriculum development, to engaging in the current debates around K-12 reform.

The fundamental question that any employer wants answered relates to the bottom line: "Is my investment in time and resources going to pay off?" While individuals may act upon some philanthropic or moral imperative, employers in general will not act without a more tangible return. The development of large-scale social policy needs to reflect that reality. If the benefits resulting from improved articulation between the nation's economic and education systems can be realized by participants and nonparticipants alike, why would any particular firm commit time and resources, since it would reap the rewards in any case?

In this article, we use the 1997 National Employer Survey (NES) to examine these questions. Specifically, we show that there are real and substantial benefits to be gained by individual employers that participate in activities related to school reform and the educational process. While the realization of such rewards does not seem to mitigate the current disconnect between employers and schools generally, establishments that regularly work with schools report that their local high schools do a better job of producing work-ready graduates.

THE NATIONAL EMPLOYER SURVEY

The NES was designed by the Institute for Research on Higher Education and administered by the U.S. Bureau of the Census as part of the U.S. Department of Education's research interest in the educational quality of the American workforce. First administered in 1994, the NES shed new light on the practices and expectations of employers in their search for a skilled and proficient workforce. More specifically, the 1994

NES documented a fundamental disconnection between employers and schools: although employers discounted schools and measures of student performance when making hiring decisions, those establishments that hired more educated workers had more productive workplaces in the long run.

The 1997 administration of the NES explored this disconnection further. In addition to capturing longitudinal information on many of the employers first surveyed, the 1997 NES posed new questions to gauge the link between work and school and to relate employers' impressions of schools and the quality of their graduates. As in 1994, the sampling frame for the 1997 NES included all private establishments with 20 or more employees (excluding corporate headquarters). The 1997 response rate was 78 percent, representing responses from more than 5400 establishments.

SCHOOL PARTICIPATION AND YOUTH TURNOVER RATES

One of the key additions to the 1997 NES was a section in which employers were asked about the different ways in which they worked with local schools. Table 1 displays employer responses to these items, along with the percentage of establishments that reported participating in each activity. Although donating materials to schools represents the most common activity by far, the most interesting findings highlight the substantial rates at which employers are engaging in K-12 reform, through industry associations, advi-

TABLE 1

PERCENTAGE OF ESTABLISHMENTS REPORTING PARTICIPATION IN VARIOUS SCHOOL-RELATED ACTIVITIES

Type of Activity	Percentage of Participating Establishments
Employees visit students in school	28
Students visit the work site	34
Employees tutor students	9
Employer sponsors before-school or after-school programs	12
Employer sponsors youth clubs	10
Employer sponsors student scholarships	24
Employees teach in the classroom	10
Employer assists school-based enterprises	8
Employer assists with professional development of school personnel	6
Employer assists with curricular development	9
Employer assists in communicating business practices	19
Employer donates materials to schools	53
Employer sponsors teacher scholarships	6
Employer works on K-12 reform through	
industry associations	28
advisory committees	23
community forums	30
local media	31
company communications	35
other methods	2

sory committees, community forums, local media outlets, or corporate communications functions.

In order to gauge the effects of relatively weak versus extensive participation, we split the 1997 NES sample into four roughly equal groups according to the number of activities in which an establishment reported participating. The bottom quartile of establishments participated in one or none of the activities. Those that participated in two, three, or four activities were placed in the second quartile. Establishments that participated in five, six, or seven activities were placed in the third quartile, and those that participated in eight or more in the top quartile.

When comparing the annual quit and fire rates of young workers (aged 18 to 25) to employers' school participation, we were struck by the strong relationship that emerged. Employers that actively participated with local high schools (in eight or more activities) have a young-worker turnover rate that is half the youth turnover rate for employers that do not actively participate with high schools (Figure 1). By actively engaging with their local education systems, establishments may be helping to generate a future labor force that is more stable, more work ready, and presumably better matched to the workplace of the future.

THE CONTINUING DISCONNECT: DISREGARD AND NEUTRALITY

Despite the benefits employers receive through substantial and active participation, the disconnection between schools and employers persists. When employers were asked once again, in 1997, to rank the factors involved in making hiring decisions, their responses were virtually identical to those given in 1994 (Table 2). Employers continue to ignore schooling factors when hiring youths; in fact, the reputation of a job applicant's school actually fell in importance.

The 1997 NES also asked employers to evaluate their local high schools using criteria that reflect the school's performance in producing work-ready graduates. An exploration of employers' perceptions reinforces the perennial disappointment they express concerning the quality of local high schools; the best way to summarize these attitudes is as "middling" satisfaction.

When employers were asked to rate how well local high schools prepared their graduates for work, based on the establishments' experiences with hiring these graduates, they overwhelmingly placed their answers in the middle of the scale (Figure 2): 62 percent of establishments rated high schools' preparation of their students for work as adequate. The remaining employers were split almost evenly between the two extremes: 20 percent reported that high schools' preparation of students was outstanding or more than adequate, and 19 percent reported that it was barely acceptable or unacceptable.

OVERCOMING AMBIVALENCE: EMPLOYER ENGAGEMENT AND LOCAL CONTEXT

When we looked at the factors influencing employer attitudes, however, an interesting story emerged regarding the triangular relationship between employers, schools, and young workers. Several factors relating to three general categories— employer's participation with schools, the nature of the employer's workforce, and the nature of the labor market in which the employer operates—are associated with more

FIGURE 1
YOUTH EMPLOYEE TURNOVER VERSUS EMPLOYERS' SCHOOL PARTICIPATION

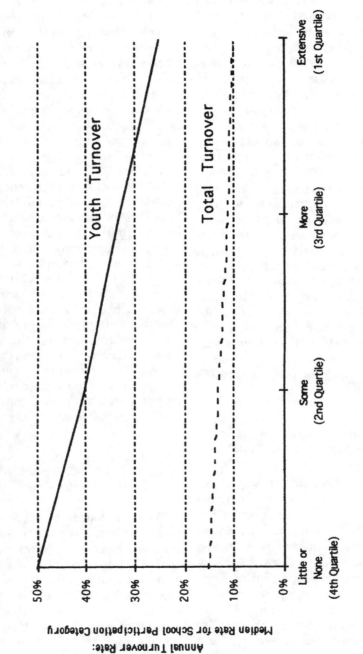

TABLE 2

**RELATIVE RANKING OF THE
IMPORTANCE OF VARIOUS FACTORS
IN MAKING HIRING DECISIONS**

Characteristics	1994 Ranking	1997 Ranking
Applicant's attitude	4.6	4.6
Applicant's communication skills	4.2	4.1
Previous employer references	3.4	3.9
Previous work experience	4.0	3.8
Industry-based credentials	3.2	3.2
Years of completed schooling	2.9	2.9
Academic performance	2.5	2.5
Score on tests administered as part of the interview	2.5	2.3
Teacher recommendations	2.1	2.0
Experience or reputation of applicant's school	2.4	2.0

NOTE: 1.0 = not at all important; 5.0 = essential.

extreme opinions of graduates' work readiness.

We used logit models to examine the characteristics that tended to pull employers toward rating high schools as other than adequate in their preparation of students for work. The results of those models are presented in Tables 3 and 4. Table 3 examines the factors associated with establishments that believe high schools are doing an admirable job in preparing students for the world of work. Table 4 examines the factors associated with establishments that view high schools as inadequate in this respect. In both models, negative signs indicate a poorer view of high schools' performance. The characteristics that appear in both models are indicated by an asterisk. The variable of academic experience may require definition: it is a composite variable that includes the impor-

tance, to the establishment when it is making hiring decisions, of school reputation, grades, and courses taken.

To better identify the relationships between these variables, we superimposed the significant factors pulling establishments away from an "adequate" rating onto the employer ratings displayed in Figure 2. The result is presented in Figure 3. Which factors are most likely to be associated with a more positive view of high schools' performance in preparing students for work? The establishment characteristics fall into three general categories. The first is employer participation with schools, where the establishment is more likely to work with local schools and considers transcripts important sources of information when evaluating job characteristics. The second involves the nature of the workforce: the establishment is more likely to have frontline workers with more education, to claim that it has highly productive employees, and to have a higher turnover rate. The third category is the nature of the labor market in which an employer operates; establishments are more likely to have a positive view of students' work readiness if their labor market has more workers with just a high school education and if they have to interview more job candidates before making a frontline hire.

Which characteristics are associated with a more negative view? These attributes fall along only two dimensions. The first is the nature of the employer's workforce: the establishment has more frontline workers using computers, has a higher turn-

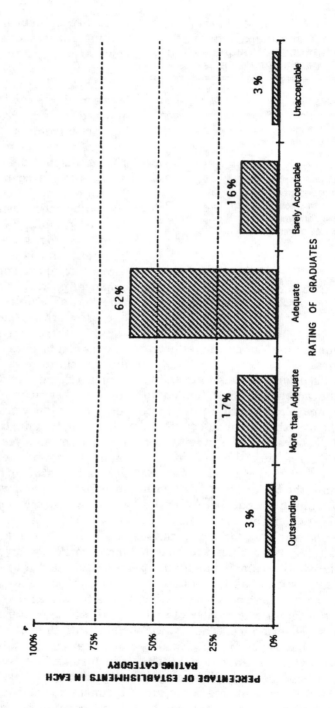

FIGURE 2
EMPLOYER RATINGS OF LOCAL HIGH SCHOOL GRADUATES' WORK READINESS

Question: Based on your experience with hiring their graduates, how would you rate your local high schools'
overall performance in preparing students for work in your establishment?

TABLE 3

LOGIT ANALYSIS PREDICTING THE LIKELIHOOD OF RATING LOCAL HIGH SCHOOLS AS "MORE THAN ADEQUATE" OR "OUTSTANDING"

Variable	Parameter Estimate	Standardized Estimate	Probability > Chi-Square
Ratio of young hires to total permanent employees	−0.204	−0.488	0.030
Establishment is growing	−0.423	−0.114	0.001
September 1997 local unemployment rate	−0.118	−0.112	0.004
Weeks to fill a production job	−0.077	−0.105	0.007
Number of candidates for production job*	0.029	0.090	0.005
Transcript is important information source	0.144	0.093	0.006
Turnover rate*	0.009	0.156	0.000
Percentage of local workers over 18 with at most a high school diploma*	0.029	0.161	0.000
Establishment self-identifies as a high-productivity workplace	0.665	0.183	0.000
High level of school participation	1.188	0.296	0.000
Frontline schooling	0.459	0.316	0.000

*This variable appears also in the model presented in Table 4.

TABLE 4

LOGIT ANALYSIS PREDICTING THE LIKELIHOOD OF RATING LOCAL HIGH SCHOOLS AS "UNACCEPTABLE" OR "BARELY ACCEPTABLE"

Variable	Parameter Estimate	Standardized Estimate	Probability > Chi-Square
Manufacturing dummy	−1.111	−0.252	0.000
Percentage of frontline workers using computers	−0.014	−0.310	0.000
September 1997 local unemployment rate	−0.174	−0.165	0.000
Percentage of local workers over 18 with at most a high school diploma*	−0.019	−0.107	0.008
Weeks to fill a production job	−0.064	−0.088	0.005
Turnover rate*	−0.005	−0.079	0.016
Establishment is growing	−0.287	−0.078	0.024
Number of candidates for a production job*	−0.019	−0.061	0.043
Academic experience	0.098	0.164	0.000
Establishment self-identifies as a high-productivity workplace	0.693	0.191	0.000
High schools important as an applicant source	0.326	0.242	0.000

*This variable appears also in the model presented in Table 3.

over rate, and is growing. The second is the nature of the labor market in which the employer operates. The local unemployment rate is high. The local labor market has more workers with just a high school education. It takes longer for the establishment to fill a frontline job, and it has to interview more job candidates before making a frontline hire.

FIGURE 3

EMPLOYER RATINGS OF LOCAL HIGH SCHOOL GRADUATES' WORK READINESS

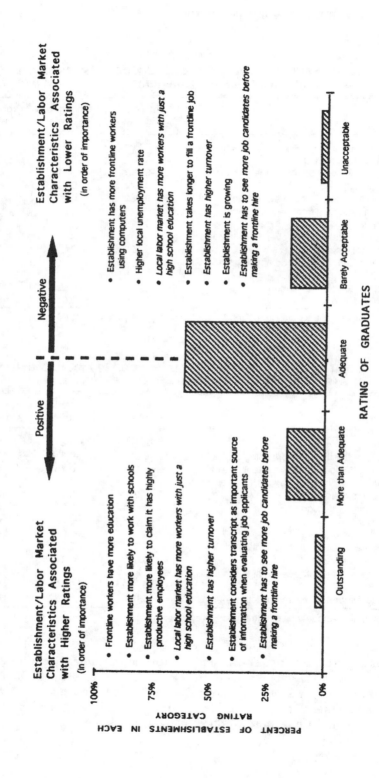

Disappointment with young high school graduates is associated with factors that are limited to the nature of the firm and the context in which it operates: its skill needs, its hiring needs, and the conditions of the local labor market. Ironically, these establishments look much like the ones that tend to rate high school graduates' work readiness more positively, with a few minor differences. They have increasing skill needs for frontline workers, have increasing needs to hire these workers due to both expansion and high turnover, and are situated in a labor market that is insufficient to satisfy their requirements. In fact, three of the characteristics appear on both sides of the divide: the establishment's local labor market has more workers with just a high school education; the establishment has a higher turnover rate; and the establishment has to interview more job candidates before making a frontline hire.

The most obvious difference is that no school participation dimensions are associated with a more negative assessment of high schools' preparation of students for the labor market. What does this finding imply? These establishments—which are representative of employers across the nation—are facing the same constraints regarding increasing skill needs, even for their frontline workforces, but are having difficulty identifying and retaining qualified employees. Where they diverge is in their approach to the problem: employers who actually engage schools and use transcripts to make hiring decisions are happier with the employees they recruit.

TOWARD CLEARER CONNECTIONS

Given the cross-sectional nature of the NES, one cannot draw a causal arrow between participation with local schools and a decrease in the turnover of young workers. Does the experience of working with schools change establishment practices so that young hires are better matched to their jobs? Does a positive experience with the youth labor force encourage employer participation with schools? Is it possible that both factors—working with schools and having a low youth turnover rate—are the result of some third attribute not examined in the current analysis? Further research may shed light on these questions.

Regardless, the 1997 administration of the NES demonstrates a key connection where none was observed before: when an establishment participates substantially in school activities, it is more likely to have lower youth turnover and better experiences when hiring high school graduates. Not only does this finding provide a clear incentive for employers to engage their local schools; it also suggests that such participation may actually contribute to students' work readiness, as well as to the fit between a young worker and his or her job—the underlying goal of efforts to connect school and work.

On Connecting
School and Work

By RALPH S. SAUL

ABSTRACT: Few American employers see schools as effective partners in their search for skilled workers. This growing disconnection between the nation's schools and its businesses threatens to undermine the educational quality of the workforce, on which American productivity depends. The challenge is to develop initiatives that require neither new funds nor another government agency; rely on the market to create incentives for firms to invest in human capital; and lower the costs to employers of screening and hiring workers. Given these problems and constraints, this article proposes the following solution: to foster education and training; to forge better, more substantive exchanges between employers and schools; to create internships that are administered at the state and local levels; and to make grades and school reputation important criteria when hiring young workers.

Ralph S. Saul is former chairman of the Board of CIGNA Corporation and chairman of the Advisory Board of the National Center on the Educational Quality of the Workforce. He is a graduate of the University of Chicago and Yale Law School. He has served as president of the American Stock Exchange and as co–chief executive officer of the First Boston Corporation.

NOTE: This article is a further interpretation of National Center on the Educational Quality of the Workforce, Advisory Board, *Making Good Jobs for Young People a National Priority* (Philadelphia: University of Pennsylvania, National Center on the Educational Quality of the Workforce, 1995). The work reported herein was supported under the Educational Research and Development Center Program, agreement number R117Q00011-91, CFDA 84.117Q, as administered by the Office of Educational Research and Improvement, U.S. Department of Education. The findings and opinions expressed in this article do not reflect the position or policies of the Office of Educational Research and Improvement or the U.S. Department of Education.

THE American economy is in the midst of a historic transition. The evidence is all around: in the increase in skill requirements as work organization and production systems grow more sophisticated; in the growing importance of competencies that allow employers to train and retrain their most productive employees; and in the broad diffusion of technologies that require simultaneous investment in a firm's stock of human and physical capital.

What this restructuring makes clear is that people do make a difference—the point that new research on business strategies has increasingly driven home. A firm's competitiveness is being defined not so much by its market strategy (how it positions itself vis-à-vis its competitors) as by its internal competencies and capacity to make the most of its unique resources, principally its workforce and its workers' skills.

Yet, as the research of the National Center on the Educational Quality of the Workforce (EQW) shows, the transition to an economy founded on new production and employment systems is neither complete nor ensured. Too many missed connections remain between firms and their workers, between workers and new technologies, and, most of all, between employers and schools.

Our primary concern, however, remains the condition of American education—and the growing perception that our schools and colleges are failing to produce work-ready citizens. In increasing numbers, Americans have come to perceive that students from the nation's public schools lack problem-solving competencies, that too often they know little or nothing about the world of work, and all too often they appear, particularly to would-be employers, as undisciplined and uninterested in work itself.

This is a perspective that the nation can ill afford. The productivity of American businesses is intrinsically linked to the success of the nation's schools and the educational attainment of its students and workers. As firms transform themselves—shedding outdated production systems, recasting older forms of work organization, adopting new technologies, and instituting high-performance systems—they will have to depend increasingly on schools to supply a workforce capable of adapting to these new modes of working. This reliance will require that firms articulate their skill needs to schools. Similarly, to dismiss schools from their share of the responsibility—to let them off the hook—is to lessen the capacity of American enterprises and American workers to compete successfully in an increasingly challenging global economy.

BASIC LESSONS

EQW's research findings demonstrate the linkage between investments in education and training and the restructuring and reorganization of work.

1. What often drives the competitiveness of firms is their capacity to make investments in the human capital of their employees. Indeed, a firm's competitiveness is more likely to be a function of the core competen-

cies of its workers than of its ability to adopt the practices of a successful competitor.

2. High-performance work systems—typically involving job rotation, increased employee involvement, group-based pay, and enriched individual tasks—can yield significantly higher levels of individual performance.

3. New forms of work organization also cause shifts in the types of skills a proficient worker needs. These new skills are not occupation specific but are broader and more general, mainly involving interpersonal and problem-solving capabilities.

4. Investments in employee training are a necessary condition for developing the teamwork skills and other abilities central to the success of high-performance work systems.

5. When firms have skill shortages, they also experience difficulty transforming their organizations. Some firms that have skill shortages also find it difficult to attract new workers with the requisite skills, and employers who have shortages in one area of skill tend to find they have shortages in all areas.

6. Firms often miss the mark when implementing training programs, usually by not putting their money where their skill problems are. For example, the training offered by manufacturing employers frequently fails to match the skill shortages they report. Firms that report more problems with employees' communication and English-language skills are less likely to spend money on training in any area, possibly because workers with basic skill problems might not benefit from training in other competencies.

To confirm and extend this understanding of how businesses invest in and use the skills of their employees, EQW surveyed a nationally representative sample of just over 4000 establishments, each employing 20 or more workers. The sum of these responses to the EQW National Employer Survey (EQW-NES) adds important detail to our understanding of the restructuring of the American economy, as follows:

1. A deskilling of work has not occurred. Quite the contrary, only 5 percent of establishments indicated any reduction in the skill requirements of their jobs, while 56 percent reported increasing skill requirements.

2. Although the use of high-performance work systems may still be more the exception than the rule, such work practices—represented by benchmarking, job rotation, and formal total quality management (TQM) programs—are becoming the hallmarks of the establishments most likely to invest in the skills of their employees.

3. The establishment that makes no training investment in at least some of its workers is a true rarity: 97 percent provide informal (on-the-job) training, and 81 percent provide formal training. Indeed, over half (57 percent) of the establishments reported an increase in formal training over the last three years.

The most important contribution of the EQW-NES, however, lies in its documentation of the link between productivity and successful business adaptation, on the one hand, and investments in education and training, on the other. A basic complementarity can be found between investments in human and physical capital; one cannot proceed without the other. Establishments that train workers, invest in new work organization, and enhance the technologies used by front-line workers in both manufacturing and nonmanufacturing industries have one thing in common: workforces with more years of schooling. Those establishments with more educated workforces—as represented by the average number of years of schooling completed by their employees—are likely to be more productive than firms of the same size competing in the same industry with less educated workforces.

In short, there is a double payoff for investments in education. The payoff for workers in terms of increased wages for additional years of schooling has long been recognized. Now, we have equal reason to believe that an increase in the average education of an establishment's workforce has a payoff for employers by enhancing their capacity to change modes of operation and by increasing productivity.

A FUNDAMENTAL DISCONNECTION

Yet what employers reported in their responses to the EQW-NES about schools and schooling also suggests that those benefits are now at risk. The survey captured something that most Americans intuitively understand: there is a growing disconnection between the nation's schools and its businesses. Although most employers require workers with higher levels of skills, most do not see schools as effective partners in developing that workforce.

Evidence of this is in the little attention that employers pay to measurements of school performance when making hiring decisions. Less than 10 percent of the employers surveyed value teachers' recommendations when considering new job applicants. Just 15 percent think grades are important. Less than 20 percent consider the reputation of an applicant's school.

Additional evidence is that most establishments have little or no contact with schools. Two out of three employers do not provide funds, donate equipment, serve on educational advisory boards, or participate in private industry councils. Less than 30 percent offer internships, apprenticeships, or a similar form of on-site work experience, either paid or unpaid.

How does the finding that education is important for enterprise productivity square with the fact that employers devalue schools? It does not, and that is the paradox that lies at the rift between employers and schools. How is it that employers can benefit from the educational attainment of their employees yet dismiss the schools responsible for providing that education? What will happen if this disconnection continues?

The result, we fear, will be a significant erosion of education's capacity to contribute to establishment productivity. That was the point that

Albert Shanker (1995) made in his response to the EQW-NES. Writing in his weekly column, "Where We Stand," the president of the American Federation of Teachers noted:

It's obvious that the less attention employers pay to school performance, the less incentive kids have to achieve and the more poorly prepared they will be. . . . Until businesses can have confidence in student transcripts and recommendations, they will go on disregarding them—and students will continue to conclude that what they do in school does not count.[1]

In the same way that employers' attitudes toward schooling send the wrong messages to students, so do the failures of high-level partnerships involving schools and business leaders make a negative impression on employers. Many business leaders entered these partnerships with the best of intentions, but, by and large, the accomplishments of these partnerships have been marginal, and they have not tackled the systemic problems of urban public education.

In retrospect, perhaps too much was expected of business-school partnerships to improve student performance in the public schools. Most partnerships had diffuse and unquantifiable goals, while the worst, I hesitate to say, were only exercises in public relations. Too often, business participation was part-time at best and handicapped by a lack of knowledge about the workings of the public schools. Even some of the most effective partnerships left school bureaucracies unaccountable for failure and had no effective mechanisms for monitoring and evaluation.

We are left with the uneasy feeling that most employers—convinced that partnerships with schools do not contribute in real ways to the functioning of their businesses and preoccupied with making their firms competitive—no longer rank school reform high on their agendas. What would make employers change their minds about schools? How can employers be convinced that partnerships can succeed, benefiting employers, schools, and students?

ESSENTIAL ANSWERS

The answer is a simple one: what is required to end the disconnection between schools and employers are more direct, substantive, and businesslike transactions between the two. Employers who disregard schools miss an important opportunity. They must come to understand that schools are often the principal supplier of their workers. When employers discount schools and their graduates without trying to improve them, they ultimately increase their own costs, having to rely on hearsay and crude measures like an applicant's age and number of previous employers to identify potential workers with good attitudes and useful skills. As a result, too many employers spend too much time screening applicants, only to have them not work out during the first months on the job.

Schools, for their part, will have to see employers as customers whose needs must be directly gauged and whose goodwill and confidence are important to maintain. A necessary step in this process is for schools to accept that a graduate's performance in the labor market is a measure of the school's effectiveness.

The first policy statement of the EQW Advisory Board (National Center 1995) made two recommendations to improve the linkage between schools and employers. In this policy statement, we proposed initiatives that

— require neither new funds nor another government agency;
— rely on the market to create the incentives for firms to invest in human and physical capital; and
— lower the costs to employers of screening and hiring new workers.

Driving our recommendations is a simple axiom: be practical and think locally. What the nation needs now are concrete, low-cost initiatives— administered at the state and local levels—that foster education and training and that forge better, more substantive exchanges between employers and schools. To this end, we urge employers to make grades and the reputation of the applicant's school important criteria when hiring young workers and to create internships.

Grades and school reputation

Using a young person's performance in school as a criterion for employment is both good business and good public policy; it reduces the cost of recruiting and training new workers and teaches students that hard work in school pays off in the labor market. The 15 percent of employers who use grades when screening job applicants share an interesting set of characteristics: they are more likely to have workforces with above-average years of schooling, more likely to report increased job skills, and more likely to use high-performance work practices, particularly job rotation. Establishments that use school grades as screening mechanisms in the hiring process also have more stable workforces and are more likely to rate their employees as fully proficient in their jobs. Not surprisingly, employers in the service industry who check grades before hiring a young worker have more productive workforces.

Internships

The EQW-NES revealed that one in four businesses offers programs that bring students into their places of work, principally as interns or apprentices. Taken together, these establishments also share an interesting set of characteristics: their workforces are more educated and more likely to use computers as part of their jobs; they are more likely to use high-performance work systems (as indicated by job rotation, benchmarking, and TQM practices); and they are more likely to report increasing skill requirements for current jobs.

These findings parallel the results of an earlier EQW-sponsored study designed to determine the incentives that would persuade employers to participate in work-based learning or formal school-to-work programs. The first part of this study involved a series of focus groups with employers who had little or no experience with young employees. In general, these employers looked beyond the nation's schools for credible job applicants. Most reported having no contact with a school—in part, because employers sense that most schools are so overwhelmed by the task of getting through the day that they have neither the time nor the energy for contact with employers. These same employers had even less enthusiasm for young people, who they found to be undisciplined, uncommunicative, uninterested in work, and either unwilling or unable to take a job seriously.

The second part of the study was a survey of firms that participated in work-learning programs, such as apprenticeships and internships. Among employers participating in these programs, there was a wellspring of support both for the initiatives and for the quality of the young workers they attracted. Most participating firms found their students to be productive and contributing employees. Although they often echoed other employer complaints about the high schools with which they worked—citing that too often the participating schools were not sufficiently organized or did not attach high priority to the program—a clear majority of these employers also reported that they would take additional students later and would recommend the programs to other small-business owners.

More employers need to become involved in this kind of school-business partnership—the kind that works, that contributes to business productivity, that can help restore employers' faith in the performance measurements that schools provide, and that gives students the incentives to apply themselves in school by making explicit the connection between school and work. We believe that internships—whether for pay, for credit, or, preferably, for both— are a proven means of making that connection. Internships bring students into the world of work and into the kinds of plants, offices, stores, and service agencies where they are likely to spend their working lives. Internships have the added advantage of creating an informal but effective communication channel through which employers learn about schools and their students and through which schools learn about the needs and practices of employers.

CONCLUSION

The lesson that many of the employers with more educated workforces are learning is that what businesses need is reliable information about the quality of the schools from which they recruit new workers. School grades, along with information on previous and successful work experiences, offer a more effective way of screening job applicants than relying simply on the applicant's age and previous work history. Interns, because they both know and represent their schools, can be the best source of that kind of reliable information.

For the schools, the testimony of successful interns may similarly prove to be the most reliable information about the nature and changing demands of the workplace. What has not worked is the formal consultative processes by which employers are asked to specify the kinds of skills their workers either need now or will likely need over the next decade or more. It is not a question to which most employers have a ready answer, nor do they have the experience of casting what they know into the terms expected by those who design curricula. Business schools have learned this lesson well, often drawing on the experiences of the managers they enroll in their executive education programs to teach their faculty about how the business of the business is changing. We think this is a lesson that all schools need to learn.

Note

1. Reprinted with permission. Copyright by the American Federation of Teachers.

References

National Center on the Educational Quality of the Workforce. Advisory Board. 1995. *Making Good Jobs for Young People a National Priority*. Philadelphia: University of Pennsylvania, National Center on the Educational Quality of the Workforce.

Shanker, Albert. 1995. Linking School and Work. *New York Times*, 23 Apr.

Report of the Board of Directors to the Members of the American Academy of Political and Social Science for the Year 1997

MEMBERSHIPS AND SUBSCRIPTIONS
AS OF DECEMBER 31

1987	5,151
1988	4,674
1989	4,903
1990	3,932
1991	4,378
1992	3,639
1993	3,472
1994	3,661
1995	3,455
1996	3,141
1997	3,124

PUBLICATIONS
NUMBER OF VOLUMES OF *THE ANNALS* PRINTED (6 PER YEAR)

1987	43,629
1988	53,497
1989	40,269
1990	39,000
1991	37,246
1992	34,900
1993	31,000
1994	29,000
1995	28,200
1996	29,900
1997	29,909

FINANCES
SIZE OF SECURITIES PORTFOLIO
MARKET VALUE AS OF DECEMBER 31

1987	387,997
1988	345,634
1989	284,732
1990	139,451
1991	164,537
1992	150,560
1993	161,117
1994	124,644
1995	157,103
1996	180,754
1997	204,578

NUMBER OF VOLUMES OF *THE ANNALS* SOLD
(IN ADDITION TO MEMBERSHIPS AND SUBSCRIPTIONS)

1987	5,314
1988	13,283
1989	4,802
1990	5,005
1991	3,766
1992	3,681
1993	3,538
1994	2,344
1995	2,449
1996	2,795
1997	2,372

STATEMENT OF ACTIVITIES FOR THE YEAR ENDED DECEMBER 31, 1997

Revenues, gains, and other support
- Royalty—Sage Publications ... $150,000
- Royalties and reprint permissions ... 924
- Sales of review books ... 2,208
- Rents ... 29,960
- Grant income ... 10,000
- Contributions ... 2,100
- Interest income ... 7,934
- Net gain from investments ... 27,603
- Miscellaneous ... 785
  - Total revenues ... 231,514

Expenses and losses
- Program ... 105,665
- Administrative ... 79,395
  - Total expenses and losses ... 185,060

Change in net assets ... 46,454
Net assets—January 1 ... 112,426
Net assets—December 31 ... 158,880

Report of the Board of Directors

During 1997, the six volumes of THE ANNALS dealt with the following subjects:

January   *The Americans with Disabilities Act: Social Contract or Special Privilege?*, edited by William G. Johnson, Professor, Arizona State University, Tempe

March   *NAFTA Revisited: Expectations and Realities*, edited by Paul Rich, Titular Professor of International Relations, University of the Americas, Puebla, Mexico, and Fellow, Hoover Institution on War, Revolution and Peace, Stanford University, California, and Guillermo De Los Reyes, Assistant Professor, University of the Americas, Puebla, Mexico, and Research Associate, Hoover Institution on War, Revolution and Peace, Stanford University, California

May   *Globalization and the Changing U.S. City*, edited by David Wilson, Associate Professor, University of Illinois at Urbana-Champaign

July   *Strengthening Transitional Democracies Through Conflict Resolution*, edited by Raymond Shonholtz, President, Partners for Democratic Change, San Francisco, California, and Ilana Shapiro, Central and Eastern Europe Regional Coordinator, Partners for Democratic Change, Prague, Czech Republic

September   *Transport at the Millennium*, edited by Stanley G. Long, Associate Professor Emeritus, University of Pittsburgh, Johnstown, Pennsylvania, and Visiting Research Associate, the Pennsylvania State University, University Park

November   *The Role of NGOs: Charity and Empowerment*, edited by Jude L. Fernando, doctoral candidate, University of Pennsylvania, and Alan W. Heston, Professor, University of Pennsylvania

The publication program for 1998 includes the following volumes:

January   *Israel in Transition*, edited by Gabriel Ben-Dor, Professor, University of Haifa Mount Carmel, Haifa, Israel

March   *Gambling: Socioeconomic Impacts and Public Policy*, edited by James H. Frey, Dean, College of Liberal Arts, University of Nevada, Las Vegas

May   *Children and Television*, edited by Amy B. Jordan, Senior Research Investigator, Annenberg Public Policy Center, University of Pennsylvania, Philadelphia, and Kathleen Hall Jamieson, Dean, Annenberg School for Communication, and Director, Annenberg Public Policy Center, University of Pennsylvania, Philadelphia

July   *Americans and Religions in the Twenty-First Century*, edited by Wade Clark Roof, J. F. Rowny Professor of Religion and Society, University of California, Santa Barbara

September   The Changing Educational Quality of the Workforce, edited by Robert Zemsky, Professor and Director, Institute for Research on Higher Education, University of Pennsylvania, Philadelphia, and Peter Cappelli, Chair, Department of Management, and Codirector, Center for Human Resources, Wharton School, University of Pennsylvania, Philadelphia

November   *The Future of Fact*, edited by Jeffrey J. Strange, research psychologist and media consultant, Philadelphia, and Elihu Katz, University Professor of Communication, Annenberg School for Communication, University of Pennsylvania, Philadelphia.

During 1997, the Book Department published 163 reviews. The majority of these were written by professors, but reviewers also included university presidents, members of private and university-sponsored organizations, government and public officials, and business professionals. More than 450 books were listed in the Other Books section.

One hundred and ninety-one requests were granted to reprint material from THE ANNALS. These went to professors and other authors for use in books in preparation and to nonprofit organizations for educational purposes.

OFFICERS AND STAFF

The Board reelected the following officers: Marvin E. Wolfgang, President; Kathleen Hall Jamieson, Vice President; Anthony J. Scirica, Secretary; Mary Ann Meyers, Treasurer; Henry W. Sawyer, III, Counsel.

Respectfully submitted,
THE BOARD OF DIRECTORS

Elijah Anderson
Lynn A. Curtis
Lloyd N. Cutler
Frederick Heldring
Kathleen Hall Jamieson
Richard D. Lambert
Ira A. Lipman
Sara Miller McCune
Mary Ann Meyers
Henry W. Sawyer, III
Anthony J. Scirica
Elmer B. Staats
Marvin E. Wolfgang

Philadelphia Pennsylvania
7 November 1997

Book Department

INTERNATIONAL RELATIONS AND POLITICS

COLEMAN, JOHN J. 1996. *Party Decline in America: Policy, Politics, and the Fiscal State*. Pp. xii, 253. Princeton, NJ: Princeton University Press. $39.95.

The tribulations of American political parties draw endless scholarly attention. Several usual suspects are routinely rounded up as possible debilitating culprits: a more sophisticated electorate less dependent on partisan clues, a robust for-hire campaign industry, the decline of patronage, public cynicism, media-centered campaigns, forced permeability of party structure, the rise of ideological amateurs, the generational replacement of hard-core New Deal–era partisans, and the proliferation of independent wealthy candidates. Propelling renewal are reinvigorated, financially flush national party committees, fresh infusions of energizing blood in wearied organizations, and the partisan labors of figures such as Newt Gingrich. Despite disagreements over the fine points, most would accept this list (and some variants) as a decent account.

John J. Coleman's *Party Decline in America* fingers a new suspect: the nature of policy facing government (actually Congress, since "party" to Coleman means party-in-Congress). Simply put, where parties dominate vital policy, they thrive. When authority is removed, however, parties atrophy, and voters drift off. Thus, to explain ebbs and flows, look at what government (Congress) does. When Congress once battled over attention-getting trade policy, parties flowered. By contrast, in the post–World War II "fiscal state," power largely flows to executive branch experts, and (congressional) parties deteriorate. This is especially true when macroeconomic choices are placed on Keynesian autopilot.

To convince, Coleman offers mountains of documentation guaranteed to please the most exacting dissertation committee. Itemized historical accounts of economic policymaking are juxtaposed with microscopic statistical analysis of legislative voting. No pertinent study escapes notice. If scholarship were simply assessed by meticulousness, agonizing over methodology, statistical virtuosity, and similar surface features, this would constitute a worthy contribution. Unfortunately, alas, the argument hardly convinces.

Technically, Coleman is correct: when parties abdicate, they lose political relevance. OK, we will add this novel suspect to our already crowded lineup, though I remain largely unconvinced of the net explanatory gain. More consequential, however, is elucidating why parties slumber along, avoiding attention-getting hot-button policy. Why did Congress shun morality—abortion, school prayer, crime, pornography—or affirmative action or school busing? Surely, a market long existed for opportunistic partisans. Did a secret constitutional amendment impose a cowardice test for national legislative office? To say that parties declined when they fled controversy and hid by bickering over secondary financial details only whets our appetites. Policy surrender is not a preordained iron law. *Party Decline in America* offers up a long, often tedious though inconclusive tale fitting nicely with a burgeoning political science literature on the state. As for some useful insights into what drives our parties—why the enduring slumber followed by sudden policy-driven animation (as in 1994)—it comes up well short.

ROBERT WEISSBERG

University of Illinois
Urbana

IRIYE, AKIRA. 1997. *Cultural Internationalism and World Order*. Pp. xii, 212. Baltimore, MD: Johns Hopkins University Press. $32.50.

This book is a landmark in the historical study of foreign relations. Over the past 30 years, Akira Iriye has been the foremost scholarly proponent of assigning culture a more significant place in international history. This volume finally provides the sweeping and systematic historical overview of the role of culture that until now has been missing from his work.

Iriye here tells the story of how cultural internationalism, carried primarily by "ideas and cross-national movements, rather than nations and governments," has made headway over the past two centuries in the face of some stiff historical headwinds. Ironically, catastrophes like World War I, the Great Depression of

the 1930s, and World War II, in which parochial forces temporarily held the upper hand, were indispensable helpmates of this fitful process, as they led more and more people to appreciate the practical wisdom of international understanding. Although political and economic internationalism were also important responses to these disasters, even more significant for Iriye were the flowering of cultural activity in the 1920s and the explosion of intercultural relations in the post–World War II era.

Besides contending with nationalism and power politics, cultural internationalism also had to master some serious internal divisions. Racialist ideas, which heavily influenced politics through World War II, were deeply embedded in liberal thought. Until they were excised, the prospects for a global culture remained dim. During the Cold War, the competing vision of a socialist internationalism made for potentially catastrophic discord. As each of these challenges was in its turn surmounted, Iriye argues that "recent years have brought culture to a central position in national and international affairs." The irony, as he notes, is that culture, once seen as a cure for power politics, has of late itself become a battleground between universalists and multiculturalists.

Not many scholars possess the extraordinary range needed to write a book of this sort, which makes use of a dazzling variety of sources from Japan, China, Russia, Germany, France, Great Britain, and the United States. This research virtuosity, combined with a sophisticated conceptual framework that shows how culture and power have interacted over the long term, makes for an impressively unique work of scholarship.

In a personal sense, this book is the fruit of a spectacular scholarly career. From a broader professional standpoint, however, it marks a new beginning for culture. Once a stepchild, tolerated but unwanted and clearly never a member of the inner family circle of international history, culture has had a difficult time in finding its place. This book makes clear that it can look forward to a mature and productive adulthood.

FRANK NINKOVICH

Harvard University
Cambridge
Massachusetts

MESSNER, MICHAEL R. 1997. *Politics of Masculinities: Men in Movements.* Pp. xviii, 137. Thousand Oaks, CA: Sage. $35.00. Paperbound, $14.95.

One of the most unexpected developments on the political scene in recent decades is the emergence of public gender politics among men. From men's liberation and gay liberation to Robert Bly and the mythopoetic movement, the White Ribbon campaign, the Promise Keepers, and the Million Man March, something is happening, Mr. Jones, and I doubt Bob Dylan knows what it is.

In this up-to-date and crisply argued book, Michael Messner tells us what it is. *Politics of Masculinities* provides an excellent account of public masculinity politics in the contemporary United States, the first extended survey of its kind.

The book is one of the early products of the "gender lens" series from Sage. As well as a broad gender perspective, it draws on the recent "explosion of research on men and masculinity" (as the series editors put it), a field to which Messner himself has been a leading contributor.

This background gives the book its key take on masculinity politics. There is no one men's movement. There is, rather, a range of different movements arising from the encounters that diverse groups of men have with issues in gender relations. Messner classifies them into four groups: essentialist retreats, sex-role reform and restoration, pro-feminist engagements, and racial and sexual identity politics. He describes their character and stances, explains their emergence, develops a map of the political terrain that they occupy, and reflects on the contradictions within them and the interplay between them.

No such movement just expresses a preformed masculinity (though the essentialist movements think they do). Rather, Messner shows, in offering solutions to problems encountered by groups of men and boys, these movements construct particular masculinities. They draw on, and transform, existing gender ideologies, and struggle to have their particular constructions become widely accepted. In this sense, even the therapeutic and religious movements are truly political, as their projects involve the remaking of gender relations, the redistribution of social benefits and costs.

This insight drives Messner's own proposal for resolving the contradictions of men's engagement in gender politics: a coalition-building politics of social justice, informed by the emerging multiracial feminism of recent years.

The book is conceptually sophisticated but also clearly written, engaged, and witty. A first-class introduction to its subject, it sets a high standard for the work that must follow.

R. W. CONNELL

University of Sydney
New South Wales
Australia

SCHNEIDER, ANNE LARASON and HELEN INGRAM. 1997. *Policy Design for Democracy.* Pp. xii, 241. Lawrence: University Press of Kansas. $35.00. Paperbound, $15.95.

Political scientists who study public policy tend to emphasize the processes by which policies are made and implemented rather than the substantive content and impacts of the policies themselves. Neither of the most notable attempts to integrate process and content conceptually—Theodore Lowi's focus on the coerciveness of policy instruments and the specificity of their targets and James Q. Wilson's focus on the concentration of costs and benefits—has proven adequate frameworks for promoting either effective cumulation of empirical research or normative reflection on the appropriateness of policy processes within democratic polities. In recent years, Stephen Linder, B. Guy Peters, and other scholars have urged that more attention be given to policy designs as objects in order to better understand policy designs as processes. Prominent among those in the design school are Anne Schneider and Helen Ingram, who present and extend their particular framework in *Policy Design for Democracy*.

After considering the contributions and limitations of the pluralist, policy sciences, public choice, and critical theory perspectives on public policymaking, Schneider and Ingram provide a set of constructs intended to connect process and content in a more conceptually useful way. They begin by setting out the mechanisms through which societal contexts affect issue contexts, issue contexts affect policy designs and, closing the loop, policy designs affect societal contexts. Central to understanding these connections is the notion that the targeted social groups fall into four groups depending on whether they are socially constructed as deserving (advantaged and dependents) or undeserving (contenders and deviants) and whether they are politically strong (advantaged and contenders) or politically weak (dependents and deviants). They see two sorts of degeneracy in poli-

cymaking that reinforce social inequities: benefits given to the advantaged, and burdens imposed on deviants. Providing benefits or imposing burdens on other target groups is politically risky, so elected officials are willing to open the door for influence by scientific analysis. A consensus among experts allows the threshold to be crossed—though the experts often bring with them values of relevance primarily to the sciences themselves.

Although one might challenge the authors' contention that policy has been largely degenerate over the last 30 years, and fault them for a few omissions, most notably the advocacy coalition approach of Hank Jenkins-Smith and Paul Sabatier in their discussion of the social construction of knowledge, *Policy Design for Democracy* makes a valuable contribution to the macro-level study of public policy.

DAVID L. WEIMER

University of Rochester
New York

YUVAL-DAVIS, NIRA. 1997. *Gender and Nation*. Pp. x, 148. Thousand Oaks, CA: Sage. $65.00. Paperbound, $23.95.

While books about gendered institutions have proliferated in recent years, this is the first comprehensive volume to examine the concept of the gendered nation. "Gendered structures" is a term that refers to the ordering of processes, practices, images, ideologies, and distribution of power by differentiating between women and men, typically to the disadvantage of women. In this exceptionally well-written book, Nira Yuval-Davis explores the complex relationship between gender and nation and illuminates the much-neglected processes through which nationalist projects have oppressed women but also occasionally created spaces for women's empowerment. She develops "a framework for discussing and analyzing the different ways in which the discourse on gender and that on nation tend to intersect and to be constructed by each other."

Yuval-Davis makes the important distinction between nation and state, showing how the assumption of correspondence between the two is almost always a myth. From a deconstructionist perspective, she also rejects the idea that a nation is a unitary entity and that gender has essential qualities. Rather, she views both as multidimensional and historically situated.

The book analyzes nation in relation to gender in the context of nationalist ideologies and movements and the institutions of the state, situated in specific historical moments. It is within this context of intersection of gender and nation that Yuval-Davis examines discourses and debates in such areas as women's roles as biological reproducers of nations, women's contributions to the cultural constructions of nations, the gendered nature of citizenship, and the gendered nature of militaries and wars. Throughout, she is careful to point out how class, race, and sexuality interact with gender and affect, and are affected by, nationalist projects.

In the concluding chapter, Yuval-Davis explores the relationship between feminism and nationalism and introduces the concept of "transversal politics" as a model of feminist politics that takes account of national as well as other differences between women. Transversal politics—as differentiated from identity politics, which is based on assumptions of universalism (a homogeneous point of departure)—involves participation in a dialogue where each woman "brings with her the rooting in her own membership and identity, but at the same time tries to shift in order to put herself in a situation of exchange with women who have different membership and identity." What is to unite women engaged in transversal politics? According to Yuval-Davis, compatible goals and values—rather than national (or any other form of) identity—should be the bases for political action among women.

Gender and Nation is a scholarly gem. Not only does it provide a comprehensive review and critique of writings on nationhood, nationalist movements, the state, citizenship, and gender, but also it presents an original analysis of the processes of interaction between gender and nationalist projects. It also raises and clarifies some of the major questions and debates of our time regarding nationalism, multiculturalism, the state, and the continuing oppression of women. It should be read by anyone interested in these topics.

JILL M. BYSTYDZIENSKI

Franklin College
Indiana

AFRICA, ASIA, AND LATIN AMERICA

HUNT, MICHAEL H. 1996. *The Genesis of Chinese Communist Foreign Policy*. Pp. xiv, 343. New York: Columbia University Press. $34.50.

Are China's relations with the world driven by Marxist ideology, hyperpatriotism, measured realpolitik, or perhaps some combination of the three? This is one of the most important questions facing American policymakers at the end of the twentieth century. Until the sources of China's foreign policy are better understood, America's posture and attitudes concerning a wide range of issues that confront U.S.-China relations—human rights, arms proliferation, economic practices, the fate of the Korean peninsula, and, most important, the future of Taiwan—are bound to produce misunderstanding and tension. What method is best suited to investigating this question? Michael Hunt argues persuasively that we cannot understand China's recent behavior unless we examine the historical origins of Chinese Communist foreign policy.

Hunt's investigation of the origins of the foreign policy of the Chinese Communist Party (CCP) reaches well beyond the formative struggle with Chiang Kai-shek's Nationalist government and imperial Japan during the 1930s and 1940s. Hunt travels as far back as the Han and Tang dynasties to identify what he calls an "embarrassment of traditions" conditioning China's engagement with the world. Perhaps most important were the lessons that early-twentieth-century Chinese reformers took from the long and painful decline of the imperial state during the Qing period. The humiliating experience of foreign intrusion, which continued even after the 1911 revolution, provoked a searching examination by China's increasingly radicalized intellectuals. These reformers—seeking ways to strengthen and unify China so that it could stand strong in international affairs—were impatient with the more cautious approaches that had failed during the Qing period. Many of these intellectuals found the cure for China's weakness in the tenets of Marxism-Leninism.

Hunt's narrative suggests that Chinese patriotism was the real fuel behind Communist Chinese foreign policy and that Marxism was a more or less effective tool for the state building that was necessary to propel China to international status. A model that includes Chinese patriotism provides a rationale for many CCP actions that could not be explained through the Marxist-Leninist perspective alone: Mao's desire to secure American aid during the 1940s, the willingness of the CCP to distance itself from Moscow, and the CCP's imperialistic attitudes toward non-Chinese people in Tibet and Xinjiang. Ideology certainly mattered, but Hunt argues that, for leaders like Mao, ideology was only one part of an equation that ultimately included a patriotism with deep historical roots and balanced assessments of a rapidly changing international environment.

Perhaps the most important service Hunt provides in this fine study is in the form of the historigraphical and methodological essay at the end of the book. Hunt gives us a detailed state of the field and argues strongly in favor of utilizing a historically grounded approach in any future examination of Chinese Communist foreign policy. This final chapter will be enormously helpful to scholars seeking promising avenues for future historical inquiry.

FRANCIS J. GAVIN

Harvard University
Cambridge
Massachusetts

THURSTON, ROBERT W. 1996. *Life and Terror in Stalin's Russia, 1934-1941.* Pp. xxi, 296. New Haven, CT: Yale University Press, 1996. No price.

At the beginning of chapter 5, Robert Thurston writes, "Stalin, or rather Stalin with a great deal of help, killed millions or facilitated their untimely deaths. He was one of history's leading murderers, and his crimes were truly grotesque." Although Thurston was capable of making this sound judgment, nevertheless he decided to write a book that would undercut, explain away, and rationalize that judgment.

He makes the following arguments: Stalin was a more complex character than the usual depiction of him in the literature. He did not plan everything but often reacted to circumstances. He was genuinely frightened of his supposed enemies. The Party and the government did not succeed in controlling the population. The Soviet people by and large supported the system even at the height of terror. The latter is the most insistent argument made.

In a modest formulation, these propositions are not only true but banal. Surely, Stalin mourned his wife. (And Hitler loved German shepherds, did not smoke, and was nice to his secretaries.) Yes, Stalin was afraid of enemies. (And Hitler was afraid of the Jews. Didn't Chaim Weitzman declare war on Germany in 1939?) No one has ever argued that Stalin foresaw the future at the time of coming to power; of course, he reacted to events as much as he created them. Indeed, the Soviet system—or for that matter any other totalitarian regime—did not function smoothly. Lack of publicity, lack of clearly established chain of command, and lack of functioning institutions inevitably create confusion and administrative morass. (The argument that the Soviet Union was not totalitarian because the Party could not control every aspect of the citizens' behavior is central to all revisionist thinking. The revisionists, to their own satisfaction, time and again demolish an argument that no one in his or her right mind has ever made.)

Thurston's purpose is more ambitious than making these banal points. What he intends to show is that the Soviet Union was not as bad as it was supposed to be and that the murder of a few million did not really affect all levels of Soviet society; that this country was more or less similar to all other regimes around the world. He overlooks the fact that terror existed within a context: contact with the rest of the world was cut, a vast propaganda organization functioned, newspapers were devoid of content, and cultural life was destroyed. In his view, the regime possessed legitimacy because the majority of the people supported it. In a totalitarian system, however, by definition alternatives cannot be developed and presented to an electorate, and therefore the concept of support becomes meaningless. Quite possibly the majority of Cambodians supported Pol Pot, and at one point the Germans most definitely supported Hitler. Such support did not make these regimes legitimate or less murderous. Indeed, it is the genius of totalitarianism to make everyone or almost everyone into an accomplice.

The controversial issue is not and never has been the character of Joseph Stalin. The dictator was not a particularly interesting person, and even if he loved his second wife, he was, without a shadow of a doubt, a thoroughly bad human being. What matters and needs discussion is the system: how it came into being and how it functioned, and about these matters Thurston has almost nothing new to tell. To what extent Stalin was personally responsible for totalitarianism is open to discussion. No doubt centuries of Russian history, ideology, circumstances, and accidents all contributed to the development of it.

In my view, it is morally reprehensible to whitewash such a regime, as it is morally reprehensible to explain away the crimes of Nazism or of Pol Pot's Cambodia. Thurston attempts to accomplish his unsavory task by making inappropriate comparisons and by defining terror and torture downward. Stalinism should be compared to Pol Pot Cambodia rather than to McCarthyism. McCarthyism probably claimed one innocent victim (Ethel Rosenberg), but Stalinism murdered millions. In the author's view, terror ended in 1938. Now if he told us at the outset that by "terror" he means a minimum of 1 million native Russian victims a year, at least we would understand one another. He could say that the deportation of a million and a quarter human beings from the newly occupied territories in 1939 and 1940, and a concentration camp population of millions, were simply understandable reactions to the threat of war. (The murder of Polish officers at Katyn nowhere appears in this book.) In Thurston's opinion, Alexander Weissberg was not tortured. Again, it is a matter of definition: Weissberg only had to stand for days and was not allowed to sleep. Unfortunately, I could continue to give similar examples of tendentious presentations.

It may be that the majority of historians teaching at elite British and American universities find Thurston's views congenial. But the issues under consideration should not be decided by a vote among the experts, nor will new revelations from archives make a difference. How we write about mass murder will ultimately be determined by our political and ethical commitments.

PETER KENEZ

University of California
Santa Cruz

TOPIK, STEVEN C. 1997. *Trade and Gunboats: The United States and Brazil in the Age of Empire.* Pp. viii, 301. Stanford, CA: Stanford University Press. $55.00.

This excellent and timely work examines the internal politics and diplomacy of trade at the end of the nineteenth century. Historian Steven Topik of the University of California, Irvine, analyzes the causes and consequences of the Blaine-Mendonca Accord of 1891, the first reciprocal trade agreement in U.S. history and an important precursor to the "special relationship" between the United States and Brazil that anchored inter-American relations for more than half of the twentieth century. Although largely forgotten, policymakers and business leaders hailed the accord as a major triumph and the cornerstone of Secretary of State James G. Blaine's pan-Americanism.

While Topik expertly analyzes the internal political maneuvering in both Brazil and the United States, as well as the diplomacy of the accord, this work's major contribution results from its discussion of the macroeconomic and strategic factors that led to the policy innovation. The partitioning of Africa and Asia by the European powers, the emergence of pan-Germanic and pan-Slavic movements, and the crisis in American business caused by overproduction of industrial and agricultural products forced Americans to be more aggressive and creative in their search for Latin American markets and allies. The accord was the first step in what was to be a pan-American customs union and the replacement of Britain as the major power in South America. To Brazilians, fresh from the overthrow of a monarch popular with Europeans, the accord was to shore up its damaged international reputation, secure U.S. support vis-à-vis Argentina (with which Brazil had a boundary dispute), and assist the regime's internal stability by giving sugar elites a stake in the regime's survival.

Unfortunately, several factors conspired to derail the accord. North American opponents of reciprocity, led by Congressman William McKinley, were more concerned with protection than trade and believed the state was exceeding its legitimate scope by brokering trade agreements. Brazilians who opposed the military also opposed the accord, as did Brazilian proponents of industrialization. Finally, the depression of 1893 proved that the proponents of reciprocity had oversold its benefits.

Based on archival materials in five countries and including the papers of prominent businessmen as well as traditional diplomatic sources, *Trade and Gunboats* fills a major gap; there are no recent studies in English of Brazilian trade, politics, and diplomacy of this period. With the renewed emphasis on trade and investment and the call for an expanded North American Free Trade Agreement, Topik's study also draws lessons for today. Few works in the history of U.S. foreign relations offer as much breadth and depth as this. *Trade and Gunboats* should be a model for those who aspire to write diplomatic history.

W. MICHAEL WEIS

Illinois Wesleyan University
Bloomington

EUROPE

DALEY, ANTHONY. 1996. *Steel, State, and Labor: Mobilization and Adjustment in France*. Pp. xix, 309. Pittsburgh, PA: University of Pittsburgh Press. $49.95. Paperbound, $22.95.

France has long fascinated political scientists as the site of Western Europe's most developed experiment in state-led industrial adjustment. Anthony Daley has written a superb case study of industrial adjustment, centering on the French steel industry and examining the interplay of state, business, and labor in the adjustment process. Along the way, he punctures many of the most enduring myths of French political economy and provides an innovative and compelling alternative account.

The core of Daley's theoretical contribution lies in his account of the interaction of interests, and the conditions under which those interests change over time. Thus he argues that familiar generalizations about France's "strong state" or "weak labor," and attempts to squeeze France into the pluralist or corporatist camps, fail because they cannot explain why the state is sometimes successful and sometimes not in its pursuit of indus-

trial adjustment or why organizationally weak unions can be influential in policymaking. Daley's examination of the interaction between state planners, steel owners and managers, and the steel unions yields a rich and complex story of industrial adjustment.

The French state has been intimately involved in the steel industry throughout the postwar period, and steel producers relied upon it for both subsidies and protectionism. Despite the leverage enjoyed by the state, its efforts to get business and labor to cooperate in restructuring steel consistently failed. They did so in large part, Daley argues, because the state acquiesced in business's demand for the exclusion of labor from policymaking, and French planning institutions never developed appropriate labor market tools. The result was that industrial adjustment came at a huge social cost, and, while labor was not able to influence industrial policy, it was able to paralyze change through industrial protest.

Paradoxically, it required the victory of the Socialists in 1981 to break the deadlock and permit restructuring; the most brutal indication of the restructuring has been the collapse of employment in the steel industry. Socialist governments developed much better labor market tools than their predecessors, and the turn to Europe from 1984 onward made rationalization a necessity. Most important, changes in workplace relations and the weakening of traditional trade unionism permitted new adjustment strategies.

Daley's book should be read by all those interested in the comparative politics and political economy of advanced industrial societies. It provides a nuanced account of how strong states can fail, and weak labor movements succeed, in the process of economic restructuring.

CHRIS HOWELL

Oberlin College
Ohio

UNITED STATES

ALDEN, JOHN R. 1996. *George Washington: A Biography*. Pp. xii, 315. Baton Rouge: Louisiana State University Press. Paperbound, $14.95.

In his 40 years as a profound student of the era of the American Revolution, John R. Alden contributed a dozen scholarly books. This 1984 biography, now available in an attractive paperback edition, was both the capstone of Alden's career and the epitome of his craftsmanship. Symbolically, Alden chose the 1772 portrait of his subject for the cover and frontispiece. Washington posed in the uniform of the First Virginia Regiment, in which he served during the French and Indian War. That strife, and often Washington's public career and private fortunes, focused on control and development of the West, then the Ohio Valley. Armed with both sword and rifle, as well as adorned with a gorget indicating that he was an officer, Washington might then have been pondering where his loyalties lay, with Britain or with the rising chorus of champions of American rights.

Contrary to most academics, Alden always wrote for a larger audience. Thus the 24 chapters, ranging from 8 to 17 pages apiece, take the reader swiftly through the development of Washington's character and the parallel evolution of an American nation. Each chapter is superbly structured with introductory and concluding paragraphs that summarize the interpretation. The portrayal is balanced in two aspects. First, the coverage is equally apportioned to three periods: 1732-75, 1775-83, 1783-99. There is judicious use of primary sources, of which the author has a thorough command. Second, he repeatedly offers correctives: Washington was not an avid Mason, nor was he taller than six feet, nor was he bled to death. In Alden's handling of evidence on Washington's 1758 suitoring of Sally Fairfax, she "saved him from disgrace and preserved a great future for him." Frequent rhetorical questions induce readers to challenge the deductions of the biographer. Among quibbles from recent researchers would be the question of the benign portrayal of slavery at Mount Vernon. The chapter on 1787-88 fails to prove Washington's critical contributions. Yet Alden succeeds superbly in his admiring rendition of "a great man, a majestic figure, unquestionably the principal, the essential founder and champion of the American republic." This biography, as well as the more recent *Age of Federalism*, a monograph by Stanley Elkins and Eric McKitrick, stresses the cultural emphasis on one's character. In the 1772 portrait as well as throughout his life, Washington, ever willing to grow, appeared to have mastered himself and his surroundings.

LOUIS W. POTTS

University of Missouri
Kansas City

CLINTON, ROBERT LOWRY. 1997. *God and Man in the Law: The Foundations of Anglo-American Constitutionalism*. Pp. xiv, 298. Lawrence: University Press of Kansas. $35.00.

In this provocative and wide-ranging work, conservative legal scholar Robert Clinton argues that we now face a stark choice in contemporary constitutional theory. We can either return to a traditional, conservative, God-centered constitutional jurisprudence or we can continue on our present course of constitutional degeneration. The consequences of choosing the latter path, Clinton predicts, will be dire.

Like Robert Bork, whose conservative political and legal views he largely shares, Clinton rejects currently influential liberal theories of constitutional interpretation and argues for a return to a more traditional jurisprudence, one strongly rooted in respect for democratic processes and traditional cultural and legal values.

Specifically, Clinton argues for a theory of constitutional adjudication that includes the following central features. First, it is grounded in an explicit recognition of, and respect for, the common law origins of the American Constitution. Second, it rests on a broadly Thomistic "naturalistic" vision of the universe that sees all legal order as ultimately rooted in a transcendent order of eternal and natural law. Third, it regards original intent (understood as the framers' "objective" general purposes, rather than their "subjective" specific intentions) as the touchstone of correct constitutional interpretation. Fourth, it attaches significant weight to the principle of stare decisis in constitutional decision making. Fifth, it requires judges to look to conventional and traditional values, rather than their own personal values, in determining how the framers' general purposes should apply to contemporary cases. Finally, it limits judges to the relatively modest task of constitutional "interpretation"—defined by Clinton as the act of giving legal effect to clear and determinate constitutional language. Constitutional "construction"—the act of supplying meaning to otherwise indeterminate constitutional provisions—is essentially a policymaking function that Clinton argues is largely unsuitable for unelected judges in a democratic society.

This is a serious and thought-provoking study of a broad range of issues bearing on constitutional interpretation and the moral and religious foundations of Anglo-American law. To his credit, Clinton recognizes clearly that to do constitutional theory well, it is often necessary to move beyond narrow academic specializations and delve deeply into such fields as political philosophy, ethics, history, so-

ciology, epistemology, metaphysics, and philosophy of language.

The main weakness of the book is that Clinton tries to say too much about too many disparate subjects in too few pages. As a consequence, the argument is often only an inch deep at precisely those points where depth matters most. On finishing the book, I could not help wishing that it had been twice as long.

GREGORY BASSHAM

King's College
Wilkes-Barre
Pennsylvania

DELLI CARPINI, MICHAEL X. and SCOTT KEETER. 1996. *What Americans Know About Politics and Why It Matters*. Pp. xiii, 410. New Haven, CT: Yale University Press. No price.

For centuries, students of democracy have asserted that governing should be carried out by citizens who are both knowledgeable about their society and capable of using their knowledge to make wise collective decisions. In recent decades, we have heard the lament, over and over, that Americans are woefully uninformed about the facts of contemporary political life. However, the evidence supporting this claim has usually come not from comprehensive and systematic studies but from quick and idiosyncratic snapshots of the public mind. In *What Americans Know About Politics and Why It Matters*, Michael Delli Carpini and Scott Keeter have given us just what we need: a programmatic investigation of political knowledge that draws thoroughly from preexisting survey data sets dating back to the 1940s and from newly collected data as well.

We are told by the authors that Americans know most about the institutions and processes of politics, the least about the people and players, and moderate amounts about domestic and foreign affairs, geography, and social and political history. We learn that most people are moderately knowledgeable; only very small groups of citizens are very well informed or know next to nothing. Furthermore, we see that levels of political knowledge have remained remarkably stable since the 1940s.

We are told as well that people are not specialists, well-informed about idiosyncratic subdomains of politics; rather, people are "generalists," falling somewhere on a single continuum from completely lacking knowledge to knowing a great deal. The more cognitively and behaviorally engaged in politics one is, the more one knows about all of politics; the more one belongs to groups that lack political influence (for example, people with low education or low income; minorities; and women), the less one knows. This suggests that rising educational levels and dropping engagement in politics during the past 40 years have counterbalanced one another, leaving public knowledge levels at about the same level.

Finally, we learn that people who know more about politics are most likely to possess the qualities that theorists believe are necessary for effective democracy. These people are more tolerant of opinions with which they disagree, vote more often, participate more in political campaigns, have more stable opinions on more policy issues, manifest more constraint with respect to their policy preferences, and manifest more consistency between those preferences and their values, their candidate preferences, their party identifications, and their demographic characteristics.

However, these cross-sectional correlations do not make a fully convincing case that political knowledge is indeed essential for effective democracy, because no evidence is presented to support the causal claim that knowledge produced these qualities. Furthermore, to support Delli Carpini and Keeter's claim that democratic systems function more effectively when their citizens are more knowledgeable, we would need to see evidence regarding system-level outcomes, which is not provided here at all. Even the authors' own evidence can be seen as challenging their conclusion: whereas the authors claim that knowledge helps people to pursue their own interests, the most knowledgeable people are shown to be the least inclined to cast votes in efforts to maximize their own economic gains.

Even more important, it is not clear exactly what knowledge is required for people to be effective democratic citizens and whether the surveys analyzed here measured that knowledge. No attempt is made to define the universe of necessary knowledge, nor is any attempt made to sample from such a universe in any systematic way. Consequently, the results reported are contingent upon the apparently arbitrary set of items that pollsters happened to ask over the years, a fact that threatens the value of some findings.

For example, the majority of Americans would have appeared to be minimally knowledgeable if the item pool had included lots more very difficult questions on topics that had received little media attention. Had many more easy questions been asked instead, most people would have seemed to be highly knowledgeable. Without a clear specification of the universe of necessary knowledge and a systematic sampling of it, it is impossible to know what to make of the distributions or factor structures that do appear.

Other questions about causal direction are raised by the cross-sectional correlational nature of the evidence. For example, we are told that the frequency of discussing politics is a determinant of knowledge levels, yet we are told that political participation is an effect of knowledge. Could just the reverse not be true of both variables? We also are told that attitudes on women's rights are causes of knowledge, whereas stands on other policy issues are effects of knowledge. Stronger evidence would be needed to support such claims convincingly.

Contrary to the authors' conclusion that knowledge is unidimensional, the book is filled with evidence that knowledge is instead multidimensional. The explicit tests of dimensionality in Appendix 4 show that multidimensional models fit significantly better than unidimensional models. And these factor models show that separate dimensions of knowledge share only about 50 percent of their variance. Furthermore, people appear to be more knowledgeable in some domains than in others, and whereas some types of knowledge are shown to grow with age, others decline. Finally, gender, race, and political tolerance are correlated with knowledge on some issues but not on others. I am not sure what additional evidence would be required to make a compelling case for the multidimensional view.

In sum, this thorough and engaging book has pushed our understanding of political knowledge in America ahead significantly. It also raises important questions to be explored in future research. It is essential reading for any student of public opinion or democracy.

JON A. KROSNICK

Ohio State University
Columbus

KEYNES, EDWARD. 1996. *Liberty, Property, and Privacy: Toward a Jurisprudence of Substantive Due Process.* Pp. xvi, 238. University Park: Pennsylvania State University Press. No price.

In this fresh and thoughtful book, Edward Keynes argues that today's courts should look backward to find the proper way of dealing with unenumerated liberties like the right of privacy. The model Keynes would use is the police power jurisprudence of the laissez-faire era (1890s to 1937). During that era, courts employed theories of substantive due process and liberty of contract to frustrate the states' efforts to regulate the economy. Critics, both then and now, have complained that these theories derived from natural law rather than the Constitution and that judges had illegitimately stifled the democratic process.

Keynes maintains that laissez-faire era judges did not create this doctrine out of thin air. He argues that the concept of due process has always been thought to have a substantive element that allowed courts to protect personal liberty against arbitrary governmental intrusion. Furthermore, he says, the concept of liberty has always been understood to include unenumerated rights as well as those rights specifically enumerated in the Constitution. That courts found one of these rights to be liberty of contract was not merely a plot to attach laissez-faire economics to the Constitution, nor was it just an outgrowth of natural law. Liberty of contract, Keynes argues, protected property rights derived from the Anglo-American common law tradition. Today that same tradition protects another set of unenumerated rights: the rights of personal autonomy and privacy.

It is not Keynes's ultimate goal to demonstrate that the doctrine of laissez-faire era was sound. Rather, he emphasizes that the method that laissez-faire era judges used to test economic regulations against individual liberty serves as a useful guide for today's courts. The police power jurisprudence of old, he says, is a valid standard to guide the courts' decisions in such subjects as abortion and privacy. The balancing test that the courts now often employ in those cases has the disadvantage of forcing judges to weigh unmeasurable competing interests. As a result, he says, judicial decisions often seem inconsistent and arbitrary. Police power jurisprudence, by contrast, asks judges to address more straightforward questions. Has a fundamental right been violated? Does the government interference with that right serve a legitimate public purpose? The result will be decisions that are less arbitrary and more consistent.

Anyone interested in constitutional history or the modern debates on privacy or the role of the judiciary will want to read this book. Keynes may paint too glowing a picture of nineteenth-century constitutional history, and I am not convinced the solution he offers is better than the balancing method he criticizes. But he seriously addresses the problem of providing judges with some relatively objective standard for enforcing individual rights against the necessary power of government. Even the nonbeliever, like me, is forced to think through the issue in his terms.

PAUL KENS

Southwest Texas State University
San Marcos

KREML. WILLIAM P. 1997. *The Constitutional Divide: The Private and Public Sectors in American Law.* Pp. xiv, 224. Columbia: University of South Carolina Press. $29.95.

William P. Kreml argues that "the primary fault line" in American constitutional law is the hitherto neglected divide between the public and private sectors. To be sure, each era articulates the divide in its own institutional fashion. For example, the Marshall Court enlisted the national legislature in a "counter majoritarian" support of the "analytical form" of private and economic contract against majoritarian state legislatures. The Warren Court overcame the "inaction" of the state legislatures and "made law" in support of the "synthetic form" of contract that advances the public status of underrepresented groups. Kreml's point is that these different constitutional interpretations are understandable and predictable when located within the "form-to-sector relationship." By contrast, the dominant scholarly paradigm—that the fundamental divide is one of institutional jurisdiction—is unable to explain coherently why liberals and conservatives switch loyalties between the courts and legislatures. Kreml's answer is clear: the sectoral argument is the crucial divide and the combatants utilize that institution which advances their agenda.

There is also a normative and dialectical dimension to Kreml's storytelling. We learn that the "progress of democracy" is achieved when the equity-based standards of the synthetic form of public contract prevail over the simple analytic form of economic contract. Although imaginative, Kreml's dramatic story contains serious conceptual difficulties. He creates alliances that would have struck the allies as odd and portrays a pattern of continuity that is strained: the "antidemocratic," private-sector-based Blackstone, *Federalist* 10, Marshall, *Dred Scott*, and the Burger and Rehnquist Courts battle the heirs to the "democratic," public-sector-oriented Edward Coke, "the Antifederalists, Andrew Jackson, Holmes," and, most important, the Warren Court. To Kreml, Articles I through VII of the Constitution reflect the private sector, antidemocratic bias of the Madison forces. Fortunately, "the Antifederalist dissenters" corrected this imbalance and permitted democracy to "restart its evolutionary progress": "their Bill of Rights" secured the public synthetic contract. But to Kreml, the contrary notwithstanding, the Federalists envisioned the Constitution as a publicly empowering document while the Antifederalists viewed the Bill of Rights as a vital restraint on government. Besides, Madison, not the Antifederalists, fathered the Bill of Rights! Kreml has creatively recycled the Beard thesis that the Constitution is an economic and antidemocratic document designed to secure oligarchic property rights. His engaging mystery story turns largely on this long-discredited interpretation of the American founding by earlier progressive historians.

GORDON LLOYD

University of Redlands
California

LENDLER, MARC. 1997. *Crisis and Political Beliefs: The Case of the Colt Firearms Strike.* Pp. x, 186. New Haven, CT: Yale University Press. No price.

Workers at Colt Firearms in Hartford, Connecticut, had been on strike for almost two years when Marc Lendler began the research that ultimately led to this perceptive study of how and why "the political thinking of ordinary citizens changes in times of crisis." Lendler intends this book primarily as an empirical contribution to the literature on dominant ideologies, those patterns of thought that secure citizens' acquiescence to unequal, if not patently unjust, social and political relations. Here, his particular target is James Scott's contention that the powerless never fully acquiesce to the unequal arrangements that oppress them. In this view, the more open resistance manifested in strikes and other forms of collective action merely expresses already existing skepticism with the extant power relations.

Were this theory to hold true for American laborers, one would expect to find no change in the Colt strikers' political beliefs before and during the strike, only the public "ventilation" of truths already privately acknowledged. Lendler presents convincing if not conclusive evidence from his interviews, on-site observations, and survey data that no such continuity existed in this case. The strikers' political beliefs and attitudes changed as a result of the strike; their worldview was transformed.

Lendler further argues that such transformation lends support to the version of the dominant ideology thesis generally associated with Barrington Moore, in which the most powerful force prompting persons to accept situations of inequality or domination is habit or routine. Strikers came to view political and economic institutions differently as a result of a dramatic break in the seemingly natural course of things, one that began with the deterioration of labor-management relations in the 10 months before the strike (spent working without a contract). A corollary of this thesis, but one that Lendler was unable to test, is that the reestablishment of routine (following the successful conclusion of the strike) would also have some effect on the strikers' political beliefs.

What sort of citizens emerge in "exceptional times"? If their views are different from normal, is the change for better or worse? Here, Lendler wisely resists the temptation to equate "better" with increased adherence to left or progressive political agendas. (The book is at its weakest when attempting to marshal evidence of this sort.) Rather, individuals thrust into exceptional circumstances of "high intensity conflict" become better citizens because they develop more "thematically consistent political reasoning," pay greater attention to public affairs, and deploy collective rather than individual definitions of self-interest in evaluating political problems. Exactly why this is so Lendler cannot tell us. But his study usefully reminds us that the democratic deliberators of whom political theorists are so enamored are forged not in civility but in disruption, crisis, and conflict.

SHELLEY BURTT

Yale University
New Haven
Connecticut

PIPER, J. RICHARD. 1997. *Ideologies and Institutions: American Conservative and Liberal Governance Prescriptions Since 1933*. Pp. ix, 449. Lanham, MD: Rowman & Littlefield. $74.00. Paperbound, $27.95.

Since the founding of the country, the relationship between public policy and the institutions of government has been a concern of students of American politics. The Founders believed that the separation of powers, federalism, an independent judiciary, and other elements of the constitutional system would allow free but energetic government. Yet the young republic was often torn over the questions of whether and how this would happen. As J. Richard Piper shows in this helpful volume, such questions remain at the heart of American politics.

Piper sets out to give an account of the relationship between policymaking and theories of governance since the New Deal. He accomplishes his task. Drawing from an array of academic and journalistic sources, Piper outlines the underlying assumptions of liberalism and conservatism, the two dominant ideological movements in twentieth-century America. He then divides the years in question into four periods: the New Deal (1933-45), the postwar era (1945-66), the "new politics" era (1966-81), and the Reagan-Bush years (1981-93). For each period, Piper describes the competing ideologies and what their specific governance prescrip-

tions were. The prescriptions fall into five categories: constitutional interpretation, federalism, the role of the administrative state, congressional-presidential relations, and the role of the judiciary. His division between the periods and his choice of institutions are reasonable and well defended.

Not surprisingly, Piper finds that liberals and conservatives tend to hold their governance prescriptions more for instrumental reasons than as ends in themselves, though this is not uniformly the case. He finds that, across the periods, liberals have advocated a "living constitution," downplayed states' rights, and favored a strong administrative state. Conservatives have advocated the opposite. In the areas of congressional-presidential relations and the role of the judiciary, liberals and conservatives have changed their emphases, largely as a result of medium-term calculations of policy or power gains. For example, liberals in the first two periods advocated stronger presidential government. Since the rise of a more conservative presidency, however, liberals have tended to emphasize the importance of the Congress. But Piper also shows that neither liberals nor conservatives are entirely Machiavellian in their governance prescriptions. Indeed, he shows both the noble and the expedient in both camps. For this, he should be commended.

There is one main criticism of the book. Piper's study would be aided by a deeper analysis of the philosophical origins of modern liberalism and conservatism. Admittedly, however, this would substantially increase the size and scope of the work. In any case, this is a good book for those—especially undergraduates—in need of a clear overview of the ideological views of government institutions in modern America.

SCOT J. ZENTNER

California State University
San Bernardino

RICHARDSON, WILLIAM D. 1997. *Democracy, Bureaucracy, and Character: Founding Thought*. Pp. xii, 202. Lawrence: University Press of Kansas. $29.95. Paperbound, $15.95.

William Richardson examines the Founders' thinking on the character traits of Americans and what this thinking suggests for public administration in our democracy. He argues that the Founders' thought provides "a mandate" to administrators to "promote policies and administrative arrangements that take account of, are in accord with, and reinforce those attributes of human nature upon which the regime lies." Richardson notes the Founders favored energetic administrators and expected them to play an important role "in cultivating citizen character."

This means, for Richardson, that administrators should respect and protect the "acquisitivism" and the "individualism" of the American character, which the Founders saw as "the primary bases of a commercial republic." However, they should also seek to channel them in ways that promote the public good. According to Richardson, administrators should "work actively to uphold the character traits that are central to the regime" and "be alert to the ways in which administrative programs may be used to encourage citizens to see how their self-interest may be related to broader public interests."

Such a role for public administrators seems to require a significant measure of virtue on their part. Richardson draws on the Founders to argue that such virtue can be nurtured by harnessing the administrator's concern for reputation and honor to the public interest and by providing an education that stresses not just practical knowledge but also matters such as constitutional history and law, political theory, and ethics. The Founders, Richardson argues, believed that "the end of education" was "to produce virtuous citizens who would serve the public."

While stressing virtue, however, Richardson also recognizes the Founders' belief that public administrators could not be relied upon to be "disinterested guardians of the public welfare." In order to remain true to the Founders' thought, he argues that we should also be concerned "with constitutional, organizational, legal, political, professional, and other external ways of improving the chances that public servants will act in a manner that promotes the public interest."

Richardson perhaps exaggerates the role virtue plays in the Founders' thought. Also, he expects perhaps too much in terms of virtuous public administration. Furthermore, Richardson's attempt to justify New Deal policies in terms of the Founders' thought seems rather a stretch. Overall, however, this is a readable book that makes a significant contribution to the growing literature on the Founders' thought and its relevance for public administration.

MICHAEL W. SPICER

Cleveland State University
Ohio

RUDENSTINE, DAVID. 1996. *The Day the Presses Stopped: A History of the Pentagon Papers Case*. Pp. x, 448. Berkeley: University of California Press. $34.95.

This is a conventional narrative of the landmark ruling on prior restraint, with a contrarian twist. Rudenstine, a law professor at Yeshiva University, finds that the defeated government case deserves more respect.

The Day the Presses Stopped carefully tells the story of how the Nixon administration began to unravel in the summer of 1971 in this dispute over publication of a historical document on Vietnam. At first, both Nixon and his defense secretary thought that the *New York Times*'s use of classified material about previous administrations could strengthen their hand. Just who talked the administration into a fight on the Pentagon papers is of great historical importance because the tactics used by Nixon operatives led to the fall of that government in the Watergate scandal three years later. Rudenstine finds that Henry Kissinger, the national security adviser, and Assistant Attorney General Robert Mardian were key. In this constitutional crisis, the ignition points seem to have been office politics and the zeal of subordinates.

Rudenstine's revisionism begins with the motives of the Nixon administration. "National security considerations were at the heart of their concerns," he argues, not their simmering anger at the press. This seems a distinction without much of a difference, because Rudenstine finds top Republicans bent upon destroying journalists only days after their loud talk about protecting the nation. Similarly, Rudenstine's useful discovery that the Pentagon papers "contained information that could have seriously harmed the national security" is an anticlimax. We learn that journalists never had these parts of the papers or were careful not to publish what they had.

The Day the Presses Stopped shows a fight over the Constitution that was messy and human. National security witnesses fumbled their lines in court. The 47 volumes kept showing up unexpectedly with armed guards, throwing confusion over both bench and bar. This was trial by rookies: Professor Alexander Bikel got his first experience as a litigator in making the first case that Judge Murray I. Gurfein heard. This was the last case for Supreme Court Justices Hugo Black and John M. Harlan, with a strange coda. Chief Justice Warren E. Burger summarized the Court's decision on the First Amendment in words that Rudenstine properly calls "ludicrous."

The Day the Presses Stopped will not help legal writing against the familiar charges of stodginess. There is life in this narrative, but it is sometimes choked by events that "begin at a much earlier point in time" or are "fairly imminent" as people "proceed with the endeavor." A wider focus on the end of prior restraint in this period would have given more force to the book. Rudenstine pays little attention to the spread of information technology. The Internet, which emerged from the Pentagon during the Vietnam war, probably ended the days when the presses can be stopped.

THOMAS C. LEONARD

University of California
Berkeley

TAYLOR, BOB PEPPERMAN. 1996. *America's Bachelor Uncle: Thoreau and the American Polity.* Pp. xi, 180. Lawrence: University Press of Kansas. $25.00.

Taylor takes to task those critics he feels have ignored or misunderstood Thoreau's political focus in his writings, claiming that "Thoreau is one of America's most important political critics." It is as "critic of American society and politics" that Thoreau performs as a "bachelor uncle." Taylor deals with most of Thoreau's writings (though the *Journal* and his correspondence are strangely absent). At his best, Taylor shows how each of Thoreau's works addresses a specific aspect of the American national identity: *A Week* is "a sophisticated meditation on the realities and consequences of the American founding"; *The Maine Woods* deals with "the whites of European ex-

traction who settle the American frontier"; *Cape Cod* contrasts the Pilgrim set-
tlers with modern pioneers; *A Yankee in
Canada* allows Thoreau to make a "positive evaluation of his native land" by contrasting it with another country; *Walden*
criticizes the "emerging capitalist economy"; and his shorter essays deal with
specific "topical and polemical" matters
rather than more universal ones.

Dealing with all of Thoreau in such a
short book (only 129 text pages) is a real
challenge, and, in many ways, this book
represents an article that got carried
away with itself. There are a number of
suggestive readings here, but the work is
in no way comprehensive (how can it be,
when *Walden* is plumbed in about twenty
pages?); the "bachelor uncle" conceit appears at the beginning and end of the
book but not as a thematic element
within it; the development of the argument is often little more than a summary
of Thoreau's own points, many of the conclusions are hardly new (for example,
"Thoreau employs his literary skills for
the purpose of showing, shocking, sham-
ing, seducing, and inspiring us"); and the
book fails to take on the political, nation-
alistic Thoreau in as detailed a manner
as such works as Joan Burbick's have
done. Moreover, Taylor has a distracting
habit of disagreeing with nearly every
critic who has written on the subject,
using them as targets in his text and
abusing them at length in his notes
(which, at nearly 40 pages, contain too
many such attacks and too many "ibids"
to be useful), rather than weaving them
into his overall discussion. The more Taylor chastises, the more he shows his own
inability to distinguish between truly significant writers on Thoreau and those
who have proven to be ephemeral. This is
a disappointing work.

JOEL MYERSON

University of South Carolina
Columbia

SOCIOLOGY

ATHENS, LONNIE. 1997. *Violent Criminal Acts and Actors Revisited.* Pp. x,
175. Champaign: University of Illinois
Press. $24.95. Paperbound, $14.95.

The original analysis of interviews
with 47 male and 11 female "violent offenders" in prison, of "a couple dozen or
so *substantial* violent acts" that he witnessed, and of "less than a half dozen"
people he knew well, never imprisoned,
whom he knew also to be or have been
violent, was published in 1980. Lonnie
Athens considers "violent" only what
would be seen legally as aggravated or
sexual assault or as criminal homicide.
The last 50 pages of the present volume
are "a second look" at the study, beginning with further justification of the
study and answers to critics, and then
summarizing his "interpretive" theory of
how "offenders'" definitions of themselves and the violent situation are "con-
gruent with" the violence, in the event
and over time, and stating theoretical
and policy implications of his findings.
Athens's approach to understanding violent offenders is inspired by Herbert
Blumer, who writes a highly laudatory
foreword and talks about the importance
of the work.

Athens took notes and reconstructed
rich, elaborate verbatim accounts by pris-
oners of their acts, of what went through
their minds throughout the encounters
leading to the violence, and of their history of violence and how their self-images
had changed. He went to great lengths to
validate the essentials of the interviews
he completed and used, as by checking
accounts against police records. He constructed a complex typology of offenders'
violence as defined by their interpretations of their acts, and of their self-images. As he introduces each subset in his
typology, he offers rather substantial ex-
cerpts from his interviews to illustrate.

Many of the illustrations are riveting. I am accustomed to hearing and reading accounts of victimization. Nonetheless I found myself fascinated by so broad an array of accounts of what goes through the minds of people doing savage things to others. I was also deeply impressed by the effort and attention that went into collecting and mulling through the data. Athens argues well that any hope of control rests on knowing not only what people do but what they mean by it and what they make of the circumstances in which they do it. It is a tribute to the care and precision with which he presents his data that I find myself questioning his categorization of his data. Where he saw "frustration," for instance, I in a number of instances saw "self-defense." All in all, I appreciated the data but found the theory wanting and the implications unsupported.

HAL PEPINSKY

Indiana University
Bloomington

HAWKINS, MIKE. 1997. *Social Darwinism in European and American Thought, 1860-1945: Nature as Model and Nature as Threat*. Pp. x, 344. New York: Cambridge University Press. $69.95. Paperbound, $27.95.

The conventional view is that several late-nineteenth-century thinkers—Herbert Spencer in England and William Graham Sumner in America—took a number of themes and tags from Charles Darwin's theory of evolution via natural selection and constructed a crude theory of human social evolution called "social Darwinism." These tags included "the struggle for survival," "the survival of the fittest," and so on. This ideology proved very useful for legitimating the actions of wealthy industrialists and financiers, but the antithetical ideologies of social-

ism and social democracy (Fabians in England, Progressives in the United States) placed the emphasis not on competition but on cooperation and succeeded in discrediting social Darwinism, which barely survived into the twentieth century.

Mike Hawkins has a different story to tell. The pegs on which he hangs his fascinating narrative include the following: Darwin was himself the first social Darwinist; there were, in addition to the individualist-competitive strain represented by Spencer and Sumner, socialist Darwinists in Germany (Ludwig Buchner, Ludwig Woltmann) and elsewhere, liberal reform Darwinists in England and America, racial Darwinists in Europe and America, and other sorts of social Darwinists as well. Far from going extinct, social Darwinism has mutated and multiplied. It has supplied the deeper ideological background of the eugenics movement (for sterilizing "unfit" humans) and modern sociobiology and evolutionary psychology. *Social Darwinism in European and American Thought* is a wide-ranging survey of these and other movements. Its scope and sweep are both this book's main virtue and its chief vice: virtue, because it covers a vast and ofttimes interconnected terrain; and vice, because the treatment of each topic tends to be a bit brief, although almost always suggestive.

Perhaps the most suggestive yet least satisfactory chapter is the last, "Nazism, Fascism and Social Darwinism." Hawkins rightly sees Hitler as indebted to earlier racialized social Darwinism (which viewed the struggle for survival as proceeding along racial lines). But one of the chief sources for Hitler and other Nazi ideologues, Ludwig Woltmann, is missing from the story, having been classified among the socialist Darwinists. But Woltmann, as Hawkins himself notes, began to move in a markedly more racist direction. Hawkins mentions Woltmann's *Die Darwinische Theorie und der Sozialismus* (1899) but takes no note of two subsequent works, *Historical Materialism: A Critique of the Marxist World-View* (1900) and *Political Anthropology* (1903), both of which advance a racist interpretation of Darwin's significance for social and political theory and practice that antedates Hitler's sketchier and less systematic version of that same view.

Still, what Hawkins's book lacks in depth he makes up for in breadth. We are fortunate to have this sweeping and accessible survey.

TERENCE BALL

University of Minnesota
Minneapolis

ROSSI, PETER H. and RICHARD A BERK. 1997. *Just Punishments: Federal Guidelines and Public Views Compared.* Pp. x, 243. Hawthorne, NY: Aldine de Gruyter. Paperbound, $19.95.

Responding to widespread complaints of bias, disparities, and leniency in sentencing, the U.S. Congress passed the federal Sentencing Reform Act of 1984, creating the U.S. Sentencing Commission. The Federal Sentencing Guidelines proposed by the commission were approved by Congress in 1987.

In constructing the guidelines, the commission chose a narrow range around average sentences actually served recently by convicted offenders. In 1993, the commission engaged Peter Rossi and Richard Berk to determine whether the public agreed with the guidelines. *Just Punishments* reports Rossi and Berk's research on that question.

Rossi and Berk are eminently qualified to evaluate the degree of public consensus around the guidelines. With Stephen L. Nock and other collaborators, they were the first to apply factorial survey design to the measurement of judgments about complex social issues.

In this study, 40 vignettes describing federal crimes were posed in face-to-face interviews to a nationally representative sample of 1737 adults. Respondents chose a punishment type and amount for each vignette. The inclusion of environmental, civil rights, white-collar, product-tampering, and immigration crimes, along with drug and street crimes, is unique among such studies.

Substantial agreement existed between average public preferences and guideline sentences for most crimes, though wide dispersion existed among those preferences. Sentences for drug-trafficking crimes were an exception; the public disagreed with the guidelines' far more severe sentences for selling crack, compared to powder cocaine or heroin. Environmental, civil rights, and extortion crimes are also punished more severely under the guidelines than the public prefers. Some characteristics of respondents—such as race, region, education, and prior contact with the criminal justice system—were related to their sentencing preferences.

Respondents were not told about the actual costs and benefits of various punishments, despite substantial evidence (acknowledged by the authors) that people state different preferences when so informed. The implications of this discrepancy between opinions held by informed and uninformed citizens deserve attention from policymakers. One objective of punishment policy is reducing crime at the lowest cost, so the public is ill served by policymaking that is constrained by the public's ignorance.

Political staff members responsible for monitoring public opinion and graduate students in public administration, criminology, and criminal justice should read this book. In addition to containing the very best available information on the topic, it provides an excellent model for evaluating how the various components of any complex social issue contribute to the formation of public opinion about that issue.

JOSEPH E. JACOBY

Bowling Green State University
Ohio

RULE, JAMES B. 1997. *Theory and Progress in Social Science*. Pp. xiv, 257. New York: Cambridge University Press. $54.95. Paperbound, no price.

Anyone familiar with academic sociology for the past several decades is bound to have wondered on occasion, Whatever happened to small group analysis? Or to ethnomethodology? These are two examples of theoretical approaches discussed by James Rule in his splendid book that loomed large for a time only to have disappeared by the 1990s or at least been relegated to the outer margins of the discipline. Nor will it have escaped notice that recently dominant approaches have hardly been independent of the headlines, that is, of historical developments in the real world freighted with ideological significance. Feminist sociology is Rule's major example of an obvious response to salient historical events: gender would certainly not have become a major sociological concern in the absence of the revived feminist movement of the early 1970s. The notion once forcefully advanced by Talcott Parsons in sociology's salad days right after the war that the field was increasingly shaped only by its internal theoretically guided trajectory could hardly be more thoroughly refuted.

Rule explores the full implications of these considerations. Theory in sociology, he notes, does not manifest any discernible progress; it is not, in short, cumulative as true sciences are supposed to be.

The recent history of the field is littered with half-forgotten approaches that turned out, despite their initial extravagant claims to the contrary, to reflect quite transitory interests, some of them mere fads or fashions, others responses to real problems and issues that no longer command our attention. He recognizes that there is genuine progress in techniques and methods of empirical study, but these are independent of progress at the level of theory. The application of new methods enabling the discovery of new facts may mean that we possess a great deal more factual information about a subject than in the past, a form of modest progress that Rule perhaps does not sufficiently recognize. This additional knowledge, however, does not necessarily lead to greater theoretical understanding. We obviously know a great deal more about civil violence (riots, rebellions, revolutions), the subject of Rule's previous book, owing both to new methods of studying it and additional historical experience, but our theoretical understanding is hardly superior to that of past thinkers. Scholars, for example, today favor Tocqueville's early nineteenth-century interpretation of the French Revolution over later once-preferred interpretations.

Rule is not just restating the case against the insistence of positivism on the primary and even exclusive value of lawlike universal propositions, for he is well aware of the onslaughts within sociology against positivism since the 1960s. But he also wisely observes the transitoriness of concerns of two of its major critics, Barrington Moore, Jr., and C. Wright Mills, who called for a sociology oriented to the "world-historical" conflicts and dilemmas of capitalism and democracy. Rule illustrates changing perceptions of "relevance," that battle cry of student rebels of the 1960s, with Moore's citing as typical of the "trivial problems" filling the pages of academic journals a study from the 1950s deploying elaborate quantitative methods to research male sexual aggression against their dates on college campuses. Years before feminists had made a major issue of the sexual harassment of women, Nathan Glazer, having spotted Moore's example, had expressed doubts that the women victims themselves would have thought the problem so trivial. Rule is a bit unfair to Moore and Mills in suggesting that their political radicalism dictated their sense of significance in theory: Mills recognized a number of conservatives—Mosca, Lippman, Schumpeter—as exemplars of the "sociological imagination," and Moore held that social science should study "what history places on the agenda for us," which he did not confine to issues of primary concern to the Left.

But Rule is more than a mere debunker of the pretensions of social science. He concedes that "expressive" theorizing articulating the sentiments and worldviews of the theorist has a legitimacy of its own and is subject to critical evaluation, resembling in this respect realist novels rather than painting or music. It is not necessarily what philosophers call a category mistake to ask whether one such theory is better than another, as it would be to argue over whether Rembrandt was a greater painter than Picasso. Rule goes beyond this qualified recognition of the inevitably context-bound nature of social theories in his striving to steer a course between ahistorical universalism and extreme postmodernist relativism. Social theory, he argues, cannot be dismissed as just an expression of its authors' particular tastes, ideological preoccupations, and/or social identities, for there are enduring questions—he calls them "first-order questions"—that transcend the particulars of time and place, as well as "coping questions" that, although limited to specific contexts, are sufficiently pressing

that attempts to solve them are not reducible to "mere" expressiveness. He assesses the strengths and weaknesses of three current claimants to the role of crucial theoretical breakthroughs: rational choice theory, network analysis, and feminist analysis. He is particularly judicious on the last, rejecting the radical claim that feminist analysis should "shape all forms of social inquiry" on the grounds that "there are simply too many other theoretical issues having little directly to do with gender that intrude themselves on our attention" while acknowledging that "as long as women's roles remain subjects of public controversy and struggle, the demand for intellectual commentary in these conflicts will continue." Gender is by now securely ensconced as a major topic of social investigation.

Rule, like me, is a sociologist. He mentions psychoanalysis, once a major cross-disciplinary influence, which nowadays is defended for its inherent "richness" and "suggestiveness" when confronted with empirical objections. It exemplifies today, Rule argues, an "internalist" legitimation exhibited by other once more ambitious theoretical programs. He also notes the enchantment of neoclassical economists with the "marvel" of their complex formal models. He cites a few cases from political science, especially the field of international relations, but the vast majority of his copious examples are drawn from sociology.

This raises a question about his use of the term "social science" in the very title of the book and throughout. All but two of his seven examples of transhistorical "first-order questions" refer to subjects primarily dealt with by sociology as a discipline. Sociologists often use "sociology" and "social science" almost synonymously. Critics might complain that they do this because they lack a delimited subject matter of their own and/or because they have an inferiority complex over the relatively low status of their field. Sociologists could credibly respond that the very boundlessness of their field, embracing everything people do in association, equips them to become philosophers and epistemologists of all of the social sciences. Rule fails to make such a case for his invocation of social science in general, which is a pity for it might have guaranteed him greater attention than he may receive for this absolutely first-rate and superbly written contribution to the philosophy of social science.

DENNIS H. WRONG

New York University

VISSING, YVONNE M. 1996. *Out of Sight, Out of Mind: Homeless Children and Families in Small-Town America*. Pp. xii, 271. Lexington: University of Kentucky Press. $39.95. Paperbound, $16.95.

When the Stewart B. McKinney Act was being considered in the U.S. Senate, a prominent member from Illinois introduced an amendment that would have restricted federal funding for the homeless to urban states. The senator justified his actions by stating that homelessness is an urban problem, that there are so few rural homeless that any allocation of funding would be a waste of resources. The stereotype held by this senator, that there are no homeless in small towns or rural America, characterizes past research on and subsequent information about the homeless in America. Researchers and writers have basically ignored rural America, leading audiences to conclude that homelessness is indeed an exclusively urban dilemma.

In her book *Out of Sight, Out of Mind*, Yvonne Vissing dispels many of the traditional myths about homelessness in small-town and rural America. Although the research reported by Vissing focuses primarily on smaller communities in New Hampshire, much of what she concludes can be generalized to the bulk of rural America. Vissing, a professor of sociology at Salem State College in Massachusetts, convincingly dispels the traditional impressionistic imagery of the media and constructs a model of rural and small-town homelessness that is based on evidence as she skillfully mixes hard data and case studies.

In her detailed description of family problems, the deplorable state of health care, the abundance of mental health problems associated with the inadequacy of programming, the scarcity of low-cost housing, the lack of good jobs, and the generally bad economic conditions that plague the poor in rural and small-town America, Vissing presents a well-balanced combination of important qualitative and quantitative data. In an engaging manner, she provides the knowledgeable as well as browsing reader with an immense amount of evidence that details the plight of homeless children, critiques their condition, and offers probable community-based solutions.

This very readable book offers a valuable addition and counterpoint to the abundance of literature about the homeless in urban America. For those who are looking for solutions to the problem, this work offers a wealth of suggestions and step-by-step action plans. For those seeking a theoretical analysis of rural homelessness that will supplement our knowledge of the urban scene, this work is a must. Yvonne Vissing has provided us with a valuable addition to the literature of the field.

R. DEAN WRIGHT

Drake University
Des Moines
Iowa

WILLIAMS, VERNON J., JR. 1996. *Rethinking Race: Franz Boas and His Contemporaries*. Pp. ix, 152. Lexington: University Press of Kentucky. $34.95. Paperbound, $15.95.

Recently, President Clinton called on the American people to engage in a serious and lengthy examination and dialogue on race relations in the United States. This text could be a valuable component of that dialogue.

Williams correctly points out that for much of the twentieth century the subject of race has been in the academic purview of social scientists and intellectual historians, many of whom were caught in a web of cultural and historical racial bias. Others, such as Franz Boas, attempted to extricate some of the racial-determinist assumptions of the prevailing social sciences.

Commonly referred to as the father of modern American anthropology, Boas was no philosophical egalitarian. Yet his empirical research allowed him, at least partially, to escape being a prisoner of his times. Certainly he provided the American conscience with a scientific antiracist foundation.

Most intriguing in this work is Williams's demonstration of the impact that Boas had on African American intellectuals, including Booker T. Washington, W.E.B. DuBois, Carter G. Woodson, and others. Also of note are the substantive chapters on the thought of Washington, DuBois, and Robert Ezra Park. Williams enlightens the reader as to the gulf that still remains between the myths that are utilized to support claims of African American racial inferiority (whether in academic circles or in our popular culture) and the true complexity of this topic as revealed by scholars like Franz Boas. Thus the current, or at least pending, dialogue would be served extraordinarily well by the inclusion of this work.

In regards to structure and style, I would give the text high marks for clarity and substance. The work flows smoothly, although some segues seem a bit abrupt. The appendix on ecumenical myth history is fascinating; the bibliography is first-rate.

In conclusion, I would imagine that the reader of this book would be best served if he or she had some prior knowledge of African American historiography or sociological research in this subfield. Without this background, a reader might be hard-pressed to appreciate fully Williams's reference to an extensive list of theories on race and race relations.

JAMES McKEE

Christian Brothers University
Memphis
Tennessee

ECONOMICS

ROOT, HILTON L. 1996. *Small Countries, Big Lessons: Governance and the Rise of East Asia*. Pp. xxi, 246. New York: Oxford University Press. $19.95.

This slim volume seeks the sources of East and Southeast Asia's spectacular economic success over the last several decades. Hilton Root, senior research fellow at the Hoover Institution working under the sponsorship of the Asian Development Bank, argues that the key to riding the international market to higher rates of growth and positive social development is to be found in state behavior. Those that succeed promote bureaucratic competence and incorruptibility, apply consistent, predictable legal and administrative rules of the economic game, develop lines of communication between the state and important economic sectors, and make decision makers somehow accountable. Sketches of Korea, Taiwan,

Singapore, Hong Kong, Malaysia, Indonesia, and the Philippines show the variations on this theme.

Root sees his main target as the overweening faith in the free market that blinds its advocates to the importance of getting governance right in the first place if those markets are to work. He disagrees with their insistence on democracy and state nonintervention, and instead makes the case that authoritarian regimes can open and manage markets at least as well as democratic ones and that some degree of state intervention is essential to launching and sustaining market-driven growth. If there is one consistent variable, it is, Root contends, not democracy or nonintervention but social equality, which figures in the Asian cases as both a precondition and an outcome of successful economic strategies.

Those with some knowledge of the region will wonder how Root would fit China and Vietnam into the generalizations offered here. Both have climbed into the high-growth range in the face of formidable obstacles and under the control of an intrusive Communist party. Moreover, while Root is right to draw attention to the political dimensions of development, he shies away from probing more deeply—into the stubborn societal and cultural patterns and the subtle influence of historical experience that may render the lessons drawn here less uniform and universally applicable. The most successful cases with the brightest outlook seem to have an ethnically or culturally homogeneous population where a consensus on economic goals most easily emerges. Those cases also operate under the long shadow of Confucius and the constellation of values associated with him. South Asia, sub-Saharan Africa, and Latin America may, as Root contends, need to practice market-friendly governance, but before that is possible they may need to find a way to address something much tougher—deep societal divisions and sturdy systems of class predation.

MICHAEL H. HUNT

University of North Carolina
Chapel Hill

SAPPINGTON, DAVID E. M. and DENNIS L. WEISMAN. 1996. *Designing Incentive Regulation for the Telecommunications Industry*. Pp. xvi, 388. Cambridge, MA: MIT Press; Washington, DC: AEI Press. No price.

This book is part of the American Enterprise Institute's new Studies in Telecommunications Deregulation series. This series of books covers a wide range of important topics in the rapidly changing telecommunications industry, and they are written to be accessible to a wide range of readers outside of the industry, particularly policymakers, public officials, and other members of the interested public. This book by Sappington and Weisman will surely stand as one of the more thoughtful and academically rigorous, yet still easily accessible, volumes in the series.

Sappington and Weisman have written about a fundamental change that has taken place in the regulation of telecommunications, both at the Federal Communications Commission for the regulation of interstate telephone service, and at state public service commissions for the regulation of local and in-state telephone service. Over the past few years, there has been a major shift away from the traditional regulation of profits, accomplished by the regulation of costs and a fair rate of return on investment, and to incentive or price regulation, which focuses on the prices that customers must pay for telephone service. This regulatory change has been driven by the increasing awareness of the perverse incentives resulting from cost-plus profit regulation, the unsuitability of a cumbersome cost-based regulatory mechanism for a rapidly changing competitive market, and the improved incentives and simplicity of price regulation. Incentive or price regulation allows the telephone companies to keep any profits they can earn as long as they meet certain price targets. As a result of this and other improved incentives for efficiency and innovation, incentive regulation is likely to have a significant effect on the performance of telecommunications companies.

The book has 12 chapters. The first chapter provides an introduction to incentive regulation and a brief discussion of the advantages and disadvantages of rate-of-return regulation. Chapters 2 and 3 provide an overview of the telecommunications industry in the United States and a review of existing regulatory plans. Chapter 4 discusses regulatory goals. Chapters 5 and 6 explain selecting performance criteria and designing such incentive regulation plans. Chapter 7 addresses how credible incentive plans can be put in place when regulators may not have the ability to make longer-term commitments to the plans. Chapter 8 relates the benefits of competition and deregulation to incentive regulation, and chapter 9 evaluates the issues associated with allowing the Bell telephone companies to provide long-distance service. Chapter 10 describes the pitfalls in measuring the effects of incentive regulation, and chapter 11 evaluates empirical studies of the effects of incentive regulation. Chapter 12 concludes the book with 25 specific policy recommendations for incentive regulation.

It is hard to think of a better book to provide an introduction to the issues surrounding the change to incentive regulation. Not only has this change become pronounced in telecommunications, and therefore a topic that commands attention, but the concept of incentive regulation is also beginning to be applied in the electricity and natural gas markets. The Sappington and Weisman book will provide a good foundation for that analysis as well.

STANFORD L. LEVIN

Southern Illinois University
Edwardsville

OTHER BOOKS

ABU-LEBDEH, HATEM SHAREEF. 1997. *Conflict and Peace in the Middle East: National Perceptions and United States-Jordan Relations*. Pp. xviii, 185. Lanham, MN: University Press of America. $52.00. Paperbound, $32.50.

AFRICAN DEVELOPMENT BANK. 1997. *African Development Report, 1997*. Pp. viii, 221. New York: Oxford University Press. Paperbound, $29.95.

ALLISON, WILLIAM. 1997. *American Diplomats in Russia: Case Studies in Orphan Diplomacy, 1916-1919*. Pp. xi, 190. Westport, CT: Praeger. $59.95.

BACCHI, CAROL LEE. 1996. *The Politics of Affirmative Action: "Women," Equality and Category Politics*. Pp. xv, 190. Thousand Oaks, CA: Sage. $75.00. Paperbound, $21.95.

BAGCHI, AMIYA KUMAR. 1997. *The Evolution of the State Bank of India: The Era of the Presidency Banks, 1876-1920*. Vol. 2. Pp. 664. Walnut Creek, CA: Altamira Press. $45.00.

BARKER, EILEEN, ed. 1995. *On Freedom: A Centenary Anthology*. Pp. xx, 357. New Brunswick, NJ: Transaction. Paperbound, $24.95.

BARRETT, CHRISTOPHER and JEFFREY W. CASON. 1997. *Overseas Research: A Practical Guide*. Pp. xvi, 142. Baltimore, MD: Johns Hopkins University Press. $35.00. Paperbound, $12.95.

BELL, CARYN COSSE. 1997. *Revolution, Romanticism, and the Afro-Creole Protest Tradition in Louisiana, 1718-1868*. Pp. xv, 325. Baton Rouge: Louisiana State University Press. $35.00.

BEM, SACHA and HUIB LOOREN DE JONG. 1997. *Theoretical Issues in Psychology*. Pp. ix, 194. Thousand Oaks, CA: Sage. $69.95. Paperbound, $22.95.

BENCKE, MATTHEW J. VON. 1996. *The Politics of Space: A History of United States-Soviet Russian Competition and Cooperation*. Pp. viii, 264. Boulder, CO: Westview Press. $49.95.

BENJAMIN, LOIS, ed. 1997. *Black Women in the Academy: Promises and Perils*. Pp. xii, 360. Gainesville: University Press of Florida. $49.95.

BERMAN, PEARL S. 1997. *Case Conceptualization and Treatment Planning: Exercises for Integrating Theory with Clinical Practice*. Pp. xvi, 191. Thousand Oaks, CA: Sage. $52.00. Paperbound, $24.95.

BOSE, SUMANTRA. 1997. *The Challenge in Kashmir: Democracy, Self-Determination and a Just Peace*. Pp. 211. Thousand Oaks, CA: Sage. No price.

BRANDT, NAT. 1996. *Harlem at War: The Black Experience in WWII*. Pp. xv, 277. Syracuse, NY: Syracuse University Press. $28.95.

BRINKLEY, ALAN, NELSON W. POLSBY, and KATHLEEN M. SULLIVAN. 1997. *New Federalist Papers: Essays in Defense of the Constitution*. Pp. xii, 179. New York: Norton. $23.00. Paperbound, $13.95.

BROHMAN, JOHN. 1996. *Popular Development: Rethinking the Theory and Practice of Development*. Pp. ix, 398. Cambridge, MA: Basil Blackwell. $59.95. Paperbound, $24.95.

BUCHANAN, PAUL G. 1996. *State Labor Capital: Democratizing Class Relations in the Southern Cone*. Pp. xix, 395. Pittsburgh, PA: University of Pittsburgh Press. $49.95.

BULLARD, MONTE R. 1997. *The Soldier and the Citizen: The Role of the Military in Taiwan's Development*. Pp. xiv, 223. Armonk, NY: M. E. Sharpe. $62.95. Paperbound, $24.95.

BURRELL, GIBSON. 1997. *Pandemonium: Towards a Retro-Organization Theory*. Pp. 244. Thousand Oaks, CA: Sage. $65.00. Paperbound, $23.95.

BUTLER, JUDITH. 1997. *The Psychic Life of Power: Theories in Subjection.* Pp. 218. Stanford, CA: Stanford University Press. $39.50. Paperbound, $14.95.

BUWALDA, PETRUS. 1997. *They Did Not Dwell Alone: Jewish Emigration from the Soviet Union, 1967-1990.* Pp. xviii, 297. Baltimore, MD: Johns Hopkins University Press. $38.00.

CASTORIADIS, CORNELIUS, ed. 1997. *World in Fragments: Writings on Politics, Society, Psychoanalysis, and the Imagination.* Pp. xxxix, 507. Stanford, CA: Stanford University Press. $65.00. Paperbound, $22.95.

CLAWSON, DAVID L. 1997. *Latin America and the Caribbean: Lands and Peoples.* Pp. xvii, 382. Dubuque, IA: Wm. C. Brown. Paperbound, $66.00.

COHEN, ARIEL. 1996. *Russian Imperialism: Development and Crisis.* Pp. xiv, 180. Westport, CT: Praeger. $55.00.

CORDESMAN, ANTHONY. 1996. *Perilous Prospects: The Peace Process and the Arab-Israeli Military Balance.* Pp. xv, 316. Boulder, CO: Westview Press. $69.00. Paperbound, $25.00.

COULTER, MATTHEW WARE. 1997. *The Senate Munitions Inquiry of the 1930s: Beyond the Merchants of Death.* Pp. xii, 182. Westport, CT: Greenwood Press. $57.95.

CROWE, IAN, ed. 1997. *The Enduring Edmund Burke: Bicentennial Essays.* Pp. 221. Wilmington, DE: Intercollegiate Studies Institute. $24.95.

CUTRONA, CAROLYN E. 1996. *Social Support in Couples.* Pp. xvi, 150. Thousand Oaks, CA: Sage. $38.00. Paperbound, $16.95.

DAINES, BRIAN, LINDA GASK, and TIM USHERWOOD. 1997. *Medical and Psychiatric Issues for Counsellors.* Pp. xiii, 156. Thousand Oaks, CA: Sage. $49.95. Paperbound, $19.95.

DANIELS, ROGER. 1997. *Not Like Us: Immigrants and Minorities in America, 1890-1924.* Pp. xi, 179. Chicago: Ivan R. Dee. $22.50.

DATT, GAURAV. 1996. *Bargaining Power, Wages and Employment: An Analysis of Agricultural Labor Markets in India.* Pp. 224. Thousand Oaks, CA: Sage. $32.00.

DAVIS, KATHY, ed. 1997. *Embodied Practices: Feminist Perspectives on the Body.* Pp. ix, 210. Thousand Oaks, CA: Sage. $75.00. Paperbound, $26.95.

DAWISHA, KAREN and BRUCE PARROTT, eds. 1997. *Politics, Power and the Struggle for Democracy in South-East Europe.* Pp. xx, 472. New York: Cambridge University Press. $64.95. Paperbound, $24.95.

DENG, FRANCIS M., SADIKIEL KIMARO, TERRENC LYONS, DONALD ROTHCHILD, and I. WILLIAM ZARTMAN. 1996. *Sovereignty as Responsibility: Conflict Management in Africa.* Pp. xxiii, 265. Washington, DC: Brookings Institution. $42.95. Paperbound, $18.95.

DIAMOND, LARRY, MARC F. PLATTNER, YUN-HAN CHU, and HUNG-MAO TIEN, eds. 1997. *Consolidating the Third Wave Democracies: Regional Challenges.* Pp. xlvii, 332. Baltimore, MD: Johns Hopkins University Press. $45.00. Paperbound, $14.95.

DiJOSEPH, JOHN. 1996. *Jacques Maritain and the Moral Foundation of Democracy.* Pp. xv, 173. New York: Rowman & Littlefield. Paperbound, no price.

ELLIS, DESMOND and NOREEN STUCKLESS. 1996. *Mediating and Negotiating Marital Conflicts.* Pp. xi, 164. Thousand Oaks, CA: Sage. $42.00. Paperbound, $17.95.

ELSHTAIN, JEAN BETHKE. 1997. *Real Politics: At the Center of Everyday Life.* Pp. viii, 375. Baltimore, MD: Johns Hopkins University Press. $29.95.

EMMERIJ, LOUIS, ed. 1997. *Economic and Social Development into the Twenty-First Century.* Pp. x, 579. Baltimore, MD: Johns Hopkins University Press. Paperbound, $24.95.

ENGLANDER, DAVID, ed. 1997. *Britain and America: Studies in Comparative History, 1760-1970.* Pp. xviii, 317. New Haven, CT: Yale University Press. $45.00. Paperbound, $20.00.

FELTHAN, COLIN, ed. 1997. *Which Psychotherapy.* Pp. viii, 207. Thousand Oaks, CA: Sage. Paperbound, no price.

FERNANDEZ-MORERA, DARIO. 1996. *American Academia and the Survival of Marxist Ideas.* Pp. 204. Westport, CT: Praeger. $59.95.

FISH, M. STEVEN. 1995. *Democracy from Scratch: Opposition and Regime in the New Russian Revolution.* Pp. x, 300. Princeton, NJ: Princeton University Press. No price.

FOWLER, BRIDGET. 1997. *Pierre Bourdieu and Cultural Theory: Critical Investigations.* Pp. vi, 200. Thousand Oaks, CA: Sage. $69.95. Paperbound, $23.95.

FOX, RICHARD LOGAN. 1996. *Gender Dynamics in Congressional Elections.* Pp. xxxi, 229. Thousand Oaks, CA: Sage. $46.00. Paperbound, $21.95.

GALTUNG, JOHAN. 1996. *Peace by Peaceful Means: Peace and Conflict, Development and Civilization.* Pp. viii, 280. Thousand Oaks, CA: Sage. $75.00. Paperbound, $26.95.

GARBER, MARJORIE. 1997. *Dog Love.* Pp. 346. New York: Touchstone. Paperbound, no price.

GARRATT, DAREN, JEREMY ROCHE, and STANLEY TUCKER, eds. 1997. *Changing Experiences of Youth.* Pp. vi, 165. Thousand Oaks, CA: Sage. $55.00. Paperbound, $19.95.

GEORGE, SHANTI. 1997. *Third World Professionals and Development Education in Europe: Personal Narratives, Global Conversations.* Pp. 325. Thousand Oaks, CA: Sage. $38.00.

GIBSON, EDWARD. 1996. *Class and Conservative Parties: Argentina in Comparative Perspective.* Pp. xx, 274.

Baltimore, MD: Johns Hopkins University Press. No price.

GIFFARD, SYDNEY. 1997. *Japan Among the Powers, 1890-1990.* Pp. xxi, 218. New Haven, CT: Yale University Press, 1997. $35.00. Paperbound, $15.00.

GINZBERG, ELI. 1997. *New Deal Days: 1933-1934.* Pp. 109. New Brunswick, NJ: Transaction. $29.95.

GOLDING, PETER and PHIL HARRIS, eds. 1997. *Beyond Cultural Imperialism: Globalization, Communication and the New International Order.* Pp. xii, 259. Thousand Oaks, CA: Sage. $56.00. Paperbound, $26.00.

GOLDSCHEIDER, CALVIN. 1996. *Israel's Changing Society: Population, Ethnicity, and Development.* Pp. xix, 271. Boulder, CO: Westview Press. $55.00.

GREEN, CHARLES, ed. 1997. *Globalization and Survival in the Black Diaspora: The New Urban Challenge.* Pp. xiv, 396. Albany: State University of New York Press. Paperbound, $21.95.

GUPTA, R. K. 1996. *Anti-Dumping and Countervailing Measures: The Complete Reference.* Pp. 298. Thousand Oaks, CA: Sage. $39.95.

HANSON, SANDRA L. 1996. *Lost Talent: Women in the Sciences.* Pp. xii, 220. Philadelphia: Temple University Press. $39.95.

HANUS, JEROME J. and PETER W. COOKSON, JR. 1996. *Choosing Schools: Vouchers and American Education.* Pp. ix, 179. Lanham, MD: American University Press. $39.50. Paperbound, $19.50.

HAQ, MAHBUB UL. 1997. *Human Development in South Asia, 1997.* Pp. ix, 153. New York: Oxford University Press. $30.00. Paperbound, $23.00.

HARDY, MELISSA A., ed. 1997. *Studying Aging and Social Change: Conceptual and Methodological Issues.* Pp. ix, 229. Thousand Oaks, CA: Sage. $44.00. Paperbound, $19.95.

HASELAGER, W.F.G. 1997. *Cognitive Science and Folk Psychology: The Right Frame of Mind*. Pp. viii, 165. Thousand Oaks, CA: Sage. $69.95. Paperbound, $23.95.

HASSANEIN, ASHRAF M. and BARBARA F. ATKINSON. 1997. *Pathology Review*. Pp. xvii, 398. Thousand Oaks, CA: Sage. Paperbound, $24.95.

HEATH, ROBERT L. 1997. *Strategic Issues Management: Organizations and Public Policy Challenges*. Pp. xiv, 410. Thousand Oaks, CA: Sage. $56.00. Paperbound, $26.95.

HENKIN, LOUIS. 1997. *The Age of Rights*. Pp. xix, 220. New York: Columbia University Press. Paperbound, $16.50.

HIGGINBOTHAM, ELIZABETH and MARY ROMEO, eds. 1997. *Women and Work: Exploring Race, Ethnicity, and Class*. Pp. xxxii, 269. Thousand Oaks, CA: Sage. $55.00. Paperbound, $24.95.

HIRSCHHORN, BERNARD. 1997. *Democracy Reformed: Richard Spencer Childs and His Fight for Better Government*. Pp. xxiv, 233. Westport, CT: Greenwood Press. $59.95.

HOPMANN, P. TERRENCE. 1996. *The Negotiation Process and the Resolution of International Conflicts*. Pp. xi, 353. Columbia: University of South Carolina Press. $39.95.

HOWE, CHRISTOPHER. 1996. *The Origins of Japanese Trade Supremacy*. Pp. xxvii, 471. Chicago: University of Chicago Press. $49.95.

JARDINE, LISA, ed. 1997. *Erasmus: The Education of a Christian Prince*. Pp. xxviii, 150. New York: Cambridge University Press. $44.95. Paperbound, $12.95.

JENKS, CHRIS. 1997. *Childhood*. Pp. viii, 146. New York: Routledge. $55.00. Paperbound, $16.95.

KAO, HENRY S. R. and DURGANAND SINHA, eds. 1997. *Asian Perspectives on Psychology*. Pp. 396. Thousand Oaks, CA: Sage. $32.00.

KAPUR, RATNA and BRENDA COSSMAN. 1996. *Subversive Sites: Feminist Engagements with Law in India*. Pp. 352. Thousand Oaks, CA: Sage. $28.00.

KEECH, WILLIAM R. 1995. *Economic Politics*. Pp. xiii, 241. New York: Cambridge University Press. $49.95. Paperbound, $14.95.

KHADEMIAN, ANNE M. 1996. *Checking on Banks: Autonomy and Accountability in Three Federal Agencies*. Pp. x, 195. Washington, DC: Brookings Institution. $36.95. Paperbound, $15.95.

KHUBCHANDANI, LACHMAN M. 1996. *Revisualizing Boundaries: A Plurilingual Ethos*. Pp. 255. Thousand Oaks, CA: Sage. $32.50.

KIRK, RUSSELL. 1997. *Edmund Burke: A Genius Reconsidered*. Pp. xv, 285. Wilmington, DE: Intercollegiate Studies Institute. $24.95.

KLEIN, DAVID M. and JAMES M. WHITE. 1996. *Family Theories: An Introduction*. Pp. xxii, 294. Thousand Oaks, CA: Sage. $48.00. Paperbound, $23.95.

KOLKO, GABRIEL. 1997. *Vietnam: Anatomy of a Peace*. Pp. ix, 190. New York: Routledge. Paperbound, $15.95.

KRAMER, HILTON and ROGER KIMBALL, eds. 1997. *The Future of the European Past*. Pp. xviii, 233. Chicago: Ivan R. Dee. $26.00.

KUZNAR, LAWRENCE A. 1996. *Reclaiming a Scientific Anthropology*. Pp. xi, 284. Walnut Creek, CA: Altamira Press. $42.00.

LANKTON, LARRY. 1997. *Beyond the Boundaries: Life and Landscape at the Lake Superior Copper Mines, 1840-1875*. Pp. xvi, 247. New York: Oxford University Press. $39.95.

LARGE, STEPHEN S. 1997. *Emperor Hirohito and Showa Japan: A Political Biography*. Pp. xii, 249. New York: Routledge. Paperbound, $18.95.

LAURISTIN, MARJU and PEETER VI-HALEMM, eds. 1997. *Return to the Western World: Cultural and Political Perspectives on the Estonian Post-Communist Transition.* Pp. xvi, 387. Tartu, Estonia: Tartu University Press. Paperbound, no price.

LEE, ROBERT EMMET. 1995. *In the Public Interest: The Life of Robert Emmet Lee from the FBI to the FCC.* Pp. ix, 274. Lanham, MD: University Press of America. $32.50.

LEE, WILLIAM T. 1997. *The ABM Treaty Charade: A Study in Elite Illusion and Delusion.* Pp. 165. Washington, DC: Council for Social and Economic Studies. Paperbound, no price.

LEFLEY, HARRIET P. 1996. *Family Caregiving in Mental Illness.* Pp. x, 259. Thousand Oaks, CA: Sage. $45.00. Paperbound, $22.50.

LEYS, COLIN. 1996. *The Rise and Fall of Development Theory.* Pp. viii, 205. Bloomington: Indiana University Press. $35.00. Paperbound, $14.95.

LICHTERMAN, PAUL. 1996. *The Search for Political Community: American Activists Reinventing Commitment.* Pp. ix, 279. New York: Cambridge University Press. $54.95. Paperbound, $19.95.

LIETEN, G. K. 1996. *Development, Devolution and Democracy: Village Discourse in West Bengal.* Pp. 252. New Delhi, India: Sage. $32.95.

MACKENZIE, G. CALVIN. 1996. *The Irony of Reform: Roots of American Political Disenchantment.* Pp. xvi, 224. Boulder, CO: Westview Press. $61.50. Paperbound, $18.95.

MAFFESOLI, MICHEL. 1995. *The Time of the Tribes: The Decline of Individualism in Mass Society.* Pp. xii, 176. Thousand Oaks, CA: Sage. $69.95. Paperbound, $23.95.

MAHAN, HAROLD E. 1996. *Benson J. Lossing and Historical Writing in the United States.* Pp. 142. Westport, CT: Greenwood Press. $52.95.

MARCUSE, PETER M. 1996. *Disease: In Search of Remedy.* Pp. x, 156. Champaign: University of Illinois Press. $21.95.

MARTINICH, A. P. 1997. *Thomas Hobbes.* Pp. ix, 156. New York: St. Martin's Press. $39.95. Paperbound, $18.95.

MARTZ, JOHN D. 1997. *The Politics of Clientelism: Democracy and the State in Colombia.* Pp. xii, 358. New Brunswick, NJ: Transaction. $44.95.

MAST, ROBERT H. and ANNE B. MAST. 1997. *Autobiography of Protest in Hawai'i.* Pp. vi, 450. Honolulu: University of Hawaii Press. Paperbound, $19.95.

McKAY, JIM. 1997. *Managing Gender: Affirmative Action and Organizational Power in Australian, Canadian, and New Zealand Sport.* Pp. xxi, 217. Albany: State University of New York Press. Paperbound, $18.95.

McKIM, ROBERT and JEFF McMAHAN, eds. 1997. *The Morality of Nationalism.* Pp. xii, 371. New York: Oxford University Press. $45.00. Paperbound, $19.95.

McSWITE, O. C. 1997. *Legitimacy in Public Administration: A Discourse Analysis.* Pp. xii, 306. Thousand Oaks, CA: Sage. $49.95. Paperbound, $21.95.

MELBOURNE, ROY M. 1997. *Conflict and Crises: A Foreign Service Story.* Rev. ed. Pp. viii, 288. Lanham, MD: University Press of America. $39.50.

MEYER, JOHN P. and NATALIE J. ALLEN. 1997. *Commitment in the Workplace: Theory, Research, and Application.* Pp. x, 150. Thousand Oaks, CA: Sage. $34.00. Paperbound, $15.95.

MICHAUX, PHYLLIS. 1996. *The Unknown Ambassadors: A Sage of Citizenship.* Pp. 173. Bayside, NY: Aletheia. Paperbound, $15.95.

MILLER, JOSEPH C. 1988. *Way of Death: Merchant Capitalism and the Angolan Slave Trade, 1730-1830.* Pp.

xxx, 770. Madison: University of Wisconsin Press. Paperbound, no price.

MITHAUG, DENNIS E. 1996. *Equal Opportunity Theory.* Pp. vii, 274. Thousand Oaks, CA: Sage. Paperbound, no price.

MOLINE, MARY E., GEORGE T. WILLIAMS, and KENNETH M. AUSTIN. 1997. *Documenting Psychotherapy: Essentials for Mental Health Practitioners.* Pp. x, 189. Thousand Oaks, CA: Sage. $39.95. Paperbound, $19.95.

MONROE, KRISTEN RENWICK, ed. 1997. *Contemporary Empirical Political Theory.* Pp. 329. Berkeley: University of California Press. $45.00. Paperbound, $16.95.

MOOIJ, MARIEKE DE. 1997. *Global Marketing and Advertising: Understanding Cultural Paradoxes.* Pp. xx, 316. Thousand Oaks, CA: Sage. $65.00. Paperbound, $29.95.

MOON, MARILYN. 1993. *Medicare Now and in the Future.* Pp. xvi, 263. Lanham, MD: Urban Institute Press. $57.00. Paperbound, $24.00.

MORSE, JANICE M., ed. 1997. *Completing a Qualitative Project: Details and Dialogue.* Pp. xiii, 400. Thousand Oaks, CA: Sage. $58.00. Paperbound, $27.95.

MOSER, RICHARD. 1996. *The New Winter Soldiers: GI and Veteran Dissent During the Vietnam Era.* Pp. xi, 219. New Brunswick, NJ: Rutgers University Press. $50.00. Paperbound, $18.95.

MOURE, RAMON DACAL and MANUEL RIVERO DE LA CALLE. 1997. *Art and Archaeology of Pre-Columbian Cuba.* Pp. xxiv, 134. Pittsburgh, PA: University of Pittsburgh Press. $35.00.

MOYNIHAN, MICHAEL. 1996. *The Coming American Renaissance: How to Benefit from America's Economic Resurgence.* Pp. 319. New York: Simon & Schuster. $23.00.

NEGASH, TEKESTE. 1997. *Eritrea and Ethiopia: The Federal Experience.* Pp. 234. New Brunswick, NJ: Transaction. Paperbound, $26.95.

NEHRING, NEIL. 1997. *Popular Music, Gender, and Postmodernism: Anger Is an Energy.* Pp. xxxi, 203. Thousand Oaks, CA: Sage. $48.00. Paperbound, $21.95.

NELSON, DAVID. 1997. *Shifting Fortunes: The Rise and Decline of American Labor, from the 1820s to the Present.* Pp. x, 181. Chicago: Ivan R. Dee. $22.50.

NIVEN, JOHN, ed. 1997. *The Salmon P. Chase Papers: Correspondence, April 1863-1864.* Vol. 4. Pp. xxiii, 479. Kent, OH: Kent State University Press. $45.00.

NIVOLA, PIETRO S., ed. 1997. *Comparative Disadvantages? Social Regulations and the Global Economy.* Pp. x, 368. Washington, DC: Brookings Institution. $49.95. Paperbound, $19.95.

O'CONNOR, STEPHEN. 1997. *Will My Name Be Shouted Out? Reaching Inner City Students Through the Power of Writing.* Pp. 382. New York: Touchstone Books. Paperbound, $14.00.

ODESCALCHI, EDMOND. 1997. *The Third Crown: A Study in World Government Exercised by the Popes.* Pp. ix, 180. Lanham, MD: University Press of America. $32.50.

PARIJS, PHILIPPE VAN. 1995. *Real Freedom for All: What (If Anything) Can Justify Capitalism?* Pp. xii, 300. New York: Oxford University Press. $35.00.

PARNELL, TERESA F. and DEBORAH O. DAY, eds. 1997. *Munchausen by Proxy Syndrome: Misunderstood Child Abuse.* Pp. xvi, 311. Thousand Oaks, CA: Sage. $52.00. Paperbound, $24.95.

PEBLEY, ANNE R. and LUIS ROSERO-BIXBY, eds. 1997. *Demographic Diversity and Change in the Central American Isthmus.* Pp. xiv, 736. Santa

Monica, CA: RAND. Paperbound, $30.00.

PERITZ, RUDOLPH J. R. 1996. *Competition Policy in America, 1888-1992.* Pp. x, 374. New York: Oxford University Press. $45.00.

PRYOR, FREDERIC L. 1996. *Economic Evolution and Structure: The Impact of Complexity on the U.S. Economic System.* Pp. xv, 399. New York: Cambridge University Press. $59.95. Paperbound, $19.95.

PUGH, MARTIN, ed. 1997. *A Companion to Modern European History, 1871-1945.* Pp. xiv, 407. Cambridge, MA: Basil Blackwell. $64.95. Paperbound, $26.95.

QUINN, PEGGY. 1997. *Understanding Disability: A Lifespan Approach.* Pp. xxiv, 232. Thousand Oaks, CA: Sage. $56.00. Paperbound, $26.00.

REJAI, MOSTAFA and KAY PHILLIPS. 1997. *Leaders and Leadership: An Appraisal of Theory and Research.* Pp. xii, 127. Westport, CT: Praeger. $49.95.

RENIAK, ANTHONY L. 1997. *We the People: To Save America.* Pp. 33. Pittsburgh, PA: Dorrance. Paperbound, $7.00.

ROSCHELLE, ANNE R. 1997. *No More Kin: Exploring Race, Class, and Gender in Family Networks.* Pp. xvii, 233. Thousand Oaks, CA: Sage. $45.00. Paperbound, $21.95.

ROZELL, MARK J. and WILLIAM D. PEDERSON, eds. 1997. *FDR and the Modern Presidency: Leadership and Legacy.* Pp. vi, 242. Westport, CT: Praeger. $59.95.

SCALES-TRENT, JUDY. 1995. *Notes of a White Black Woman: Race, Color, Community.* Pp. viii, 198. University Park: Pennsylvania State University Press. $19.50.

SCHER, RICHARD K. 1997. *The Modern Political Campaign: Mudslinging, Bombast, and the Vitality of American Politics.* Pp. xi, 206. Armonk, NY:

M. E. Sharpe. $51.95. Paperbound, $19.95.

SHAH, GHANSHYAM. 1997. *Public Health and Urban Development: The Plague in Surat.* Pp. 317. Thousand Oaks, CA: Sage. $36.00.

SHUGHART, WILLIAM F., II, ed. 1997. *Taxing Choice: The Predatory Politics of Fiscal Discrimination.* Pp. xv, 396. New Brunswick, NJ: Transaction. $39.95.

SIDDIQUI, RUKHSANA A., ed. 1997. *Subsaharan Africa in the 1990s.* Pp. xiv, 221. Westport, CT: Praeger. $59.95.

SILVERMAN, DAVID. 1997. *Discourses of Counselling: HIV Counselling as Social Interaction.* Pp. x, 244. Thousand Oaks, CA: Sage. $69.95. Paperbound, $21.95.

SIMONS, RONALD L. 1996. *Understanding Differences Between Divorced and Intact Families.* Pp. xii, 252. Thousand Oaks, CA: Sage. $44.00. Paperbound, $21.95.

SINGH, NARINDAR. 1996. *The Keynesian Fallout.* Pp. 257. Thousand Oaks, CA: Sage. $36.00. Paperbound, $16.95.

SINYAVSKY, ANDREI. 1997. *The Russian Intelligentsia.* Pp. x, 98. New York: Columbia University Press. $19.95.

SMITH, PAUL J., ed. 1997. *Human Smuggling: Chinese Migrant Trafficking and the Challenge to America's Immigration Tradition.* Pp. xv, 207. Washington, DC: Center for Strategic and International Studies. Paperbound, $21.95.

SOMIN, ILYA. 1996. *Stillborn Crusade: The Tragic Failure of Western Intervention in the Russian Civil War, 1918-1920.* Pp. viii, 236. New Brunswick, NJ: Transaction. $32.95.

STAEHELI, LYNN A., JANET E. KODRAS, and COLIN FLINT. 1997. *State Devolution in America: Implications for a Diverse Society.* Pp. xxxiii,

286. Thousand Oaks, CA: Sage. $58.00. Paperbound, $24.95.

TAYLOR, JOHN M. 1997. *History in Your Hand: Fifty Years of the Manuscript Society.* Pp. x, 171. Westport, CT: Praeger. $49.95.

TAYLOR, ROBERT JOSEPH, JAMES S. JACKSON, and LINDA M. CHATTERS, eds. 1997. *Family Life in Black America.* Pp. xiv, 377. Thousand Oaks, CA: Sage. $42.95. Paperbound, $21.95.

TENDLER, JUDITH. 1997. *Good Government in the Tropics.* Pp. xi, 221. Baltimore, MD: Johns Hopkins University Press. $36.50.

TESTER, KEITH. 1997. *Moral Culture.* Pp. vii, 164. Thousand Oaks, CA: Sage. $69.95. Paperbound, $23.95.

TOCQUEVILLE, ALEXIS DE. 1997. *Memoir on Pauperism.* Pp. 80. Chicago: Ivan R. Dee. $15.00. Paperbound, $6.95.

TORDOFF, WILLIAM. 1997. *Government and Politics in Africa.* 3d ed. Pp. xxii, 378. Bloomington: Indiana University Press. $39.95. Paperbound, $18.95.

VARMA, MADHURENDRA K. 1997. *Managing More Effectively: A Professional Approach to Get the Best Out of People.* Pp. 267. Thousand Oaks, CA: Sage. $29.95.

VAZ, KIM MARIE, ed. 1997. *Oral Narrative Research with Black Women.* Pp. x, 262. Thousand Oaks, CA: Sage. $46.00. Paperbound, $21.95.

VERMA, J. C. 1997. *Venture Capital Financing in India.* Pp. 374. New Delhi, India: Response Books. $28.00.

VIRMANI, B. R. and KALA RAO. 1996. *Economic Restructuring, Technology Transfer and Human Resource Development.* Pp. 288. New Delhi, India: Response Books. $38.00.

VITULLO-MARTIN, JULIA, ed. 1996. *Breaking Away: The Future of Cities.* Pp. xv, 255. New York: Twentieth Century Fund Press. $21.95.

VOEGELIN, ERIC. 1997. *History of Political Ideas.* Vol. 1, *Hellenism, Rome, and Early Christianity.* Pp. 281. Columbia: University of Missouri Press. $34.95.

VOGEL, EZRA F., ed. 1997. *Living with China: United States–China Relations in the Twenty-First Century.* Pp. 336. New York: Norton. Paperbound, $18.00.

VOGT, W. PAUL. 1997. *Tolerance and Education: Learning to Live with Diversity and Difference.* Pp. xxviii, 287. Thousand Oaks, CA: Sage. $56.00. Paperbound, $25.95.

WESTERFIELD, H. BRADFORD. 1997. *Inside CIA's Private World: Declassified Articles from the Agency's Internal Journal, 1955-1992.* Pp. xxii, 489. New Haven, CT: Yale University Press. $40.00. Paperbound, $18.00.

WETSTEIN, MATTHEW E. 1996. *Abortion Rates in the United States: The Influence of Opinion and Policy.* Pp. xv, 153. Albany: State University of New York Press. Paperbound, $16.95.

WETZEL, DAVID and THEODORE S. HAMEROW, eds. 1997. *International Politics and German History: The Past Informs the Present.* Pp. viii, 180. Westport, CT: Praeger. $55.00.

WINTERS, JEFFREY A. 1996. *Power in Motion: Capital Mobility and the Indonesian State.* Pp. xvi, 241. Ithaca, NY: Cornell University Press. $35.00.

INDEX